IN THE EYE
OF THE NEEDLE

At the May 1999 Drug Summit held in the NSW Parliament. Among those celebrating the resolution to establish a medically supervised injecting were: (*back row from left to right*) Assistant Commissioner Mal Brammer of NSW Police Internal Affairs (back to camera), Tony Trimingham from Family Drug Support Organisation, Dr Ingrid van Beek of KRC (centre), Rev. Ray Richmond of Wayside Chapel (side on to camera), Richard Walsh (ACP); (*front row from left to right*) Annie Madden from AIVL (side on to camera), Dr Alex Wodak from St Vincent's Hospital (side to camera), Federal Member for Sydney Tania Plibersek (back to camera) and former member of the NSW Legislative Council Anne Symonds. (PHOTO BY STEVEN SIEWERT, COURTESY OF FAIRFAXPHOTOS)

IN THE EYE
OF THE NEEDLE

Diary of a Medically Supervised Injecting Centre

DR INGRID VAN BEEK

ALLEN&UNWIN

First published in 2004

Allen & Unwin
83 Alexander Street
Crows Nest NSW 2065
Australia
Phone: (61 2) 8425 0100
Fax: (61 2) 9906 2218
Email: info@allenandunwin.com
Web: www.allenandunwin.com

National Library of Australia
Cataloguing-in-Publication entry:

Van Beek, Ingrid.
  In the eye of the needle : diary of a drug injecting centre.

  ISBN 1 74114 381 0.

  1. Narcotic addicts - Services for - New South Wales -
  Sydney. 2. Narcotics, Control of - New South Wales -
  Sydney. I. Title.

362.2937099441

Set in 13/10 pt Stone Serif by Bookhouse, Sydney
Printed by Griffin Press, Adelaide

10 9 8 7 6 5 4 3 2 1

Contents

would like to dedicate this book to my father, who died two weeks before the NSW Parliamentary Drug Summit; he would have enjoyed this latest episode in my professional life. But my (now) 84-year-old mum has been there all along, giving out information about the MSIC to other residents in her apartment building nearby and at the street stall in Kings Cross, and hand-delivering that big bunch of tulips to congratulate staff on the very cold, wet night after the MSIC opened. Dad would have been proud.

I would like to thank Richard Walsh whose idea it was to document this journey, guiding me at every step of the way. His contribution to this book was integral.

For privacy and/or legal reasons none of the clients in this book are referred to by their real names. Where the names of other people have been changed, the first time they are mentioned their adopted name is placed in inverted commas, thus 'Michael' etc.

Prologue

It was Thursday, 5 April 2001. Karen Nairn and I were sitting in my room at the Ashoke Hotel in Delhi, looking anxiously at the phone, knowing that at any minute it would ring from Sydney to let us know the outcome of the court case. We were in New Delhi attending the 12th International Conference on the Reduction of Drug-Related Harm.

The Kings Cross Chamber of Commerce and Tourism, under the florid leadership of its Vice-President, Malcolm Duncan, in a further attempt to stop us opening Australia's first Medically Supervised Injecting Centre, had challenged the validity of our licence to operate. If there was a result against us, it would be worse than all the other setbacks we'd had to endure over the preceding twelve months. So there we were in Delhi, sitting in my hotel room with an increasing sense of impending doom; all the confidence we'd sustained until then had just about ebbed away.

Finally the phone rang. The Chamber of Commerce had been unsuccessful on all counts and costs had been awarded against them. Immediately after Judge Brian Sully delivered his verdict, the Chamber had sought a 'stay' (which is tantamount to an injunction) to prevent us from opening the service until they could lodge an appeal. But apparently the judge had emphatically denied the stay, which meant that we could proceed to open the service immediately. Karen and I had finally come to the end of what had been a very arduous journey for us both. We left the hotel room feeling absolutely elated.

The first person we came across was Annie Madden, the executive officer of the Australian Injecting and Illicit Drug Users' League, an organisation that represents injecting drug users (IDUs) at a national level. We had consulted with her often during the course of the project's development so she was very personally involved. When we shared the news with her, she was just as elated as we were. The three of us stood there in the corridor of the conference venue hugging, with tears rolling down our cheeks.

There were other people there, including Jo Kimber from the National Drug and Alcohol Research Centre (NDARC), and Margaret MacDonald from the National Centre in HIV Epidemiology and Clinical Research, who were going to be part of the team that would formally evaluate the injecting centre if it ever got up and running. Like us, they had essentially been on hold for many months and thus acutely aware of the difficulties we'd encountered.

At the closing ceremony of the Delhi conference that evening, Dr Gerry Stimson, the conference program director, announced that in Australia there had been a momentous result. Before he could actually proceed to explain what this was, there was a shriek of 'Oh, no!' from an Indian delegate. We were of course perturbed (having assumed we were surrounded by supporters), but we soon learnt that she thought Gerry was about to announce that Australia had won the cricket Test against India. (India won, so we discovered the following day!).

There was thunderous applause among the many hundreds of delegates when Gerry announced the result regarding the Medically Supervised Injecting Centre (MSIC) in Sydney. After all, our victory was also a win for all of us who support the harm reduction approach. The Australian contingent, who had assembled near the back, added lots of whooping and catcalling to the applause in typical Aussie style.

At the end of what was a great day for us, we celebrated with our friends and colleagues at the hotel bar with tiny bottles of champagne. We were ready to start. The enabling Act would be declared on 1 May and we had 18 months from then to the end of the trial.

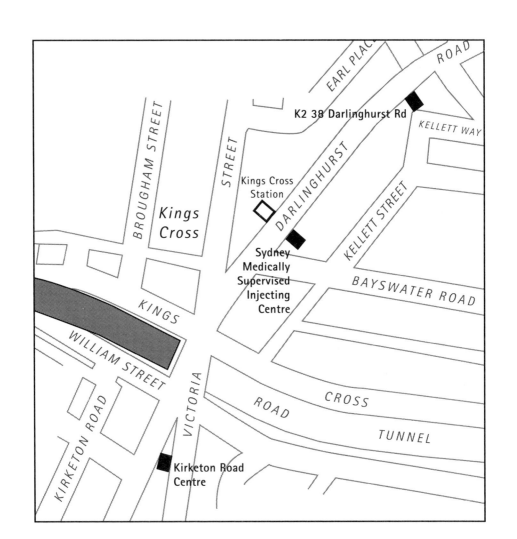

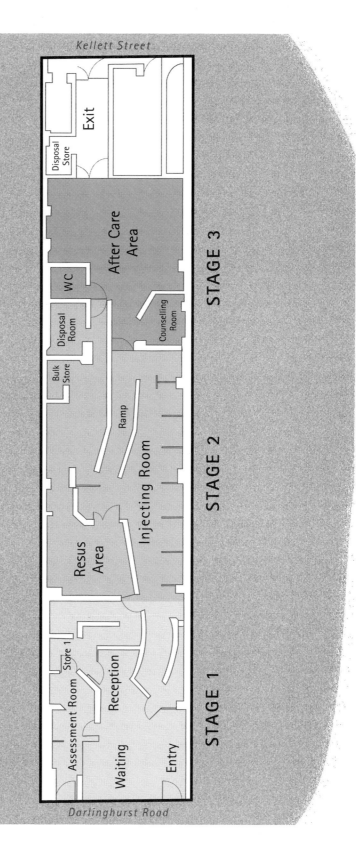

Kellett Street

Exit

Disposal Store

After Care Area

WC

Disposal Room

Bulk Store

Counselling Room

Ramp

Injecting Room

Resus Area

Store 1

Assessment Room

Reception

Waiting

Entry

Darlinghurst Road

STAGE 1   STAGE 2   STAGE 3

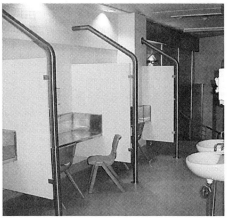

one

In the beginning

The whole idea of a supervised injecting centre originated in Kings Cross in 1990 when the local police commander at that time, Jim McCloskey, contacted me in my capacity as director of the Kirketon Road Centre (KRC), an off-site unit of Sydney Hospital located above the Darlinghurst Fire Station at Kings Cross. Established in 1987 in response to a recommendation of a parliamentary inquiry into prostitution in New South Wales, KRC provided a comprehensive range of primary health care services to meet the health and social welfare needs of 'at risk' youth, sex workers and IDUs.

Superintendent McCloskey told me that the ambulance service had let him know that there had been an increasing number of call-outs to drug overdoses at some of the commercial sex premises on Darlinghurst Road, the main street of Kings Cross.

This wasn't all that surprising when you consider that almost all street-based sex workers are drug-dependent, injecting mainly heroin at least several times a day, and they need to do this somewhere in the course of things. In some instances, it wasn't only the sex workers who were using these premises to inject drugs—sometimes they would be recruited to procure drugs for their customers too. These premises had then increasingly begun to transform into rooms rented solely for the purpose of injecting drugs, because this way a faster turnover could be achieved.

Superintendent Jim McCloskey was a progressive-thinking commander who appreciated that, if he went in 'boots and all' and closed these premises down, this activity would simply return to the back streets. He also understood that this would probably increase drug users' risk of death from overdose and reduce public amenity because of the increased visibility of drug injecting and its associated paraphernalia left lying around on the streets. So he sought my advice as to whether he should proceed with a purely policing approach to this new situation, or whether some other arrangement might be more appropriate.

But then there was a change of patrol commander at Kings Cross. The next commander was unwilling to form any relationship with KRC, so there was no real dialogue between Health and Police regarding drug-related matters for at least a year or so until, in 1994, Mal Brammer took over as commander of the Kings Cross police service. Mal, like Jim McCloskey, held the view that drug use was better dealt with as a health and social issue with drug supply left to the police. Several decades directly involved in drug law enforcement had convinced him of that. But Mal felt that informal arrangements with what came to be called 'illegal shooting galleries' were problematic. He was concerned that, when the police were required to use their discretion without a way of ensuring accountability for this, it opened the door to accusations of corruption. I could see his point. So Mal and I spent six months working on a proposal which had already gained considerable support as it made its way slowly upwards through the health and police bureaucracies only to have it killed off overnight as a result of a media leak that caught the Premier, Bob Carr, on the back foot.

The NSW Health Department then decided to assess the feasibility of establishing a supervised injecting facility to be run by the Area Health Service as part of the Kirketon Road Centre, which also operated the primary needle syringe program (NSP) for IDUs in the area. Dr Alex Wodak, the director of the Alcohol and Drug Service at St Vincent's Hospital in Darlinghurst, and I worked up a proposal and submitted it to the Health Department.

At this time the 1996 Wood Royal Commission into the NSW Police began its hearings and all of Mal Brammer's concerns about the possibility of police corruption in relation to these commercial sex premises were found to be justified. As a result of the subsequent jailing of several key operators, many of these illegal premises folded, with drug dealing returning to the streets where it was harder to police. Their closure also led to a significant shortfall in the supply of needle syringes, particularly after hours. Recognising the serious public health implications of this situation, the Health Department asked me to look around for suitable premises in the heart of Kings Cross to accommodate a NSP. The potential for these premises to be converted into a supervised injecting facility, should this be approved at some stage in the future, was also kept in mind.

Premises were eventually leased under the Pink Pussycat nightclub on the main street at 38 Darlinghurst Road, opposite Springfield Plaza, which was where most of the drug-related activity in Kings Cross was centred at this time. This site had previously been a 'pinball parlour' that operated 24 hours, 7 days a week. Apparently, despite none of the pinball machines ever working, it had been a very busy place, which was perhaps connected to the large quantities of cocaine that had been supplied from these same premises until the Wood Royal Commission.

This shop-front NSP opened in 1997, despite vocal opposition from one of the local residents' associations, and became known as 'K2'. Social welfare advice and referrals to other relevant services were also provided from this location. Operating from two in the afternoon until ten at night, seven days a week, it was soon seeing up to 200 IDUs a day.

Meanwhile, in his final report, Justice Wood tabled the following recommendation: 'At present, publicly funded programs operate to provide syringes and needles to injecting drug users with the clear understanding that they will be used to administer prohibited drugs. In these circumstances to shrink from the provision of safe, sanitary premises where users can safely inject is somewhat short sighted. The health and public safety benefits outweigh the policy considerations against condoning otherwise unlawful behaviour. Consideration should be given to the establishment of safe, sanitary injecting rooms under the licence or supervision of the Department of Health, and the amendment of the *Drug Misuse and Trafficking Act 1985* accordingly.'

In response to Justice Wood's recommendation, the NSW government established a Joint Select Parliamentary Committee to investigate what were then still referred to as Safe Injecting Rooms. Chaired by Anne Symonds MLC, the committee accepted 103 submissions and expert testimony from a plethora of people, mostly in support of establishing such a facility. Importantly, many of the relevant stakeholders in Kings Cross—including the then Chamber of Commerce, local residents, the ambulance and police services—were in favour. Yet, despite this, eventually six of the ten members of this parliamentary committee voted against the establishment of a supervised injecting centre anywhere in NSW.

So much for the proposal to NSW Health about KRC operating an injecting centre, possibly from the K2 site; it was back to the drawing board, because Kings Cross still had the problem of street-based drug use and all the public health and public order problems that arose from it. Meanwhile the rate of heroin overdose deaths was increasing very significantly—almost matching the national road toll—right across the country but particularly in Kings Cross, where there was the highest number of overdose deaths anywhere in Australia, particularly because drug use was so street-based.

In mid-1998, the Reverend Ray Richmond from the Wayside Chapel, a parish of the Uniting Church, called together a small group to consider what alternatives might exist. Eventually a plan was hatched to stage a very public civil disobedience exercise, using the chapel's premises as a quasi-safe injecting room.

Then there was a new development. The *Sun-Herald* ran a dramatic front-page story about an allegedly under-age boy injecting heroin in the area of Redfern known as 'The Block', using injecting equipment provided by the local needle syringe program. This resulted in an escalation of the space given to the drugs issue in the media and to a polarisation of views in the community.

It was now just weeks out from the 1999 state election, and in response to this news story Premier Bob Carr announced that, if re-elected (which he was), he would host a Drug Summit to examine all the complexities of the drug issue in NSW. In this masterful way the by-now raging drug debate was largely deflected until after the elections. So the civil disobedience exercise was timed to take place two weeks before the Drug Summit, thereby ensuring that the question of a supervised injecting centre was placed firmly on its agenda.

At the Drug Summit in May 1999 the resolution to establish a medically supervised injecting centre was passed with a big majority in what was a wonderfully dramatic moment that still sticks in my memory. All of us who had been working hard, some of us for many years towards this outcome, rose spontaneously, hugging each other and shrieking in pure glee. Despite its somewhat cynical genesis, the Summit was a well-planned process, which was constructive and highly productive. There was a real sense among those of us participating that we needed to pull together, to put minor differences aside and focus on communicating the big and important picture to the politicians who made the big and important decisions about drug policy. After several horrendous months, when support for all harm reduction efforts had seemed to wane, we were now on Cloud Nine, with high hopes for the future. While the injecting centre resolution was perhaps the one which most symbolised this break-through (getting by far the most media attention), every one of the other 171 resolutions was equally important in promising a more balanced, evidence-based approach to the complexities of the drugs issue in NSW. They ranged from better policing of drug supply, to school education to prevent the uptake of drugs among young people, to greater drug treatment and rehabilitation options for those wanting to stop using drugs, and more ways of reducing harm to those who continue to use drugs. These were all in keeping with the three pillars of the harm minimisation that underpin Australia's National Drug Strategy—supply reduction, demand reduction and harm reduction. Like the needle syringe program, supervised injecting centres are an example of a harm reduction strategy.

In the ensuing weeks Robert Griew, the Chief Executive Officer of ACON (the AIDS Council of New South Wales) and I made contact with various people in the premier's office and the Department of Health to get an idea of how the supervised injecting centre was going to be implemented. We encountered a lot of vagueness about this. Apart from it being confirmed that the facility would be in Kings Cross, where both overdoses and community support for the trial were highest, it became increasingly clear that the government would prefer a non-government organisation to carry this forward, whereas KRC was a government organisation. We then proposed that perhaps Kirketon Road could form a consortium-type arrangement with the AIDS Council of NSW and maybe with the Ted Noffs Foundation, both non-government organisations. We were trying to broker an arrangement that would be acceptable to everybody but, while everyone seemed happy to hear us out, we never received any inkling that this was what they would agree to do.

At this time I also approached Alex Wodak, the Alcohol and Drug Service director at St. Vincent's, to see if he would be willing to consider an arrangement between the hospital and KRC. He also seemed reluctant to be nailed down, saying that whatever was decided in the end, we all had to stay focused on making this thing happen. That seemed to go without saying, I thought.

Then at the end of June 1999, about six weeks after the Summit, I was invited to a meeting at Governor Macquarie Tower, where all the relevant political offices are housed, to discuss the project. When I arrived, there were quite a few familiar faces there: Dr Alex Wodak and his deputy Bronwyn Crosby; Dr Tina Clifton from the Sisters of Charity Health Service; Dr Andrew Wilson, the Chief Health Officer and David Fowler from the AIDS and Infectious Diseases Branch, both of the NSW Health Department; Nathan Rees representing the Health Minister; Julie Sibraa representing Minister Della Bosca and Leigh McLaughlin representing the premier . . . It was then announced that the Sisters of Charity Health Service would oversee this project, and not KRC.

I was very taken aback; I'd always assumed that it had been a foregone conclusion that KRC would eventually get to run the centre. I told them in my (sometimes too) direct and forceful way that they were opting for a second-best arrangement. Unlike KRC, St Vincent's had no experience providing low-threshold, harm reduction services to the most marginalised, street-based IDUs who would be the clients of the new facility. As Justice Wood had highlighted in his original recommendation, an injecting centre was an extension of the needle syringe program and KRC had been providing this—

along with medical, counselling and social welfare services—to this part of the drug-using population in that area for over ten years. But it was to become clear to me in the ensuing months that it made very good political sense for the government to accept the Sisters' offer to be involved; they would be much harder to attack; even lapsed Catholics seem to retain a deep fear of the nuns of their youth!

This decision also effectively allowed the government to 'arm's-length' itself from the project—the Sisters of Charity Health Service was at least a quasi-non-government organisaton whereas KRC, as a unit of Sydney Hospital, sat squarely in the government sector. And of course they did have a very solid history of health services management in the area, a lot of credibility and an influential hospital board. However, in the course of this meeting I did manage to convince most of the others present that Kirketon Road had the more appropriate clinical practice wisdom and service expertise which would be critical to ensuring this controversial project's success. I went on to suggest that the Sisters of Charity Health Service could perhaps contract the clinical service from Kirketon Road, but retain overall control; a good compromise and win/win solution I thought, which was ultimately acceptable to everyone at the meeting. The meeing also agreed that the position of Medical Director should be advertised and recruited in the usual way. I walked out of that meeting four whole hours later in a complete daze, having first seen it all slip away for KRC and then seeing things turn back around by the end.

But the following Tuesday the Sisters of Charity Health Service held a press conference to announce that the medically supervised injecting facility would be established as part of the Alcohol and Drug Service of St Vincent's Hospital and that Dr Alex Wodak would be its medical director. Of course the government was not going to publicly refute this, but they weren't impressed that Plan A had been pushed through after all. It was also announced that the injecting facility would be conducted as an 18-month trial, to be formally evaluated by an independent team of researchers. They included Professor Richard Mattick of the National Drug and Alcohol Research Centre (NDARC), Professor John Kaldor of the National Centre in HIV Epidemiology and Clinical Research (NCHECR), Dr Don Weatherburn of the NSW Bureau of Crime Statistics and Research and Ms Helen Lapsely, a health economist from the School of Medicine at the University of NSW.

Then came a bolt from the blue. Several months later, in late October—at the very same time as the enabling legislation was being debated in the Lower House—the news broke that the Vatican had advised the Sisters of Charity to withdraw their participation in this initiative. There were various rumours as to who exactly at the Australian end was responsible for the

Vatican's involvement at this eleventh hour. Archbishop George Pell of the Catholic Archdiocese of Melbourne was the chief suspect, but the Reverend Fred Nile also claimed credit since this happened apparently only days after he had written to the Pope urging him to take such action. As I understand it, the Vatican didn't actually order the Sisters, but *advised* them, to pull out and the advice was heeded. The St Vincent's team were completely shocked and devastated. There is no doubt that they were truly committed to the initiative. Many of the more progressive among the greater Catholic congregation were too. They felt badly let down by their church, some even seriously questioning their faith.

Almost immediately Robert Griew and I recommended making representations to the government that Kirketon Road should take it over, but the government had decided that to 'replace like with like'; they were in the market for another church group. Quite fortuitously, the matter was raised by Sally Loane on ABC radio during an interview with Reverend Harry Herbert, the executive director of Uniting*Care* (then called the Board of Social Responsibility), who indicated that they might be willing to consider taking over the project. Uniting*Care* is the branch of the Uniting Church of Australia that oversees its community-based services in NSW. Minister John Della Bosca's office contacted Harry the next day, and subsequently invited Uniting*Care* to apply for the licence to operate the MSIC. So finally I had to admit defeat. KRC was not going to be involved. It simply wasn't going to be.

In January 2000 Uniting*Care* advertised the positions of general manager and part-time medical director. To begin with, I decided not to apply to be medical director; I had wanted to have KRC as an organisation involved, not me personally. Besides, the word was that it was already a done deal and that Alex Wodak was a shoo-in for the position. That no one at Uniting*Care* had encouraged me to apply seemed to confirm this. But at the eleventh hour I decided I would go for it anyway. After all, I'd spent many years thinking through all of the management aspects that this would entail. I had also visited many injecting centres in different countries, giving me a depth of understanding of their operation which I figured would be hard for anyone else to match.

The interview seemed to go well and several days later I was contacted by Harry and told that I had been successful. I was surprised and elated. Alex congratulated me, and promised to continue to support the initiative. He told others that he was in fact relieved not to have gotten the job in the end, because it was probably a poisoned chalice in the current climate. I hoped he was wrong about this, but I too had my doubts.

Meanwhile the search, first initiated by St Vincent's, went on for a suitable building for the centre. Finally, the site opposite Kings Cross train station exit at 66 Darlinghurst Road, suggested by the then President of the Chamber, was judged to best meet the various site selection criteria initially developed by the Sisters of Charity and adopted by Uniting*Care*'s Community Consultation Committee. Other members of the Chamber of Commerce raised objections, as did some members of the 2011 Residents' Association. These two groups then formed the Kings Cross Community Coalition—or the KCCC as they called themselves—which was headed up by Malcolm Duncan. It also included the Kings Cross Community Information Centre, a centre for older people in the area, the president of which was another member of the Chamber of Commerce. The KCCC held a press conference, put out media releases and at one stage even said they would apply for the licence to operate the facility themselves but retain me as the medical director!

Already a year had passed since the Drug Summit and all the other processes, such as developing the clinical and internal management protocols, were waiting upon the choice of site. So finally, after consideration of no less than 39 sites, Uniting*Care* decided that no site would ever be perfect for everyone and that the facility would be at 66 Darlinghurst Road.

It was at this point that the Chamber of Commerce and Tourism announced that it would be taking legal action to prevent the service opening at this location.

two

Preparing to
open the doors

As we celebrated in New Delhi the Supreme Court's decision allowing us to go ahead with the project, Dr Nick Crofts, a well-respected public health advocate from Victoria, said to me: 'You probably feel like I do on the day when I hear that I've had success with a research grant application—it's the one day when you can sit back and enjoy a sense of triumph. But of course, at the same time, you realise that this is the last day on which you'll be able to sit back, for now the work begins.'

Indeed, already the realisation had dawned that the real work was now going to begin. But, of course, having been on hold for so long, I also had a great sense that it was About Time. I also felt some trepidation at finally having to go forward to meet the challenge, after spending over a year saying we could do it. I'd settled into having the status of being the 'national expert on injecting centres' without in fact ever having run one. Now I was going to be put to the test.

•

We had to quickly work out what needed to be done to ensure the service opened as soon after 1 May as was possible. Probably the first priority was to recruit someone to replace Karen Nairn as general manager. Karen had been on 12 months' secondment from the Central Coast Area Health Service, where she was the HIV/AIDS and Sexual Health Coordinator, but had decided not to extend this secondment. So the first thing I did upon returning to

Sydney was to seek the secondment of Colette McGrath, from the Kirketon Road Centre, to be the Clinical Services Manager (re-jigging the general manager's role so that it also had a clinical focus). Colette had previously been the Assistant Director and the Nursing Unit Manager for several years before that at Kirketon Road. She had also been a member of the management committee of the injecting centre when the Sisters of Charity were set to run it and was very up to date on the project's progress.

I then called together Colette, the Nursing Unit Manager Andy, the Senior Counsellor Damian and the Office Manager Tracey to plot out exactly how soon after 1 May, the day the enabling Act would be proclaimed, we would be able to open.

We had to remobilise staff who had been previously recruited and then put on hold because of the legal challenge. These people had to commence their training (after they had given notice if they were working elsewhere) and commit to various shifts. Some of the people whom we had previously recruited had moved to other jobs, because, of course, most people are not in a position to just wait around until things like court cases resolve themselves. So we needed to contact those people and find out about their availability for training, as well as recruit more people so that we would have a full complement of front-line clinical staff ready to start work from day one.

We developed a staff training program to go for a full week, starting on 30 April, which would run into when we were planning to open. We decided that it would be best to open only for a four-hour session each day to begin with. At this stage we would have had trouble staffing anything more than that anyway. Our budget restricted us to operating only eight hours a day, so to maximise our impact across the day we planned to run for two four-hour sessions with a break, probably of a few hours in between. When I submitted our internal management protocols as part of the licence application process, I had flagged that we should review the appropriateness of those hours after six months operation.

So, at least for the first month, we would just open for four hours a day, from 10 am until 2 pm, which we predicted would be the quietest four hours. This way we would have the opportunity to find our feet and to get over any teething problems with the internal management protocols—of course, all of which had not yet been tested, here or anywhere.

We appreciated that there was likely to be intense media focus on our first operating day and that the media would actually want to be at the injecting centre on that day, so this was something we would need to actively manage. Tentatively we set the opening for 6 May, a Sunday, at 6 pm, when we were advised that most of the TV media would be unable to get any footage to air because there are no late evening news slots. This would not prevent the story from breaking, but it would not break in as big a way as it might otherwise do. Our particular concern was that the very first person who used the facility would be shown on national media. We felt that, even if they consented, it wouldn't be appropriate. It was, after all, a serious health facility—not a shopping mall—that was being opened. So Sunday night, 6 May became our projected opening night, and we asked staff and other people who needed to know to keep it to themselves.

It was at this stage that we also realised there was a very real risk that soon after we opened the media might attempt to enter the facility and film clients injecting. For obvious confidentiality and privacy as well as safety reasons, we wanted to prevent that from happening. So in consultation with our media consultant, Pat Kennedy, we decided to produce a demonstration tape in which our staff mocked up the procedures that clients would be involved in when they used the facility. So on 18 April this video was filmed, using Colette and Damian in the roles of nurse and counsellor. Andy Dakin played the part of an injecting drug user, wearing a dark hat and for the most part facing away from the camera so as not to be easily recognisable. The plan was to distribute copies of this to the media at the time of the opening to use as file tape, thereby minimising the incentive to enter the facility using the type of micro-camera technology that is currently available for such operations. Little did we know when we started making our plans that the *Daily Telegraph* was already occupying rooms across the road in the Crest Hotel with cameras on tripods trained on the entrance to the injecting centre.

At the same time we continued to address all the other aspects of the operation that needed to be sorted out prior to opening. This included meeting with the relevant professional/industrial organisations representing MSIC staff—the NSW Nurses' Association and the Health and Research Employees' Association (HREA), which covers the health education officers/counsellors. We also invited WorkCover representatives to attend this meeting to show them through the premises and describe what each staff member's role would be in the various stages of the centre. We also invited these organisations to look through the 373 pages of policies and procedures. As employers of staff in what would be a very controversial program, we were conscious that there might be industrial issues specific to this work environment which we had not anticipated. We were particularly mindful that any claim for work-related stress would have to be taken very seriously, so we felt it was important to be proactive and engage such organisations sooner rather than later, before things went wrong, and not just cross our fingers and hope that there'd never be a problem.

We also intensified our efforts in showing various groups of people from the community through, because we realised that after the opening we'd be more restricted. Our policy was going to be that we would not allow visitors to view the service while it was operating. This was intended to prevent the zoo-like atmosphere that we imagined an injecting centre could quickly degenerate into.

Meanwhile I also participated in a seven-minute segment for the ABC's *Stateline* with Quentin Dempster on 26 April. I was filmed showing him through each of the three stages of the facility—the reception/assessment room, the injecting room and the after care area—describing exactly what would happen in each of these stages in quite a lot of detail. This ended up going to air on 4 May and was important for gaining significant additional public support. Apparently they got lots of feedback after it was aired, with many people commenting on how impressed they were that the facility would be very clinical and professional in approach.

This was an interesting piece of psychology for me. I suppose when you work in this area full-time you forget that most other people have a limited understanding of what drug users need and want, and just how desperate their lives can be. IDUs are at significant risk of death from drug overdose on a daily, if not hour-by-hour, basis, but are concerned enough about this that many would attend an injecting facility if it were available. Or at least that was our theory and these commentators were conceding that, if our theory was borne out, this in itself might justify the necessity for the centre's existence.

I must say that, at this stage, the degree of publicity surrounding the court case, the proclamation of the Act and now the imminent opening of the service, had become utterly daunting. I was experiencing quite a rapid increase in my own personal profile, which was new for me. Working in this politically sensitive end of the drugs field in Kings Cross for many, many years, I'd always deliberately avoided raising my personal profile or that of the Kirketon Road Centre, never seeing any advantage in this, just lots of disadvantages. But this was clearly no longer an option. The profile of the injecting centre was high and increasing; it was to be the only one in Australia and the first in the English-speaking world. As its medical director, I suppose I should have realised beforehand that I would become the public face of this new and controversial service, but it had never really occurred to me until now.

Those few weeks between the court verdict and actually opening the doors, while very intense and stressful, were also of course very exciting. Now at last we were going to do what we had actually been recruited and trained to do, in my case more than a year before. So, rather than being engaged in various court and political activities, for which I was not trained, it was a relief to be finally taking the last steps in service planning and seeing what we'd been speculating about for so long come to fruition. But by now I also knew that, if this thing fell over, it wouldn't do so quietly. I read somewhere that to succeed greatly, you have to risk failing greatly—well I sure was doing that!

It was at this point that we took steps to ensure that drug user expectations in the area were somewhere close to what the realities would be, so for a few weeks we held information sessions for IDUs at nearby Kirketon Road Centre.

We also decided to pre-register as many injecting drug users in the Kings Cross area as we could prior to opening the facility. One of the concerns of the local community was that there would be people over-crowding our waiting room and spilling back out (or 'vomiting' out, as Malcolm Duncan once put it!) onto the street, and we wanted to avoid this. This registration procedure had a clinical purpose. It elicited a medical history from each individual drug user attending the facility—their previous drug use, their history of treatment and its success or failure, their history of drug overdose and psycho-social issues that might be addressed by us, including housing, employment and income. It was also an important tool for the evaluation of the service as it provided a demographic profile of the segment of the drug-using population we would be making contact with and enabled analysis of their subsequent patterns of service use. I am unaware of any other injecting facilities in the world at this time that obtained this information in as systematic a way for all clients.

In the last week we recruited a group of drug users, about eight or so, to actually show through the facility. I was quite anxious about this step in the process, having worried about the acceptability of some of our policies, particularly the No Smoking policy, which we intended to at least start with. Not only did we appreciate that virtually all heroin injectors smoke cigarettes, but our consultation with drug user organisations had informed us that smoking immediately after a shot of heroin is almost always part of the whole injecting ritual. There is even a belief that it actually enhances the effect of the heroin—I suspect this is more psychological, but it is nonetheless real to IDUs. We were concerned that, if clients couldn't smoke afterwards, they either wouldn't use the facility at all or, if they did, that they would leave straight after injecting instead of being observed until fit to leave. This might result in an overdose occurring elsewhere, which would of course undermine what is the most important objective of the service.

We wanted to start out with a No Smoking policy not because we disapproved of smoking per se. (As a now thankfully ex-smoker of far too many years myself, this would have been hypocritical indeed!) Besides we appreciated that in the total scheme of things, smoking is less of an immediate health risk among heroin-dependent people than heroin and the various other drugs people use along with it and that one has to prioritse which addictions are dealt with first up on this basis. But, because the place was virtually windowless and we use oxygen, which is highly flammable, on the premises, there were potential occupational health issues for staff. When sites were being considered for the facility, it was hoped there could be a designated smoking area, preferably outside, such as a balcony. But none of the sites considered had the potential to accommodate this. So we took the view that, if indeed the No Smoking policy did affect client attendance or resulted in overdoses occurring elsewhere, we would drop it and install smoke extractors, or devise some other solution.

So we proceeded to show the group of IDUs through each stage of the facility and, by the time we got to Stage 3, their enthusiasm was unbridled. To see how pleased they were with the whole look and feel of the facility was one of the most exhilarating moments ever for me as a service planner. They expressed exactly the pride I hoped that they might feel about the facility. When I was finally brave enough to ask what they thought of the No Smoking policy, I was very pleasantly surprised by the strong response right across the board of 'Goodness, no, you wouldn't want someone "on the nod" [drowsy from drugs] here while smoking to burn a hole in these really nice chairs.' (This would also have been a real risk; quite a few drug users have died and others have serious scars from burns which have resulted from clothes or other items having caught fire from a lit cigarette dropped during a heroin overdose.)

Later I told the story about the IDUs wanting to keep the chairs nice to a friend, who said 'How sad to think that there's a middle-class, bourgeois person in everybody.' But, on the contrary, my view would be: *Thank goodness there is.* That appreciation of better things is what we appeal to and try to nurture among drug users, hoping that this will one day translate into a vision of a better life for themselves. I believe that environments like this can potentially dignify and validate those who use them and in so doing raise self-esteem and respect, necessary for turning such hopes into reality.

Some even suggested that the environment might be 'too nice' for this clientele, that they might not be comfortable in it, given what they're used to. I also feel very strongly that, just because many people who inject drugs end up living in squalid situations, it doesn't mean they prefer to. Health facilities for them should be just as well equipped and attractive as for the rest of the population. What's more, I also believe that people live up and down to the physical environment they find themselves in. At the risk of sounding patronising, these IDUs we showed through seemed to become a little more plumped up in this setting, which is quite attractive, courtesy of its previous life as an upmarket nightclub (with all the latest light fittings and contemporary stainless-steel and copper wall panels) and Karen's bold taste in furnishings and colour.

Then—having reassured me that no, they were in complete agreement with the No Smoking policy—they went on to ask whether perhaps there could be an exception made just on this day for them while they were viewing the facility. So I agreed to that and cigarette smoke filled Stage 3 for what would be the first and hopefully last time.

three

The first days

When we finally opened our doors at 6 pm on Sunday, 6 May 2001, we saw that the *Daily Telegraph* photographers, stationed for the last two weeks at the Crest Hotel over the road, weren't in position at their window; the curtains were drawn. As it turned out, a State of Origin rugby league match was on television that night; a record one million plus viewers watched this particular game in Sydney and I gather the photographers were among them, completely missing our grand opening. Even to us it seemed unfair, given all their efforts!

Our very first client, who did not arrive until about an hour later that night, came in off the street. He was somebody we did not know from other services in the area and in fact, when I first looked at him, I thought to myself: *This person looks under the age of eighteen; I can't believe it—we're actually going to have to exclude the very first person who came in on this night, on the basis of age.* One of the legislative requirements is that we cannot admit people under the age of eighteen. However, he turned out to be nineteen years old; it seems the reason why he looked so young to me was because he was not (yet) a street-based drug user.

We proceeded to register him in Stage 1 and he then went through to Stage 2 and injected heroin. He was a young labourer, and while he was still in employment, he was using increasing amounts of heroin—it had almost become a daily event. So he was working during the daytime and using heroin most evenings. Sometimes he would be in the Kings Cross area until quite late at night but had never been to any of the services to assist IDUs in the area. So staff took the opportunity to engage this young man about his pattern of increasing drug use. He then came back another time later on, and by the end of this second visit had agreed to accept our assistance getting into a drug treatment program.

The next client came down from K2, having been registered by one of our staff stationed up there. By this stage Kelly Burke, the on-call reporter for *Sydney Morning Herald* who earlier in the evening had tried to gain access to the centre, having been tipped off that tonight was the night, had realised that she was pretty spot-on and within the hour there were at least three television cameras stationed on the opposite side of the road trained on our front door. Meanwhile I had walked around the block and gone up to K2, promptly running into Malcolm Duncan, who was to become the ever-present Everywhere Man on this our first evening—somewhat daunting in itself.

The next two clients through came as a couple and were among the people we had seen talking with Kelly Burke across the road a short time before. Pip was a sex worker whose usual spot was right in front of the injecting centre, so in the weeks before we opened, our staff had got to know her quite well. Her photo had also been published in the *Telegraph* as part of a lead-up story about the MSIC earlier that week. Pip had been pre-registered but her male friend was not registered yet.

It was on this very first night that we also came to realise the difficulties that arise when one of a pair is registered and the other isn't. We also learned that staff shouldn't walk in and out through the client door between the first (reception) stage and the second (injecting room) stage—after we had allowed Pip to enter Stage 2, her friend managed to slip through behind her when a staff member came back out through that way. We also had a second problem—he seemed drug-affected, probably by a psycho-stimulant (cocaine or methamphetamine was our assessment), which also tends to increase people's potential to become aggressive. So we already had two issues with him going through to Stage 2—he was not yet a registered client and he also seemed drug-affected, one the of the MSIC's exclusion criteria. But he was very determined about going through to Stage 2 without delay, because it turned out that Pip was carrying the drugs for the both of them. We were to discover that this could be a problem for the client left behind, and a real one at that. Not infrequently clients would deliberately go through with the booty for both, knowing full well that their unregistered mate would be held up. They would then inject the lot and quickly exit from Stage 3 out the back while their mate was still angsting throughout the registration process in reception. Friendships based on drugs aren't usually very reliable.

So already within our first hours of operation we had to deal with a situation we considered had the potential to escalate into a crisis. I grabbed Arthur, the security guard on duty, and he and I both moved through to the second stage to confront this young man about the fact that he was not eligible to inject at the premises that evening, at least not until he registered and was more fully assessed for intoxication. Thankfully our crisis management skills were sufficient to avoid any aggression while persuading him to leave the facility without injecting.

Then, having seen him talking to the journalist beforehand, we became concerned—perhaps paranoid, some might suggest—that this male might have been wearing a listening device. So we asked Pip whether her companion had been wired—meaning wired for sound—and she emphatically agreed that indeed he was wired, thus confirming our worst suspicions. Our hearts sank. But then we ascertained that she was actually referring to the fact that he was drug-affected with a psycho-stimulant, for which the slang term is 'wired' as well. We all breathed a sigh of relief when Pip reassured us that, no, they weren't carrying any listening devices. This exchange had actually been a bit scary for us; we really didn't want something like this to become the first story to emerge about the injecting centre. So we were all very relieved when the clock finally reached 10 pm, which was when we had decided we would finish up that night.

I had meanwhile gone out and bought a few bottles of champagne for us to celebrate the end of the first shift. It had certainly been a very significant occasion for us. It also felt very strange for me, as a health care worker who had worked in this area for many, many years, to be supervising people in an activity like this, which was still illegal in all other circumstances. While we had, of course, always known that our clients engaged in this activity in a habitual way, to actually to be there and witness that from go to whoa was a first for all of us.

We saw a total of only eight clients on that first night, not one of whom was captured by the television cameras. We made the late news on Channel Ten, Fox News and the early news (6 am) on Channel Nine. But, as we'd hoped when we planned it this way, the story didn't break with anywhere near the sort of bang that it might have if we had opened in the morning with the whole day ahead for the story to gather momentum.

By about 11 o'clock our celebrations had pretty much run their course when we got a phone call from the outreach staff at Kirketon Road Centre to inform us that there had apparently been a drug overdose not far from the injecting facility some time after we had closed. Immediately after I hung up, the intercom at the front door buzzed and I thought it was possible that we were being called upon to assist with the overdose.

When I opened the door it was the on-call reporter for the *Daily Telegraph,* who had finally heard that we had opened. I merely confirmed that indeed we had operated earlier that evening and this appeared verbatim in the late edition of the *Daily Telegraph* the following day. I then saw Malcolm Duncan again, looming up behind the reporter, so I referred the reporter to Malcolm, who could probably be relied upon to give a fuller media interview, and he didn't disappoint. Malcolm also commented in the press that on the first night there were more bottles of champagne drunk at the injecting centre than drug users registered, so he must have seen me in the local bottle shop too!

Pat Kennedy had lined up space in the city to hold a press conference at nine thirty the following morning. As seemed to have become the pattern, very little notice needed to be given to get a large turnout to our press conferences. I felt for Pat at times like this. He would shake his head in amazement and tell us about how when he arranged press conferences for his other clients, with lots of notice, press releases and all the rest, he'd be lucky to get a handful of media along. While Pat, as a PR consultant, was normally engaged to increase his clients' public profile, we had employed him mainly to minimise ours, which was turning out to be quite a unique challenge for him.

I returned to the centre before midday to find many, many more TV cameras trained on the entrance on both sides of the road, including right outside the front door. The weather was also particularly inclement that day, rain bucketing down, cold and blustery, so we saw even fewer people. Only two clients came but, importantly, one was the young man who had been our very first client the night before. He ran the media gauntlet to pick up a referral letter to be assessed for buprenorphine treatment at the Langton Centre in Surry Hills as we had arranged.

During our first week of operation, Pat Kennedy remained posted with us at the injecting centre, receiving inquiries from no fewer than 150 media outlets—television, radio and print media—from all over the world. I was interviewed by media from as far away as South Africa, Ireland, Indonesia, Canada, the US and Mexico. We were featured on CNN and even America's *Sixty Minutes* wanted to do a piece, the story having gone out on Reuters and Associated Press, both international newsagencies.

Pat also distributed the videotape to the various media and I particularly remember reporter Fleur Bitcon from Channel Nine News complaining: 'But, Pat, these are just actors—we don't want actors.' Nonetheless, every single TV station did use this as a file tape on that evening's news.

The next day there were only a few cameras on the doorstep and that was pretty much it, something for which we were very grateful. As the media vanished, we saw an increase in the number of IDUs registering and attending the facility. Interestingly, we saw a lot of new clients whom we had never seen before, almost all of whom had heard about the facility through the media, which had been like a huge free advertising campaign. Normally it is considered most desirable that services like this are only advertised through word-of-mouth. But of course with MSIC we didn't have a choice in the matter.

The first full weekend was very quiet, especially on the Sunday when I also worked. Less than a handful of people came through. But we already noticed that it was going to be quite difficult to uphold the licence condition that we only let clients who were using the injecting centre take needle syringes away with them and not issue them to IDUs who weren't. Instead we were to refer such IDUs to nearby NSPs such as Kirketon Road Centre and K2. This was not a major problem during the week, but because we were operating on the weekend, when the local needle syringe services were not yet open, we were inundated with requests for clean needle syringes from IDUs who we then couldn't refer elsewhere.

Particularly at a time when we were trying to establish a relationship with local IDUs and engage them with the service, denying them needle syringes—when, of course, they knew we stocked them on site—seemed churlish and mean-spirited and unsurprisingly led to a not very happy response from these drug users. Some of them were willing to register at the injecting facility, which was a good thing, but others didn't necessarily want to inject right there and then, so left angry, accusing the staff of not caring whether they got HIV from having to then share someone else's injecting equipment. We were concerned from a duty-of-care perspective. This also raised staff safety issues, should someone get aggressive about it.

We considered lining up our weekend hours to coincide with other NSPs, which do not open until 2 pm on Saturday and Sunday. This would reduce the dilemma of having nowhere to refer people with genuine needs of this kind, but it seemed a pity not to be able to exploit this opportunity to actually extend the availability of needle syringes on the weekends in Kings Cross. I had already formally communicated my disagreement with this licence condition on public health grounds to the MSIC's two licensing authorities, the Director-General of the NSW Health Department and the NSW Police Commissioner, but to no avail. I now realised I would need to raise it with them again.

The other issue that became obvious at this early stage was that, as we saw with Pip and her friend, most drug users buy their drugs jointly because they are sold in quantities that are usually enough for several injections. So, while we allowed people to use an injecting booth together, providing they arrived together, they were not allowed to divide their drugs on site because this might constitute drug supply. According to the amendment of the *Drug Misuse and Trafficking Act 1985* specific to the MSIC, people on the premises of the injecting centre (and nowhere else) are exempt from being charged with self-administration of an illicit substance or possession of a personal quantity of an illicit substance. However, supply to others most definitely remains a crime at the MSIC and, in the event of a person not ceasing and desisting, the staff are required to report this to the police, or else risk being charged themselves with aiding and abetting a crime.

I raised this issue with Peter Zahra SC, the legal expert on our Policy Advisory Committee, who advised that any exchange of drugs among clients could indeed constitute supply, even without money changing hands. However, he said that where drugs had been purchased jointly and were then divided, as in this situation, it would usually be deemed to be joint possession when it came before the courts. But, while the court magistrate has discretion in such a matter, neither we nor the police did. So the onus on staff would be to refer any such incident to the police who would then charge the person with drug supply, thereby referring it to the courts, where it was likely to be deemed joint possession and dropped. Of course, this was a path we wanted to avoid since it would have quickly made the service unacceptable to injecting drug users.

However, Peter also reminded me that the injecting centre's internal management protocols, which were approved by both licensing authorities (including the NSW Police Commissioner), clearly indicated that there would sometimes be two clients injecting in a booth together without any specific staff procedure to investigate the source of clients' illicit drugs. Given that it was not our usual practice to hover over clients when they first sat down at the booths anyway, it was unlikely that we would necessarily see the division of the drugs in the course of things, so he further advised that under these circumstances, staff would only be at risk of being charged with aiding and abetting drug supply if they ignored overt signs of supply (such as seeing drugs actually being divided, money changing hands or people moving from one booth to another carrying drugs clearly obtained from one client and being given to another).

Staff would have to be vigilant, mindful and diligent in policing such overt signs, but would not be required to do more than what was stated in the relevant section of the internal management protocols. We would also emphasise to clients that drugs shouldn't be divided and hope the clients could somehow adapt to that, although I wasn't sure how. There were few alternatives. Perhaps the dealers could start selling in much smaller quantities, but that would be fiddly—it would increase not only drug wastage but also the number of transactions and therefore the risk of apprehension of buyers and sellers by police. Perhaps people could divide up before they got to the facility, but this was also unlikely to appeal, given that drugs are usually divided by first dissolving them in water and then drawing that solution up in needle syringes, using the calibrations on the syringe to mete out the proportion for each joint purchaser. Once drawn up in a needle syringe, it would be very impractical and also risky to carry it like that to the injecting centre for the final step of injection, and way more simple to just whack it up right there and then, end of story.

Peter also advised me to make a diary entry to indicate that I had specifically consulted him and the advice he gave, this way reducing my personal liability in this regard. I really appreciate how Peter tries to protect us like this. He also tries really hard to find solutions for us rather than just identifying the roadblock. Peter is the Senior Defender at the NSW Public Defenders office and wrote a text book on Drug Laws in NSW, which we now refer to a lot. Like us, he really seems to hope this initiative will work.

But I realised that we were going to be operating in a rather grey area here and that this was the kind of issue that would ultimately need to be clarified, so I also referred it for further discussion at our next Police Advisory Committee meeting. If we were to continue beyond the 18-month trial, further legislation would need to be drafted, so hopefully at least then this new legislation could address this issue. While I knew by now that the protocols which had been so carefully prepared ahead of time had not dealt with absolutely every challenge that would face us in the weeks and months ahead, all things considered, they were doing okay so far.

four

One whole month

From the second week of the operation of the Medically Supervised Injecting Centre I began to record a taped 'diary' of this extraordinary and unique trial. What follows are edited excerpts from this log of events.

Monday, 14 May 2001

Having now already seen a significant number of clients injecting at the centre, it strikes us all that the injecting episode not infrequently becomes quite a bloody one. It is now easier to understand why there's such an ongoing high incidence of hepatitis C infection among the injecting population despite the needle syringe program. It would seem—even among quite experienced injectors and those with reasonably easy-to-inject veins—that their injecting technique is quite poor. Particularly when people are getting frustrated with not being able to find a vein or when they're withdrawing from heroin and becoming edgy, within a short space of time the needle syringe becomes full of blood, various pieces of injecting equipment end up all over the place and covered in blood, hands and arms become covered in blood and risks are taken, knowingly or unknowingly. It seems to us that, if this can happen in this controlled, injecting centre environment, goodness only knows how much worse it must be when people are injecting in a back lane, between two parked cars, in poor lighting, especially at night time with the ever-present threat of somebody, including the police, interrupting things.

The risk of coming into contact with another IDU's blood during the injecting episode has also brought home the need to promote hand-washing, both before and after injecting, and to specifically advise people not to touch one another's injecting sites or equipment—especially not with bloodied hands—because there may be a risk of hepatitis C transmission, for example. There seems to be a certain comfortable familiarity or kinship generated by the sight of each other's blood among drug users—perhaps a 'blood brother' thing, unlike for most of the population, who are usually put off by it.

I'm pleased that clients by and large have so far readily agreed to wash their hands before and after injecting. When we decided to install the basins in the hope of introducing hand-washing into the injecting ritual, I had concerns that asking people to wash their hands would be met with 'thanks, but no thanks'. But that hasn't been the case; people have been very cooperative. Perhaps because it's still early days and drug users don't have too many preconceived ideas about the service (there never having been one like this before), they seem rather tentative and quite compliant with the various policies. Like us, the clients seem to be pinching themselves to check that the service is for real. But one also gets the impression that they still don't quite trust it and wouldn't be surprised if one day the police jumped out from behind the counter and arrested them all, saying it was just an elaborate trick!

This tentativeness is something that will probably only be temporary so we appreciate the need to maximise this opportunity to try to establish healthier behaviour rituals at the injecting centre.

I suppose it should not be all that surprising that drug users don't have pristine injecting practices. While they have been advised not to share needles for years, unlike health professionals, they haven't been formally trained in how to inject into a vein. They have usually learnt to inject (badly) from their peers (who had learnt from their own peers) in far from clinical circumstances. Injecting yourself—with only one hand, sometimes with your left (non-dominant) hand—is also much more difficult than injecting someone else using both hands, as doctors do. For some people it can take a very long time; they often end up puncturing their skin in many different places, many times. Very occasionally it almost verges on self-mutilation, not uncommon in this population, especially among those who have been sexually and physically abused. We always intervene in these circumstances.

Otherwise we stand back to start with, but after a time suggest that they give it a break, or try another mode of administration, such as taking it orally or by subcutaneous (known as 'skin-popping') or intramuscular injection, depending on the drug. Unlike in Europe, these other ways to inject are rarely practised among IDUs in Australia, where the culture of intravenous injecting has always been very strong among heroin users. This situation of people running out of patent veins to inject that haven't already been damaged is also seen by us as a good opportunity to suggest that it might be timely to have a break from injecting drugs altogether.

Another aspect of our experience so far is how difficult it is for us as health professionals to actually watch people inject. It's quite agonising to see people getting frustrated, particularly when, as a clinician supervising the activity, you know that within a few seconds you could probably site that needle in the vein and the agony would be over for both you and the client.

We sought advice from Peter Zahra as to what the legal situation is as far as us assisting in this way. According to the amended *Drug Misuse and Trafficking Act*, it is not illegal for drug users to self-administer an illicit substance at the MSIC; however, 'administration of another' remains a crime here as it is elsewhere. Therefore even staff allowing clients to inject each other would be aiding and abetting a crime. This we already understood. But as far as what constitutes 'administration', we figured that it would include pushing the plunger of the syringe containing the drug, but wondered if it also included just siting the needle in the person's vein. Peter's advice is that this might indeed also be regarded as administration. He also warned that in that event, should the person subsequently overdose and die for whatever reason, we could be liable to a manslaughter charge. This clearly meant that we would have to remain completely hands-off in this regard.

We discussed all this at our team meeting and worked through the issues, finally realising that, even if we were legally allowed to site the needle in certain cases, this would to a large extent be meeting our own needs rather than the clients'. Clients in this situation have poor injecting technique; if we were to step in we wouldn't necessarily be improving this at all—in fact we may be doing the reverse.

Our guiding public health principle is that we should be promoting behaviours which not only decrease health risks at the injecting centre, but will also be translated into other situations. The injecting centre is only going to be open for eight hours a day during the trial and this necessarily means that injecting drug users who attend will be injecting in other circumstances at other times. We will have achieved very little if the benefits derived from attending the MSIC are all undone in other circumstances. A service model that assisted injection among injecting drug users might also promote a service dependency, which would also be undesirable.

So, since we need to inform people where they are going wrong in a way that doesn't involve actually demonstrating how to do it on the client, we have decided to buy an artificial arm with lifelike veins—apparently these are used in America to train health care workers. We would use it to demonstrate safer injecting techniques.

Because there is such a large range of problems with injecting technique, we have also decided that we need to approach this systematically at a broader client population level. So, rather than attempting to point out the flaws to each client as they go, which wouldn't be feasible and might also put clients off, staff will develop a different health promotional message each fortnight specifically targeting the injecting behaviours they see as being most problematic at that time. This targeted message will be communicated in various ways throughout the centre, including being depicted on laminated posters in every injecting booth. These messages will then be rotated to maximise the client base's exposure to them across time. We also hope that these will be disseminated more widely to the clients' injecting peers, who may not use the MSIC, and to other services for drug users. We will then evaluate how effective this strategy is in reducing the presence of blood and risk of hep C transmission during the injecting episode.

The feedback from clients in this regard is that they are amazed the staff at the MSIC are willing to witness this at all, and glean from this that they are truly non-judgmental. They say things like: 'You guys see us here at our absolute worst [and we do] but you're still here for us. You really must care.' This extra credibility that seems to come with this particular turf is especially important when it comes to advising clients to seek treatment for their drug dependence. They know that we do not have a moralistic agenda, but that we are purely concerned for their health, so they are more likely to trust our advice. We hope this translates into more appropriate, and therefore effective, referrals to drug treatment programs.

Thursday, 17 May

It was my special pleasure to show Dr Margaret Rihs-Middel from Bern in Switzerland through the injecting facility today. Margaret was one of the investigators on the heroin prescription trials that started in Switzerland in 1994. She was particularly impressed with the physical environment at our centre and thinks it would also suit a heroin prescription trial. I must admit that the thought had also crossed my mind that, if this trial falls over, the site could easily be converted to this purpose. However, given Prime Minister John Howard's strident opposition to such trials occurring in Australia, I doubt this would come to pass in the foreseeable future.

As a researcher in this field, Margaret is surprised that the evaluation of our service has started from the very first day of operation, rather than waiting until service utilisation by clients has reached representative levels, which, especially given the media attention we have had, may take some time yet. But the legislation only allowed for an 18-month trial, so I gather there was a view that there was no time to waste. I hope that the research team does take this into account in their evaluation.

Friday, 25 May

We have already had two separate visits from people stating that they are diabetic and wanting to inject insulin at the centre, claiming that there are very few places in Kings Cross to do this. Most public toilets in the area, and even private toilets in restaurants, have been closed as part of a strategy to reduce drug use over the last few years. Like putting in blue lighting in public places, which makes veins harder to see, this has just moved injecting to even less safe situations, but what is out of sight is out of mind.

We are sensitive to the fact that some years ago the diabetic lobby had issue with the full funding of needle syringes for drug users. At that time the government was only partly subsidising these for diabetics, although this policy changed two years ago and they are now provided free to diabetics too. Because we didn't want to inflame that situation the policy at the local needle syringe service was to provide free injecting equipment to diabetics who presented there.

On both of these occasions at the injecting centre we have not wanted to turn these diabetics away. Besides, it may well be that it is difficult to find places to inject insulin subcutaneously as insulin-dependent diabetics are required to do, sometimes several times a day. But, rather than formally registering both of these individuals as clients of the injecting centre and having them inject in the injecting room of the facility among the other IDUs, we allowed them to use the client assessment room, just off the reception area, which they did. I also wonder though, if our policies in this regard weren't being tested. We shall see.

We've had our first pet animal through the service—a rabbit called Winky, who lives in the backpack of one of our female clients. Seeing Winky hopping about among the injecting booths today was again something new and very different.

Monday, 28 May

At this early stage we're quite surprised to see the relatively high level of cocaine injecting that's occurring at the MSIC. Many heroin users are substituting cocaine for heroin since heroin became harder to come by earlier this year. I had anticipated that the facility would not suit the injection of cocaine, which usually occurs in a binge-like fashion, because of cocaine's very brief pharmacological effect and its psycho-stimulant nature. Specifically to prevent binge use occurring at the centre, our protocols only allow people to inject once per visit and for this reason I thought those wanting to inject cocaine, which typically involves multiple injections on any one occasion, would find this protocol unacceptable and inject elsewhere.

While I regarded this as a pity in a way, knowing that cocaine binges are associated with very significant harm which the MSIC might reduce, I felt that we needed to accept that we would not be able to be all things to all people and would have to draw the line somewhere. I wasn't willing to allow cocaine bingeing here because one of the harms is that people can develop acute psychosis and become a safety risk to both themselves and others. The safety of all clients and staff being of paramount importance, I thought it would be negligent to allow behaviours at the facility that had a high probability of endangering this.

While clients can only inject once per visit, they can leave the facility and then re-present and, providing they are not assessed as 'intoxicated' (one of the service exclusion criteria), they can then be readmitted to the facility. The assessment of a client's level of intoxication is made by the nurse at reception and involves careful observation of speech, gait and other psychomotor skills. By and large, people who inject cocaine, in the early stages anyway, wouldn't usually be assessed as being intoxicated as such so would be readmitted. But I had predicted that this procedure—being required to leave and literally go around the block and then re-present to the reception staff for assessment—would be very unappealing. While it hasn't happened all that often, it does seem that some people are willing to go to these lengths to use the facility. Among them, this policy of only allowing the one injection per visit has the effect of slowing things down and thereby allowing us to identify the earliest signs of psychosis. These are often manifest as becoming fearful of leaving the facility, thinking the police are out the back, or suspecting that the music speakers on the wall are a form of surveillance. So, we're able to use this as an opportunity to reality-test them. It is only in this very early stage of the paranoid state that there is still some insight, and advice may be heeded. It really is the last occasion that you have to stem the onset of cocaine-induced psychosis. Once a person has become psychotic they have necessarily lost all insight. Then, even our advice to stop the binge just feeds further into that paranoid state. So it would seem that a protocol that I thought would potentially exclude cocaine injecting at the MSIC is turning out to be somewhat therapeutic in itself, either stopping the binge altogether or at least slowing it right down to allow our intervention.

Not having predicted a heroin shortage in association with a burgeoning supply of cocaine, I'm now also having to develop clinical protocols to manage the other manifestations of cocaine overdose (or toxicity as it is often referred to). These range from headache, sweatiness, nausea and vomiting through to high blood pressure, chest pain and palpitations (from coronary artery spasm and abnormal heart rhythms) and in some instances seizures (fits). When clients develop any of these symptoms, we move them into the resuscitation area for close observation, darken the room, make it quiet, administer oxygen, and regularly monitor their blood pressure, pulse and temperature while speaking to them in a calm and reassuring way to relax them. The upside of cocaine being so short-acting is that the toxic effects usually pass reasonably quickly, generally within 30 minutes. However, if a seizure were to occur, we would call an ambulance to transport them to the local hospital for at least four hours' observation, until their level of consciousness returns to normal.

We're also arranging to get the doors between the three stages to close more slowly so they don't slam shut too loudly. We've found that people injecting cocaine, in particular, are very sensitive to noises and get quite jumpy with any sudden loud noise. I'm surprised by this. I had always assumed that because cocaine is a psycho-stimulant, those using it would like stimulating environments—loud music, dancing and so on. It's a dance party drug, isn't it? But it would seem that, when injected at higher doses, cocaine causes users to become very, very sensitive to sound. Apparently some of the European injecting rooms even provide ear muffs to prevent cocaine injectors from becoming unduly irritable which, given the other effects of cocaine, can also lead to aggressive behaviour. But at this stage we haven't seen users here get too aggressive, probably again because, unlike the European rooms, we have this policy restricting the number of injections per visit.

We've only just had a sound system installed throughout the facility, because we don't want there to be deathly silence either, so now there're various discussions among staff about what sort of music is most appropriate and some complaints that Andy puts on too much reggae!

We're pleased to note at this early stage that policing around the facility has been very appropriate—there haven't been any unwarranted patrols but nor has there been a no-go zone observed as far as policing drug supply in the immediate vicinity, which is consistent with the local policing guidelines that have been specially developed for this initiative. While there is still some concern among clients about police surveillance of the facility, this doesn't seem to be based on reality—nobody has been apprehended upon entering or leaving the facility to date.

Many of our staff work in other services nearby and they report that they are seeing people here who have never previously used those other services. It is through the injecting centre that these drug users are now gaining access to health advice for the first time. They have almost all invariably injected in the Kings Cross area before this but, perhaps because some are still relatively new to drug use, they haven't yet recognised that they already have a health problem or are at risk of developing one, so they aren't yet fronting up to the existing health services. So the injecting centre is also offering an early intervention, potentially preventing the downward spiral from eventuating amongst this hidden, hard-to-reach population—and, of course, we know that the earlier an intervention, the more likely it is to be effective. Once people become homeless, street-based, and involved in prostitution and crime, it is far more difficult to effect any sustained change in their drug-using lifestyle because they have usually already lost their existing relationships and come adrift from the previous social supports so necessary to prevent relapses to drug use.

One of the potential benefits of injecting centres is that—because they don't pitch themselves to drug users as being health services per se, but rather as places where these people can engage in an activity which elsewhere is less safe and illegal—they have the ability to 'net-widen' the population engaged with health services. The aim from a public health perspective is always to widen the net as much as possible. I had been anxious that this project wouldn't be able to achieve this because of the scrutiny it's been under, fearing that this more hidden population would also be more concerned about maintaining their anonymity and prefer to stay underground. The MSIC is anonymous, but nonetheless requires you to walk in through the front door and provide some information to staff and then sit in an open booth, with other IDUs walking through at the same time. However, it would seem this has not been a deterrent. We are finding that often these people have never previously had any discussion with a health professional about their drug use. While they may have a family GP, they often don't want to discuss their drug use with that person because they feel ashamed and worry about their confidentiality being maintained.

We're also finding that the policy not allowing neck-injecting has had to be enforced. We hadn't realised that people in the Kings Cross area injected into their necks to any extent. While only a few probably do, those who do have been attending the injecting centre in numbers because they probably figure that we will be able to provide them with expert assistance in this regard. From this we can also summise that we are probably seeing that part of the injecting population that has the more significant vein problems. However, we have had to inform them that we don't allow neck injecting.

Again, I felt that this was an 'unhealthy behaviour', that could never be made safe. Not only shouldn't it be assisted but should be actively discouraged, given all the vital neural and vascular structures in the neck. We have found that on every occasion so far, we've been able to locate another more peripheral vein to use, which also raises the credibility of the service overall among our target population of high-risk injectors.

Meanwhile we've also had a report from a member of the community that someone from the Chamber of Commerce was allegedly seen rummaging about in our garbage bin out the back, so we do seem to be of continuing interest to them!

Friday, 1 June

We had a government working group meeting today. It's a great pleasure to finally be able to report to this group how the centre is operating, after meeting for more than a year to talk about whether we would ever finally get to operate at all.

Also pleasing was the final resolution of another issue that has been difficult to negotiate. We have always wanted to ensure that people who were referred into drug treatment programs would be fast-tracked and funded so they had good access to such treatment. That has now been agreed to. We were concerned that when we did make referrals, people wouldn't actually be able to get a place in a program, given that capacity in the treatment sector is still pretty tight. Our ability to refer people to treatment is a very important indicator of success for our project and is being measured as part of our service evaluation.

At this meeting I also raised the issue of providing needle syringes to IDUs not necessarily using the MSIC at that time, particularly when other services are closed on the weekend. The Chief Health Officer, Dr Andrew Wilson, undertook to pursue this with the Director-General of Health, but his own view was that we would have a duty of care during such times, particularly when we have them there on the premises, given the public health risk that is potentially posed by IDUs then having to re-use injecting equipment.

Tuesday, 5 June

An issue that's arisen now is that people often come in groups of more than two. Stage 2 has injecting booths that accommodate up to two people; however, if a person comes on their own, it is our policy that they get a booth on their own. We don't put people together who don't arrive together because we don't want to create drug-using networks where they don't already exist. When people come as a pair, we allow them to use a booth together. This is because we encourage people to use in the company of others to reduce the risk of drug overdose death in otherwise unsupervised circumstances, even though we also appreciate that it introduces the possibility of people coming into contact with each other's blood—advertently or inadvertently—and hence HIV or hepatitis B and C transmission. But again, we want to simulate real-life (out of the MSIC) situations and then try to improve the behaviours that occur from the point of view of risk, including the sharing of injecting equipment, and have this translate to all other situations people find themselves in, thereby potentially having an impact beyond the MSIC.

But at times people come in threes and fours and want to use the same booth, which is impractical. So we're having to ensure that when more than two people arrive together we first of all break them up into pairs and allow no more than two to go through to the second (injecting room) stage at a time. The staff there also need to be able to marry up the information that's been entered onto the database in the first stage—the last drug used and what's going to be used now—with the individual presenting in the second stage, so as to be able to direct supervision towards those most at risk of overdose. With several people walking in together that's more difficult to do, so we need to hold things back in the first (reception) stage.

Today we saw two people coming in through the front door and next thing they were being pulled backwards, which was a curious sight in itself. Shortly afterwards, these same clients came back in. It turned out that the police had not realised that they were entering the injecting centre—walking in through the front door would most certainly be regarded as being 'in the immediate vicinity' of the facility, in which case, according to the guidelines, police are allowed to apply discretion as far as charging someone with possession of a personal quantity of drugs. When the two men were searched and each found to be in possession of only one cap of heroin each, they were allowed to proceed into the service.

This is the first and only incident we've had to date in which police have impeded clients' entry into the service. However, when they realised it was the injecting centre, the police rightly applied their discretion and, in so doing, sent a very strong message to our client base. It is important for us, particularly at this early stage, to gain the confidence of IDUs in the area—they need to feel that they can walk in without fear of being apprehended. By the end of their visit these two clients had told all and sundry of this unique experience they had had so, with the grapevine being such an effective communication tool in this population, it was a good outcome.

Lots of members of the community have also been coming in through the front door to let us know that they are supportive of the facility and to congratulate us on how it's gone to date. One of these was Steven Spears, who wrote the play *The Elocution of Benjamin Franklin*. He brought a bottle of champagne, no less, for the staff.

It's gestures like these that lift our spirits. I hate to admit that I would never think of doing something spontaneous like that but, when someone else does it, it reminds you that you should think of doing it yourself now and then.

Thursday, 7 June

We've made it to one month! It's now, at this one-month mark, that we are extending our hours. We will now run for a continuous eight-hour day, from 10 o'clock in the morning until 6 pm, to see how that goes.

Up to now, operating four-hour shifts has proven feasible. Staff have not found it too stressful; we are making sure to rotate staff between the different stages of the facility, so that they don't spend all their time in the injecting room part, which is the most full on.

The last of the unusual challenges of these first few weeks was when someone turned up with his heroin in a tiny balloon held in his mouth, probably the most common place drug users hide drugs, especially when the sniffer dogs are in town. When he was washing his hands over the basin prior to injecting in the second stage, he accidentally let this balloon drop out of his mouth and it washed down into the S-bend of the washbasin. He turned off the tap immediately, assured staff that he had once worked as a plumber, then proceeded to detach the S-bend and miraculously found the missing balloon of heroin. Less miraculously, he was unable to thread the S-bend back on so we had to call out a plumber to fix it. Such are the highs, lows and funny twists as we have experienced them in our first month.

Finally establishing our routine

Wednesday, 13 June 2001

Our first one-month clinical activity report shows that there's been about five hundred visits; 60 per cent of these were male and 40 per cent female. Heroin was the most common drug injected but this was only just higher than cocaine, which was injected on 39 per cent of occasions. This seems quite high, even higher than we believed the prevalence of cocaine-injecting to be in the local area.

Cocaine and heroin are substitutable drugs in Kings Cross, which is surprising given that their effects are quite the opposite of each other, heroin being a depressant and cocaine being a stimulant. But strangely, as we have seen in the past, when heroin supply has gone down, cocaine use has gone up, and vice versa. This may be an indicator of just how desperate IDUs in Kings Cross are, particularly during this heroin shortage, which started early this year. Instead of planning to use a drug based on its effects, drug users are buying whatever injectable powder is being sold from the first dealer they come across. So unfortunately the heroin shortage is far from being one big good-news story.

Clearly the supply of cocaine in Kings Cross has been unaffected during this period. Since both drugs are imported from overseas, this suggests that the heroin shortage is not a result of improved interdiction by Australian Federal Customs Police. For the same reason, it is also unlikely to be the result of policing at the local level. It is noteworthy that police haven't rushed in to take credit for the shortage either, probably realising that it may soon lift, as it always has in the past, and not wanting to then have to assume responsibility for this as well.

In the first month the most attendances by any one person was nineteen, and four heroin overdoses were successfully managed using oxygen alone. To date we haven't needed to use naloxone (more commonly known by its trade name, Narcan), the drug used to reverse the central nervous system (CNS) depressant effects of heroin. That's been because the overdoses have been very quickly recognised before the person stopped breathing completely, enabling the reversal of the respiratory depressant effects of heroin by administering oxygen by mask only. By contrast, in the community setting overdoses are not usually identified until much later, when the person stops breathing altogether, becomes blue due to lack of oxygen in the blood, and loses consciousness. By this stage administering oxygen by mask only is no longer effective because the person is not able to breathe in the oxygen needed in order for it to be delivered to the brain receptors affected by heroin.

Wednesday, 20 June

I got an urgent call late this afternoon from John Della Bosca's office informing me that the minister was before the Cost Estimates Committee and that the issue of the cost of the injecting centre was being raised and was likely to be picked up by the press. Our initial cost estimates were made soon after the Drug Summit and well before a service model was even developed. Because of the delays and the court actions, our start-up costs have exceeded those initial estimates. So I am advised to be ready for negative media tomorrow morning.

This evening we had our first community consultation committee meeting since we commenced operations and I warned members that it's likely we will be getting bad press tomorrow. I also briefed them thoroughly about the costs of the centre and assured them that our recurrent costs are quite comparable—in fact less—than those of other services in the area, such as Kirketon Road Centre, St Vincent's Alcohol and Drug Service and the Langton Centre.

We are funding just eight staff a day for an eight-hour shift and all of these staff work under state awards so there are no hidden costs. Apart from that, we do pay a hefty rent on the building but it is in fact $100 000 less than what the people we are subleasing from pay the owner of the property. So, it's well below market price for a shopfront CBD property in Kings Cross.

Thursday, 21 June

Pat Kennedy, our media consultant, rang me first thing in the morning, saying that he had already had numerous media inquiries. So we decided to deal with these at a press conference again, which is proving to be the most efficient way of handling multiple media enquiries all at one time. We scheduled this for 10 am, right after the evaluation committee meeting I needed to attend. I took this opportunity to inform members of the evaluation team what was going to take place and that we would also be reporting our one-month figures in an attempt to keep a human perspective about our costs. By the end of the day the media was no longer running a cost blowout story, but rather a four lives saved story.

While the four overdoses we have successfully managed in our first month were *potentially* 'lives saved', they don't necessarily equate to 'four lives saved' and I very deliberately avoided saying this. But already at this early stage it's apparent that the media are very comfortable with equating it. It is certainly true that, if these overdoses had occurred in unsupervised circumstances, which presumably otherwise would have been the case, then the outcomes would have been less likely to have been as benign and could well have included death. We know that when an overdose occurs in an unsupervised situation, it's really in the lap of the gods as to whether, first, it's identified and then, second, an ambulance is called and, third, whether the ambulance arrives in time to reverse the damage, especially to the brain and other vital organs. This damage commences within minutes of an overdose occurring, as a result of hypoxia (low oxygen levels) from not breathing. There is a tendency to focus only on the most devastating outcome of overdose, i.e. death, and not on the other organ damage that can occur from sustained hypoxia. There are studies which show that drug users who have multiple heroin overdoses become increasingly cognitively impaired. The early treatment with oxygen afforded by the supervised injecting centre setting also prevents this from happening.

As a result of all this, the media were back on our doorstep this morning, but we also noted that in all the TV news reports this evening there was heavy reliance on the file tape that Pat had originally provided. Again there were grimaces, particularly from Andy (who pretends to be a client on the tape), but also from Damian and Colette, that yet again their faces are appearing on TV. I am glad I opted out of being involved in that tape.

Wednesday, 27 June

At our team meeting we discussed a number of recent client injecting episodes. In one of these a client accidentally dropped his drugs into the sharps safe, which is the big yellow container where used needle syringes are disposed of after injecting. Without thinking, he thrust his bare hands into the safe to rescue his drugs, risking needlestick injury from other people's used needles. Such is the desperation around drugs. In fact on this occasion the client then proceeded to empty all of the contents of the sharps safe out onto the floor, which then put staff and other clients at risk as well. This is the kind of unexpected drama we sometimes have to deal with.

Another client, when asked at the front what drug he was intending to use, said he couldn't really say; it'd depend on what he'd be able to buy inside. Needless to say, we informed him that drugs were not supplied at the MSIC and he left.

We don't check people's drugs before they inject at centre and, even if we did, we'd have no way of knowing what they were or anything about their quality. A frequently asked question is whether we test the quality of the drugs; people are often surprised that we don't, and that we're not particularly interested in doing that either. Apart from the fact that the technology doesn't exist to do it quickly, drug quality it is only one part of the equation anyway. In line with the scientific literature, we're finding that an individual's tolerance is the most important indicator of the risk for overdose. What other drugs have been taken beforehand is very important as they can increase the effect of heroin and impair clients' ability to assess their own tolerance. This is why we ask people about what they last used, how much and when this was, and what they are injecting on this occasion.

We've also found that overdoses are more likely to occur when people have taken a long-acting benzodiazepine, such as Valium or Rohypnol, even as long ago as 24 hours earlier. They may then present to us showing no signs of intoxication, but the drug is still in their system. Using heroin, another CNS depressant, on top of this then places them at higher risk of overdose. This really impresses upon us the need to get that message out— that drug users should not just rely on how they feel, but also look at exactly what else they've used in the last 24 hours.

The same goes for alcohol. People can have had just one or two beers in the six hours before and not feel at all alcohol-affected, but this seems to be enough to tip some people over if they then have a shot of heroin on top of it.

So while excluding people from the centre on the basis of intoxication is an important first step, it's by no means the last step as far as preventing overdose. When overdoses do occur, as well as counselling them afterwards, we flag the person's registration number. Then, the next time they visit, we counsel them again about that event and how to prevent it from recurring. In this way the service is not only reducing the morbidity and mortality among overdoses by administering treatment immediately, but it is also helping to prevent them from occurring at all. By increasing drug users' awareness of these risks, we hope to also reduce the rate of overdoses at the facility and elsewhere across time.

Also this week a drug sniffer dog search occurred outside, in the entrance alcove to the injecting centre. We asked the police to move a few metres down the street so that they weren't actually impeding access to the facility, which they agreed to do. We also reported this to the local police command and they said that they would follow it up. But one of the problems in this instance is that the drug sniffer dog operations are directed from the regional level and undertaken by police who are not acquainted with the local situation so are not necessarily aware of where the injecting centre is.

We deliberately haven't put any signage on the facility to say what it is. Many people complain that they walk straight past because it is so innocuous among the various street-frontages in this part of central Kings Cross, which of course was our intention. But the downside is that the police, at least on this occasion, unknowingly chose the alcove of our entrance to conduct a body search.

It would be inappropriate for the injecting centre to interfere with policing of drug supply on the main street of Kings Cross, especially given that this is the part of Kings Cross where drug supply is the most concentrated. The very reason we argued that we needed to locate the injecting centre in a central area was because we knew that drug users inject as soon after they procure their drugs as they can. This was confirmed by the fact that the main street is where there was also the highest number of heroin overdoses and deaths in the Kings Cross area (or NSW for that matter). Now that the injecting centre is in this very central location, it would be wrong for us to expect the police to stop policing supply in the vicinity, which of course is very much their duty and in itself ought not to interfere with the operation of the injecting centre anyway. These efforts should operate together in a complementary way, in keeping with the harm-minimisation approach, which incorporates the reduction of drug supply, the reduction of demand for drugs and the reduction of harm associated with their use.

I support a high visibility community policing approach to curtail the supply of highly addictive and harmful drugs like heroin and cocaine in Kings Cross. When you see first hand the havoc they wreak in people's lives, more of these drugs being available more cheaply is a horrifying prospect.

On the other hand I see little point in criminalising drug use per se since this doesn't stop people from using drugs and instead just drives it underground, which makes it harder to address drug users' health and social issues. The prison system most definitely isn't a healthy place for drug users to end up either.

We have found that the use of drug sniffer dogs—which are better at detecting cannabis possession than any other type of drug and don't distinguish suppliers from users—has been having a very dramatic effect on the presence of drug users on the main street of Kings Cross. After a dog patrol has gone past, we sometimes don't see any clients for an hour or two. This is somewhat counterproductive but at least the effect is not sustained, certainly not from one day to the next. But we're going to have to keep an eye on how this new mode of policing drugs affects utilisation of the facility over time.

Monday, 2 July

We have now entered the third phase in establishing the hours of operation at the injecting centre. As of today we're operating from 12 midday until 4 pm. We then close for two hours and open again until 10 pm.

Every second Wednesday we hold a team meeting between the two sessions. On the other Wednesdays, we have clinical supervision sessions run by David Leary, a clinical psychologist who heads up the Come-In Youth Resource Centre in Paddington. Clinical supervision is undertaken by many services in this field, to help staff make sense of their work and its limitations at both a personal and professional level. It's a process that encourages clinicians to vent their frustrations and concerns about their work with clients, on a group or individual basis.

David and I have had a very long professional association; he's worked with this same client group for more than twenty years and has a lot of experience with clinical supervision. We have decided that, given the nature of the work and our inability to predict its effects on staff working here, we should, at least to begin with, provide clinical supervision on a group basis. Because we employ over thirty staff, all on a part-time basis, it wouldn't be practical to offer it on an individual basis. Unfortunately though, only certain staff work on Wednesdays and so this limits access to such supervision. So we are encouraging staff to come in on their days off and take the time off at another time, but we appreciate that, particularly in the interests of maintaining their psychological health, it may be better for them to just have the day off. So we'll see how it goes.

The fact that staff are all part-time and at no one time do they all come together is proving to be frustrating in lots of different ways, particularly for both communication and training. We use email, of course, to circulate minutes of all meetings, but things like clinical supervision and training cannot happen by correspondence. There's no apparent way around this, given the structure of the team and the service.

This evening I hosted a visit from a very large group of community members, which was organised by the Community Drug Action Team. Called The Walk-Around, it involves members of the community coming to visit the various frontline services for drug users in the area to inform them about how they operate. Afterwards one of the women who was part of the group drew me aside and thanked me for providing the facility. She explained that her daughter has been a long-term IDU in the area and that she's tried everything to get her daughter into a drug treatment program but so far nothing had been successful. She's most grateful that a facility like the injecting centre exists, which at least can keep her daughter alive. Of course it is only as long as her daughter is alive that there's any chance that she will undergo treatment and rehabilitation, and this is the very essence of what the MSIC is aiming to do.

We put a Client Comments book out in the After Care area following lots of requests from clients who wanted to make comments. We've had this in place now for some weeks and what clients have to say has been really interesting. I suppose the first stand-out is just how recurrent the comments are about being treated in a non-judgmental way, and feeling that they're respected. I find this dismaying—the preponderance of such comments suggests that this continues to be a very rare experience for most drug users.

Some clients have suggested having a smoking room, but, so far, we haven't found the no-smoking policy to have been a problem. Clients recognise that, if we allowed smoking, it would have to be confined to a designated area, but that there's no additional space for such an area. We haven't found that the policy has resulted in people leaving sooner than they should. On the other hand, people perhaps hang around for less time than they would have otherwise, which is also a good thing. We didn't want people to stay at the facility for the whole day, because this would also reduce client throughput.

Because, as with any service, there is an upper limit to our client capacity, we need to maximise client throughput to maximise the impact of this facility at a community level. During these early months, on average people are spending about half an hour here. They spend only two minutes at the front end, so any concern about spillage back out onto the streets has most definitely not eventuated; in fact, we've hardly ever had anyone need to sit on the five seats in our waiting room. Then they're spending about 15 minutes in each of the other two sections, but that varies a lot according to the drug being used, with cocaine injectors tending to move through more quickly than heroin injectors. It also depends on how proficient people are at locating a vein and injecting—people with poor veins can be held up for a lot longer while they search for a vein to inject into.

A little while ago we realised we would also have to provide scissors for clients to open the little, usually red or blue, balloons in which they carry their heroin or cocaine. This is the level of detail we missed in our service planning stage! So Tracey went out and bought some children's scissors, which we believed would be safe—ever mindful of not providing people with potential weapons. However, the children's scissors were not sharp enough so today we had to purchase some sharper blunt-ended scissors. Clients are supposed to give them back, but at present we are 'losing' about thirty per week!

Friday, 6 July

Today we held our first Policy Advisory Committee meeting since we've been open and I was able to inform the members of this committee too—who have a range of expertise from health and ambulance to legal, police, community and ethics—of our progress to date.

There were no major policy changes proposed to the meeting. Perhaps the only issue of significance reported was that we now also routinely ask all clients whether they have received methadone that day to help assess their risk of overdose on that visit. In Germany they don't allow people on methadone programs to use injecting centres, mainly for political reasons. This is slightly curious, as it is known that some people on methadone programs still inject drugs occasionally, especially at the beginning when still stablising their methadone dose. Excluding them from using injecting centres does not prevent this; it simply moves it somewhere else, and so increases their risk, which is not in keeping with harm reduction principles.

I also received the committee's endorsement for a form we have just initiated—the introduction of a Discharge Against Clinical Advice form for people who we assess as being too drug-affected to leave the facility but nonetheless leave. Actually, in all instances like that up to now, we have been able to convince such people to stay. But it may come to pass that someone does want to leave the facility when we feel this is not advisable, in which case we should, at the very least, document that we advised them to the contrary.

I also raised the issue of drug division possibly constituting drug supply and Clive Small, who is on a secondment from the Police Service to the Premier's Department, agreed that we should ensure that any future legislation deals with this. I suppose this is a good thing about being a trial; we get a chance to identify glitches like this and get it right should the service eventually get the go-ahead on a more permanent basis.

Wednesday, 8 August

We closed the centre all day—it is the first time we've done this—to have a training day for as many staff as we could muster. As I've already noted, we've found it difficult to provide the necessary ongoing training for all staff working at the centre, whose needs are evolving as the services evolve, hence our decision to close for a full day. We looked at the various aspects of our operation and also invited some experts to speak on specific topics.

In the evening we spent some time enjoying each other's company socially, which is also important. When you are operating a service across seven days a week with part-time staff, there are also few opportunities for team-building.

It is surprising how quickly a team operating a service like this can start to see it all as just business as usual. But I for one still find myself walking through the place amazed that this is all really happening. I'm also very pleasantly surprised that it has gone as smoothly as it has to date and that the worst-case scenarios that I had envisaged have (touch wood) so far not come to fruition. Indeed, even those objectives that I thought we might have difficulty achieving look as though they are within our reach. But we have, of course, a very long road yet to tread.

Friday, 10 August

There has been criticism that we closed the service on Wednesday. The clients weren't happy about it, even though they were notified well in advance, and someone was sighted injecting publicly. It's my public health view that, if it all falls apart because you are not there for a day, then the effect that you are having is obviously not sustainable, in which case you really have to go back and question what you're doing. No service should ever allow itself to become indispensable or create dependency especially among an already drug dependent population because there will always be unpredictable, unavoidable events that can get in the way of services like this operating. On the other hand, the need for ongoing training of staff should always be regarded as a priority.

Wednesday, 15 August

I was in Perth today, addressing the West Australian Community Drug Summit being held in their Parliament House. This is similar to the original NSW

Parliamentary Drug Summit, which gave birth to the MSIC, although it is different in that it is a 'community', not a 'parliamentary' drug summit, so all the state politicians are not necessarily in attendance as delegates as they were during ours.

The media were alerted to my attendance and, starting in West Australia but unfortunately not ending there, they took the opportunity to broadcast widely the clinical activity data for our first three months of operation that I was reporting to this summit. Even though I put many, many riders on my comments—prefacing everything I said with 'it is far too early to call this a success'—that got dropped off. The journalists' accounts tended to lead in with statements that the trial was already a great success and that lives had been saved.

Responding to this, Major Brian Watters of the Salvation Army, who is also the Chair of the Australian National Council on Drugs (ANCD), was interviewed on *The World Today* on ABC Radio National, and in no uncertain terms took the opportunity to argue that the trial was by no means a success at this stage, something I agree with. But he also went on to say that it had already spent more than $4 million attracting drug-related activities to the area and it was seeing cocaine using 'middle-class yuppies', none of which was true.

Friday, 17 August

Since yesterday I have been rung by various people around the country who heard Major Watters' radio interview yesterday. They were most upset, particularly because he was identified as the Chair of the ANCD (which reports directly to the prime minister) and the previously stated position of the ANCD has been that it would not be taking a position on the injecting centre until the results of the trial are known. So Brian's comments in the media were quite out of step with this stated position. I was urged to take this up directly with him, which I did by writing a letter to him as Chair of the ANCD. I put the facts of the matter on record and also sought a clarification regarding what the current position of the ANCD is.

Brian and I have, until now, had a tacit agreement to agree to disagree about the value of trialling a supervised injecting centre. Publicly he has always supported me, never attacking me personally or professionally, and has even said on the record that, if an injecting centre was to occur, it was best it was in my hands. To this extent we've had a good professional relationship up until now, so I am particularly disappointed by his public slamming of the project, and especially that he has yet again put into the press this misinformation about our so-called budget blow-out.

Wednesday, 29 August

We have reminded staff that they should wear closed shoes at all times for occupational health and safety reasons. At the same time we are also ensuring that clients don't come in barefoot, because of the risk of needlestick injury in these circumstances.

Meanwhile we've also decided not to allow clients to bring alcohol into the service and to add this to the client code of conduct. We started to notice the odd bottle of beer in a brown paper bag appearing in the After Care area. While we accept that our standard hospital issue tea and coffee might not be the best, we don't feel it's appropriate that people bring their own drinks, particularly not alcohol since it may result in aggressive behaviour, posing a health risk to themselves and others, including staff. I suppose this shows how clients associate injecting drugs with other social activities, but this is a health service, and not a social venue.

Just when I have started to think things might be about to settle down media-wise, a photographer has taken a photo of the drug sniffer dogs patrolling in front of the injecting centre. This has been passed on to the Sydney *Star Observer*, a gay and lesbian community newspaper which has been campaigning against this method of policing drugs more broadly since earlier this year. At that time there was a threat that drug sniffer dogs would be used at the big party following the Mardi Gras parade and they had been used on at least one occasion in various nightclubs on Oxford Street in Darlinghurst. So a page-one story, with the picture of the dogs in front of our facility, has been run in the Sydney *Star Observer* with a piece arguing that this type of policing is inappropriate.

As I've said before, our position is that we don't believe we should object to the policing of drug supply in central Kings Cross, given that we chose to establish the service here, where drug supply has been endemic for decades. There's follow-up press in the *Telegraph*, as well, so we have tried to mitigate the potential damage by contacting the police service to assure them that this story was not instigated by us.

This is one example of how some supporters of the injecting centre, who also often have other drug-related agendas, can potentially cause problems for us. Most people probably assume that we endorse our supporters' views on this and whatever other views they may hold, which is not always the case. I have been very wary of weighing into any other drug-related issues, being mindful that we already have our own band of detractors and do not really need to acquire any more by lending our voice to other issues. So, although I am almost invariably asked to comment on any matter relating to drugs these days, whether it be heroin prescription programs or drug sniffer dogs, I assiduously avoid stating any opinion publicly, instead confining myself to the injecting centre issue. This is quite controversial enough.

Ultimately both the Police Service and the MSIC were quoted as saying that we enjoy a cooperative relationship. This is the case and its maintenance is vital.

The interesting thing is that injecting drug users in Kings Cross have already adapted to this mode of policing, now almost always carrying their drugs in their mouth and no longer carrying cannabis to sell on to help fund their drug habits. In fact some actually quite like the dog patrols, following close on their heels to pick up any drugs that have been quickly discarded— and missed by the dogs—by the unprepared more 'recreational' drug-using people who live in the area. We discovered this when two of our regular clients had that smiley ecstatic look post-injection, having for the first time injected ecstasy, which they'd found on the street.

six

Of needlesticks and dogs

Monday, 10 September, 2001

This morning I got a phone call from Julie Sibraa from Minister Della Bosca's office. She had just opened the *Daily Telegraph,* where the columnist Piers Ackerman had devoted yet another whole page to the injecting centre. Headed '$4m to keep the junkies happy' Piers began: 'The Government's Kings Cross shooting gallery'—he prefers to call it a shooting gallery, as does Fred Nile, when referring to it in parliament (despite being corrected on numerous occasions, I'm told)—'is now attracting its own dealers—as predicted. They hover near the rear door aiming at junkies as they leave after their state-supervised fix. This is the honeypot effect that those opposed to the notion of the state helping addicts enjoy their addiction warned about. They were howled down at the Government's rigged drug summit but they did sound the alarm.' It is as though Watters and Ackerman are in cahoots!

I find it interesting that as a newspaper columnist Ackerman doesn't seem to have to substantiate categorical statements like this; the statement about the centre attracting drug dealers is not even backed by 'unknown sources'. He then goes on to devote most of the rest of his article to the progress report on the first three months, which has not yet been released but has obviously been leaked to him—not the first leak to this particular journalist. He is actually quite faithful to the results quoting parts of the draft report word for word and, from my reading anyway, they speak for themselves. So overall it's not a bad article. He ends by saying that whether the shooting gallery has been a success or not is certainly debatable, which I think in Ackerman language is almost tacit approval.

As always with this type of article, there was something of a flurry as we get together with Pat Kennedy and discuss how we would respond if there was any media follow-up. As is also our practice, we informed the staff about the story. We display these sorts of articles in the staff room and talk about them at team meetings.

I've gradually become more thick-skinned about articles devoted to denigrating this service I'm responsible for. But I think it's more difficult for the nurses and counsellors, who work in what is, after all, a legal government-funded service, to open the newspaper on a not irregular basis and find all sorts of people taking pot shots at it. It is the big downside of being such a high profile, controversial public entity, and the only one of its kind.

This is quite different to what any of us have experienced previously. Working in other harm reduction health services that have attracted similar controversy, such as the needle syringe or methadone programs, you take it less personally when they are pilloried, probably because you are only one of many such programs. What makes this situation different is that this is the only injecting centre in Australia, so any and all references to this as a strategy refer to this one and only this one.

Wednesday, 12 September

The greyness, the blustering rain, the sound of the fire engine sirens this morning made it seem almost as though the horrific events that occurred at the World Trade Center in New York overnight were actually happening here in Kings Cross. Inside the injecting centre, on the other hand, there was an incredibly quiet, subdued atmosphere. Activity was right down. Everybody seemed in a state of shock, including the drug users in the area.

For our clients, it often seems that world events like this have less relevance. They tend to have much more immediate needs, such as their current state of drug withdrawal, trying to find the money for the next hit or food or where to sleep that night (in about that order). Events like national elections seem to come and go without even registering with some drug users. But on this occasion it was very different—there was a real appreciation amongst everybody that something awful had happened.

We were hearing all kinds of reactions from the clients—some reasonable and some way out there. We saw this as something that had the potential to affect the atmosphere at the MSIC so the staff had to be briefed to watch out for the possibility of an escalation of emotions, which might develop into aggression or abuse. They were to defuse any adverse situations that might arise—not to fuel speculative conversations, particularly if they took odd twists and turns—and to try to settle them down. This of course was among staff who had their own debriefing needs, which had to be subordinated to the more immediate needs of the service as it continued to operate, although at a slower pace than usual. As a small treat, Tracey went out and bought cakes for the staff. At least we could share afternoon tea with each other, and hopefully regain some sense of normality in the face of this senseless world event.

In the evening I lectured to the Masters of Public Health students at the University of NSW, which I have been doing for years. There are Muslim and North American students amongst them. I usually get particular enjoyment from this aspect of my work as I hope to inspire students in Public Health. But tonight, as I faced the students, I extended my sympathies, particularly to those who may have been directly affected, and apologised that the lecture was likely to be a bit flat. Something like what happened in New York yesterday certainly puts your work into perspective. Somehow today it didn't seem all that important.

Thursday, 13 September

We received an email from a Barry Small, who states that he is a researcher for the Reverend Fred Nile, requesting statistics regarding how many people have attended the centre and how many referrals we have made. We assume the Rev. Nile's interest has been roused by Piers Ackerman's story in the *Telegraph* a couple of days ago, in which many of these statistics were discussed. We've noticed before that after stories like this, Fred will often write a letter to the editor, of course always critical of the injecting centre. So we have a certain level of anxiety as a result of this request from his researcher.

Friday, 14 September

Both Pat and I spoke to Barry Small today, to ask what the Rev. Nile planned to do with the statistics he's requested but at the same time indicating that we have every intention of providing them as part of continuing to be open and transparent about this service. We believe that we should provide as much information to people as we can, especially to those who we know don't necessarily support our work. But it does involve a risk; statistical information can easily be misconstrued.

When I spoke to Barry, he said that he understood what our anxieties might be but that, after speaking to Pat, he himself thought that perhaps what we were doing was potentially worthwhile. He agreed to my suggestion to ask Fred to come and visit the service for a proper briefing about all the operational aspects. I even offered to do this away from the media, perhaps somehow spiriting him into the service at a time when we weren't be operating. Mind you, given the profile that Fred has, this would be a challenge in itself.

I've actually had previous discussions with Fred Nile about injecting centres and heroin prescription programs. During the Drug Summit he was part of the parliamentary group that visited the Kirketon Road Centre mid-week and I found him to be very knowledgeable about these initiatives and their relative potential benefits. At least in this private circumstance, he indicated a certain openness when expressing the view that personally he would be more likely to support a heroin prescription program than a supervised injecting centre. His reason for this was that he thought a heroin program was potentially more therapeutic for drug users, whereas he considered an injecting centre, with one of its aims being to get drug users and needle syringes off the street, as being more focused on the needs of the community, which he didn't think should take precedence over the health and social welfare of drug users. While this injecting centre is very much focused on the health of drug users, indeed not all are—some seem to be mostly about managing the public nuisance associated with street-based injecting. Mind you, Australia has never had to accommodate anything even resembling the open drug scenes that have developed in some European capital cities.

I gave Barry a range of possible times. We'll wait and see whether he comes back to us in the next few days.

I let Harry Herbert know that Fred's office has been in contact, but he thinks that it's probably best that we handle this one directly, rather than involving him. There's been quite a history of differences of opinion and approach between these two reverends, Harry Herbert and Fred Nile, both being from the Uniting Church. Indeed, it's interesting to note how well the Uniting Church seems to be able to accommodate disparate views in this regard. I think it's probably both the strength and the potential weakness of the Uniting Church. In this instance, however, it was the essential difference that allowed them to operate this trial as opposed to the Roman Catholic Church which, because of its more centralised nature, didn't seem able to accommodate philosophical differences to the same extent, at least not with a high profile project like this.

Today we set a record in terms of client activity, with 83 visits in the first four hours, from twelve until four, without any hitches. We managed a couple of overdose cases, one quite serious in a person who had injected temazepam, a prescribed benzodiazepine drug like Valium, the sedating effects of which, unlike heroin, aren't reversed by Narcan. For the first time Andy was on duty for a record day. Up until now it's always been Damian, but now at last Andy breaks the record!

Wednesday, 19 September

This evening our community consultation committee met. After four months there's been no observed increase in drug-related activity in the area. If anything, there's less. There's been no sign of people congregating around either the entrance or the exit (contrary to what Piers writes). People like Tom McMahon, who owns a boutique hotel near Springfield Avenue, reported that they continue to notice less drug-related activity, particularly around Springfield Plaza where it has been rife for years,, which they are attributing to increased police activity and the injecting centre. There was no negative feedback.

We reported our latest attendance figures. In the fourth month we accommodated over 2600 visits to the injecting centre so these are continuing to increase as we'd anticipated. I'm expecting that this will continue for at least the first six months. We've registered over 1100 individual drug users since the centre started and managed more than 50 overdoses of cocaine, heroin and also temazepam.

We've not heard back from Fred Nile's office and no letters penned by Fred re the MSIC have been published in the *Daily Telegraph* in the last week.

Friday, 21 September

At 8 o'clock tonight I got a phone call from Damian to say that 'Michael', one of our health education officers, had sustained a needlestick injury while standing close to a client who was having difficulty accessing a vein. When the client unexpectedly moved the needle syringe away—a needle syringe which had fresh blood on it—it pricked the base of Michael's thumb.

The client involved was very upset by the accident and extremely apologetic. He said that he was HIV negative but hepatitis C positive. He is a regular client of Kirketon Road Centre, so we referred him back there for re-testing.

Michael was keen to continue working, having cleaned the wound with soapy water immediately and carried out the other procedures that are part of the protocol you follow in such circumstances. The fact that we were operating at the minimum staffing level today (six staff including at least three nurses) meant that if he went to the emergency centre at the hospital (which is how we usually follow up such injuries) the service would have had to close. Michael is a particularly dedicated, hard-working person who in this instance put the needs of the service ahead of his own by offering not to go to hospital until the next day. While this probably would still have been well within the necessary time-frame, as service director I couldn't allow this to happen and I instructed Damian to arrange for Michael to go down to Sydney Hospital's Emergency Centre accompanied by another staff member. As it turned out, we were able to redeploy a staff member from K2 (who also works part-time at the injection centre) to the MSIC, so it didn't have to close.

Apparently the doctor at Sydney Hospital was quite shocked that Michael would be exposed to such a risk at the injecting centre, which I suppose shows how limited people's understanding is regarding the type of work we do, even within the health sector. Michael was counselled about the risk of transmission of the various blood-borne viruses and underwent baseline testing. Michael would also have been offered what's called post-exposure prophylaxis, which is a course of medication, to reduce the risk of acquiring HIV infection, although it would not have been recommended because this type of circumstance is considered very low-risk for HIV. The risk of hepatitis C infection, while greater, is still low because the injury was only a very superficial wound from what was a very small-bore needle and the correct procedures were carried out immediately afterwards.

But even when the risk is low, this is a very traumatic event for any health care worker. I personally have had two or three needlestick injuries over the years and, even though on all of those occasions I knew I was at very low risk, it really isn't until the final test following the three-month window period (by which time the infection should have shown up on testing) that your anxiety is allayed and you start to feel your usual relaxed self again.

This episode certainly underscores the risks we take in this line of work and reminds us of the need not to get in too close to the clients while they're injecting, even to offer advice. We also need to consider whether or not health education officers/counsellors should get in close at all, since they may not have developed that sixth sense that clinically trained nurses and doctors have as to the whereabouts of sharps like needle syringes at all times. This is clearly something we need to think more about from a policy perspective.

I have also informed Colette of this incident and she undertook to phone Michael over the weekend as part of the debriefing process after a critical incident.

Wednesday, 26 September

Every two weeks on a Wednesday, between the first and second sessions, we have a team meeting. On the agenda today we had 'animal policy'—whether we would admit clients accompanied by their pets to the service.

Many street-based drug users have animals they look after; as health practitioners we generally consider this to be a positive thing. Particularly for young people who are considering becoming pregnant, looking after an animal to start with seems like a good way of giving them a sense of the seriousness of the commitment required. Most other health services don't allow pets in the waiting room, let alone the clinical areas when their owner is being seen by the doctor or other practitioner. Now this issue has arisen here in the injecting centre.

As previously mentioned, the first animal to visit us was the rabbit Winky, who lived in the backpack of a homeless female client who attended the centre. It was felt at the time that, since this rabbit didn't have anywhere else to stay, it would be okay to allow Winky to accompany his owner through the various stages of the MSIC. While it was kind of cute seeing the rabbit hop out of the backpack and around the injecting booths, the repeated attendance of Storm has become more problematical—Storm is an American pit bull terrier, which we now discover is apparently illegal to own in Australia. Some of the staff are not enamoured of dogs anyway and he does look rather frightening.

Recently Storm's owner spent a considerable amount of time at reception explaining to the staff how his dog had quite a history of aggressive behaviour towards other dogs. Understandably this concerned our staff and, even though Storm—whenever we've seen him—has seemed to be pretty calm, they felt we needed to revisit this issue.

We considered allowing dogs through on restraining leads, but then there might be more than one animal in Stage 2 at a time and a situation could arise in which their owners, particularly if they're mid-injection, can't keep them apart. After some discussion we agreed that we wouldn't allow any pets, restrained or otherwise, through the facility and we would encourage clients to make their own arrangements prior to arriving. From now on Storm will need to be tied to a telegraph pole out the front and wait for his master to return from around the block, which I gather Storm is used to anyway; we've seen him tied to various telegraph poles around the place, so this shouldn't be a problem.

This reminds me that many years ago at Kirketon Road Centre we had to develop what we called 'the rat policy'. When it was popular among drug users to have rats as pets (this was later followed by a ferret phase), we allowed clients to have rats in the clinic room with them as long as they were in a bag of some sort. Mind you, seeing a bag creep along the clinic floor was still a bit unnerving for some staff at the time. I suppose these are among the things that people working outside this field would probably never envisage!

Thursday, 27 September

You might have thought that this World Trade Center tragedy could surely not have an illicit drugs angle, but it was reported yesterday that the Taliban has stockpiles of heroin. Having last year decreed it 'un-Islamic' to grow and sell opium poppies, they have now, according to this news report, reversed that decision. Indeed, their stockpiles of heroin are reportedly being sold to fund their efforts to defend Afghanistan against an impending strike from the US post September 11. It is therefore anticipated that the so-called heroin drought that has affected Australia since January this year may well be broken by increased heroin supply from this part of the world.

I have been contacted by Kelly Burke from the *Sydney Morning Herald* (who in May broke the story of us opening) seeking a comment on how the injecting centre would respond to such an eventuality. Traditionally Australia's heroin has come from the Golden Triangle—Thailand, Burma, Laos—rather than from Afghanistan, whose supplies go mainly to Europe. It is also usually not as high in quality and of a different chemical type to that from the Golden Triangle—not the acid form that is less suitable for smoking and more readily injected.

There's been much speculation over the past months about the cause of the heroin shortage in Australia. It's been suggested that the drought in Afghanistan or the drought in Burma reduced supplies last summer. It's also been speculated that the very large and growing populations of injecting drug users in countries such as India, Thailand, China, Vietnam and Indonesia have increased demand for heroin more locally. Heroin suppliers in Asia may prefer use to just land routes and off-load more quickly instead of seeking to reach a smaller IDU population across the sea in Australia, even though it can be sold here at much higher prices. So whether any increase in supply in Afghanistan actually manages to get across to Australia is doubtful.

For nine months now we have been waiting for the usually inevitable cessation of the heroin shortage, as has always occurred in the past. At the injecting centre we have prepared ourselves for the possibility that it might happen quite suddenly, just as the shortage seemed to arise almost from one week to the next. In this event the injecting centre is in a prime position to provide an early warning system of any significant increase in supply or quality, at least in the Kings Cross area; we will be able to let other services seeing drug users know so they can warn them of the increased risk of overdose.

We anticipate that, should the quality increase suddenly, we may be faced with a spate of overdoses, possibly occurring simultaneously since the recent poor quality of heroin has also resulted in a reduction of physical tolerance to heroin and other opioids among drug users generally. They may not actually recognise this reduction in tolerance and therefore not adjust for it when and if the quality improves, given that this is not something that people are reliably informed about when they are buying heroin. When people purchase heroin and other drugs on the illicit market, it's anybody's guess as to what the quality is or indeed even whether the drugs they are seeking are contained in the substance that is being sold to them. This has complicated the management of overdoses at the injecting centre, particularly when a person has bought what they thought was cocaine, which then turns out to be heroin or vice versa. This is why all our staff are trained to assess which drug is involved in an overdose situation according to a client's signs and symptoms, rather than from what drug they've been told was going to be used.

So, as well as being in a unique position to detect any increase in the quality of heroin being sold and to issue appropriate warnings, the injecting centre is prepared to manage this spate of overdoses should it occur, as well as multiple overdoses at one time. But so far there's been no sign of this; over the four months we've continued to see occasional bursts of increased quality heroin hit the streets, but these have not been sustained. In fact the latest figures available show that for the first time cocaine has exceeded heroin as the most commonly injected drug at the injecting centre, accounting for 53 per cent of injecting episodes. So the media's insistence on describing us as the 'heroin injecting trial' is even more of a misnomer at the moment.

Friday, 28 September

This is the last Friday of the month, which means that it's one of our regular open days from 10 until 11.30 am. We've been promoting this to the local community, to other health agencies and to anyone wanting to find out more about the injecting centre. We are inundated with requests from literally all over the country and from overseas as well. At times it seems like every student from primary school to post-doctoral level, studying everything from public health and communications to architecture, has decided to do a project on the MSIC! To deal with this interest, we've decided to host these monthly open days to show people through the facility. We are also setting up a website.

This afternoon I had a meeting with a medical colleague of mine and discussed the recent needlestick injury at the injecting centre with him. He told me that on this very day a paper has been published in the *New England Journal of Medicine* reporting that, when treated with high-dose interferon (a medication that boosts your immunity to viruses) in the acute phase of viral infection, hepatitis C was cleared in all cases. It was only a small study, but significant when you consider that until now it has generally been accepted that only about a third of people will eventually get rid of the virus from their bloodstream altogether. The rest may go on to develop chronic hepatitis which, over twenty to thirty years, may have quite a significant health impact.

This study is good news for all health services like ours, where staff are at risk of contracting hep C through needlestick injury, from a post-exposure prophylactic point of view. Because these findings are considered to have significant public health implications at a global level, the paper's publication was brought forward on an urgent basis. It is particularly good news for Michael, the health education officer involved in the recent needlestick incident here. I immediately informed him of the paper and recommended that his liver function should be tested regularly over the next few weeks. At the first sign of hepatitis C, he should be considered for this high-dose interferon treatment. This will now also become the procedure for all needlestick injuries at the MSIC from now on.

seven

Death of a colleague and friend

Monday 1 October 2001

The weekend was uneventful although we now have an addition to our collection of odd places where clients carry drugs. A female client arrived with her cap of heroin stored in her ear, believing this to be a reasonably safe place. Of course there are some very delicate structures in the ear, including the tympanic membrane (ear drum), which were at risk of damage in the course of her desperately trying to get the cap out of there. Andy made five attempts to remove the cap before he was finally successful. The client was delighted with his efforts, but of course we recommended that she not use her ear for such a purpose in future.

Tuesday, 2 October

We were visited by senior bureaucrats from the the NSW Cabinet Office of Drug Policy today. We usually like to show such visitors our clients' comments, which provide telling insights into how important this service has become for them. Just as I was gathering up the client comments book from the After Care area downstairs, I saw that there had been a new entry made this very day from a client—a full-page, very long and detailed recipe on how to convert certain prescription pills into heroin! I decided that our visitors probably didn't need to read this, so I removed it from the book. We regularly check the book for inappropriate entries like this. There's just so much to be thinking about in this job!

Saturday, 6 October

I received the terrible news today that Karen, who had worked as an administrative assistant at Kirketon Road Centre a number of years ago, and who had remained a friend of mine since, died of a heroin overdose last night.

This has come as a great shock to me, particularly because I was completely unaware that she had ever used heroin at all. It was only on last Monday's public holiday that Karen and I, together with Annie Malcolm, another friend and colleague of mine from Kirketon Road, had met up, as we so often did. The three of us had walked across Waverley Cemetery to Clovelly Bowling Club. Karen was married there, overlooking the Pacific Ocean. I had marvelled at how well she was looking. She seemed very much in love and was looking forward to going overseas with her husband this Christmas, and there was mention of then possibly starting a family themselves next year.

So this was devastating news at a personal level and also at a professional level—I find it hard to believe that something as tragic and final as this could happen to someone I knew so well. And in her own home, with her husband there. Karen had been out earlier in the evening for a few drinks, then got back and around midnight had a shot of heroin. I have now learnt that this was something she did from time to time, only on a very occasional basis, because she didn't want to become heroin dependent (i.e. physically addicted), that way avoiding the cravings and other physical signs of withdrawal exprienced by regular users when they stop using. Of course, the downside of not being physically dependent is that you also don't develop a tolerance to the drug, so you are at much greater risk of overdosing. Particularly if you drink alcohol and the quality of the heroin is, for whatever reason, a bit higher than usual, this simple and not uncommon combination can lead to a potentially fatal heroin overdose. In this instance it wasn't immediate; she had her shot, then went off to sleep. Her husband woke at five in the morning. She didn't. He found her lying beside him dead.

Karen had probably slowly lapsed into a coma over a number of hours but, being ostensibly asleep, no one would have realised until well after she stopped breathing and died. People often think that in overdose situations people lose consciousness on the end of the needle, but that is not so. What happened to Karen is not an uncommon scenario and highlights the risk of injecting heroin in what is an essentially unsupervised setting. Heroin is a potentially lethal nightcap for this reason.

The fact that she actually worked in the field of illicit drugs and overdose prevention makes this seem even more shocking. I knew her as an enthusiastic supporter of licit drugs, including alcohol and cigarettes, but she had not told her friends that she had commenced using heroin, albeit in this type of 'recreational' way. She probably figured we would have disapproved and she'd have been right about that.

As it happens, yesterday at the injecting centre we noted that there were many reports from clients that the heroin was stronger than usual and they were more drug affected throughout the two shifts than was usual. I also spoke to a colleague at Cabramatta yesterday, who said that in Cabramatta too there was very strong heroin around at the moment and likewise the clients there were more drug affected than they had been for a while.

It's hard for me at a time like this to make any sense of this event, particularly given how focused my work is on preventing otherwise fatal overdoses, work that Karen supported very strongly. I can't help asking myself how a medically supervised injecting centre can help prevent something like this, particularly when it occurs among people who are well informed about the risks involved. I later read in the newspaper that the number of drug overdose deaths in Australia this month was only eleven, compared to sixty-five in the previous year. This was the lowest number since records have been kept in recent years. But Karen was one of them. Perhaps we get a false sense of security from such statistics.

Wednesday, 10 October

We had our fortnightly clinical supervision session with David. We feel that perhaps, as we predicted, the honeymoon period is over. Clients are less tentative now than they were at the beginning; they've got a greater sense of ownership of the service. While this is for the most part a desirable thing, they're also starting to test the boundaries a little more these days. We're rising to that occasion—it's extremely important in this type of work, while being empathetic at all times, to maintain order and control in the service so that it is safe for all clients and staff. It's also important that staff set limits on unacceptable client behaviours and apply policies consistently. Having said that, it's also necessary to be flexible at times as well.

We have noticed in recent times that there's been an increase in benzodiazepine use—temazepam gelcaps in particular. When injected, temazepam damages veins, leading to ulcers and abscesses. It can also result in disinhibited behaviour, which can sometimes lead to aggression. These 'pills' (as they are colloquially known) also cause amnesia, so incidents that occur don't even provide for a learning opportunity. When you later see a client who has previously been abusive or aggressive towards staff or other clients and seek to discuss this episode, the client often quite genuinely has no recollection of what you are talking about.

Thursday, 11 October

Karen's funeral was held at the Eastern Suburbs Crematorium in Botany. It was very well attended; many were people I know professionally—staff from Kirketon Road, and some who are no longer working there and have moved away from Sydney but made the effort to return for the funeral. The main wake was held by some of her friends from outside of work, but we decided to have our own Kirketon Road Centre staff wake at my place. It was like a reunion; coming together to share our grief for Karen was what we needed to do. She would have been proud of us.

This kind of event has quite a strong ripple effect. At the injecting centre we also have staff who knew Karen so we were all very sombre as we returned to work. I discussed with the management teams at both Kirketon Road and the MSIC the need for us to keep a close eye on staff and how they are coping.

I also wonder whether there is a risk that people working in this field for a long time may become desensitised to the very real risks of injecting a drug that they see used by our clients day in day out, often with such gay abandon. There is no sure-fire way to use a drug like heroin. It may not have direct toxic effects on organs, as alcohol does, but it can stop you breathing for a time and that's all that it takes to make it potentially lethal when used in unsupervised circumstances.

Those who argue that allowing heroin to be legally available would overcome this risk because the purity would be known do not seem to appreciate that this is only one factor. Your personal tolerance on the day is probably more important and even experienced heroin users can misjudge from time to time. In the wrong circumstances, once is all it takes. Heroin injection can only be reasonably safe from an overdose perspective in a supervised injecting centre or when prescribed and administered, as they do in Switzerland, because staff can resuscitate clients if and when they overdose.

While I advocate the decriminalisation of drug use regardless of the drug, I do not support the legalisation, meaning the regulated supply of heroin (and the other highly addictive drugs like cocaine) beyond a tightly controlled heroin prescription program. On the other hand I think cannabis should be regulated in line with alcohol and tobacco, which have comparable effects, but that the regulation of these licit drugs should be tightened up, especially when it come to those pretty coloured, sweet, fizzy drinks marketed to young people.

I am also a hard-liner when it comes to promoting the professional model with its strict client/practitioner boundaries for clinical services for drug users. In my experience there is a need to be ever-vigilant that staff are not starting to over-identify with the client group, even though this may sometimes lead to greater understanding of its needs. I think our clients also value the fact that we're not in there amongst it with them.

Karen's death makes me feel even more determined to remind staff at both KRC and the MSIC that overdose and other drug-related harm does not just happen to clients. I'm trying very hard to retrieve something positive from this event, but so far with no success. It shouldn't have happened. I will miss her a lot.

Monday, 15 October

Andy rang to report that a client had had a temazepam overdose and that, even though he was still conscious, he was very drowsy. In such instances we don't use Narcan, as it's only effective in reversing opioids like heroin, morphine and pethidine, not benzodiazepines. We decided that this person needed to be observed until the effects of his drugs wore off, so it would be best if he were transferred to St Vincent's Hospital. So, for the first time ever, we phoned for an ambulance transport and, even though the client was reluctant to begin with, paramedics finally transferred him to St Vincent's for observation. When clients agree to this, it is usually very significant—it indicates that they themselves realise that their level of consciousness is sufficiently diminished that they don't feel safe and we use that in itself as an indicator of overdose severity. There certainly isn't any abuse of the hospital system in this regard—drug users generally will do almost anything to avoid being transferred to an emergency centre under these circumstances. Sadly this ambivalence is often mutual.

Tuesday, 16 October

In the evening we had our monthly community consultation committee meeting. The Reverend Ray Richmond from the Wayside Chapel informed us that, since the injecting centre has been open, the number of people injecting in the toilets or elsewhere in the premises of the Wayside Chapel has more than halved. This kind of feedback is very encouraging to us. KRC has had the same experience.

Wednesday, 17 October

These things always happen in runs. Tonight we needed a second ambulance transport to St Vincent's. However, this time there was a striking difference to the episode on Monday—this client came to the injecting centre ostensibly to inject benzodiazepine but, before he actually did so, he lost consciousness. We decided, again because there seemed to be no opioids involved, that there was no point in administering Narcan, and that it would be best if he was observed in a hospital situation. This client has previously attended the injecting centre on quite a number of occasions and we know him to be a pill user who has had a previous pill overdose at the centre. But this is the first time anyone's arrived and overdosed prior to using what they have come to inject.

At Kirketon Road we have found that there are clients who manage to get up the three flights of stairs to the reception and then collapse unconscious at the very top. Our belief is that clients often know when they are at serious risk of losing consciousness—and, almost like automatons, will direct themselves towards where they will be assisted and then collapse there. Drug users realise that we have the relevant expertise, but sometimes we have trouble convincing some members of the ambulance service of this. Our most senior nurse ended up having an argument with the ambulance officers, who insisted that this was a heroin overdose and that he should have administered Narcan. Andy stood firm; he knew the history of this particular person and clinically it was his assessment that this was a benzodiazepine overdose.

Friday, 19 October

I spent some time down in Stage 3 of the injecting centre this afternoon. I always carry my mobile phone—these days I'm more difficult to track down, particularly because I'm having to spread myself between two different services. At some stage I became aware that I was no longer carrying my mobile in my pocket and that I must have set it down somewhere. Ringing the phone number, I discovered that it had already been switched off, going straight to voice mail, which was not how I had set it. I then realised that one of the clients must have come across it and taken it for a walk.

This is now the third time that I have donated a mobile phone to the client population over the last few years. I feel very foolish. This is very irresponsible of me—it's like putting cheese out for the mice and then hoping that they don't make off with it. I take the view that we have to expect this from people who live hand-to-mouth. We have some idea which client it may have been, but of course we can't prove it. In these circumstances our approach is not to pursue it further. Finders keepers!

Tonight I received a call from Nicky, one of the nurses. She was quite distressed because they have just discovered that one of our clients, Jane, who has attended the injection centre no less than 38 times, is in fact not quite seventeen years old now, well below the centre's age requirement of eighteen. She has been a street-based sex worker in Kings Cross since she was fourteen. When she first came to the MSIC, she had been injecting heroin into her neck veins two to three times a day; she had already contracted hepatitis C and recently been admitted to Westmead Hospital with infective endocarditis (an infection of the heart valves) and septicaemia. She had survived at least one drug overdose but had never been in a drug treatment program.

It was not until we effected a referral for her to be assessed for Kirketon Road Centre's methadone access program, for which age verification is required, that her real age was discovered. According to our policy, staff now have to tell her that she can't return to the MSIC, which they all feel badly about, given how high risk an injector she has been from such a young age. What's more, they believe that it is only because they have had the opportunity across 38 visits to engage her that this referral to methadone treatment has been achieved.

Of course I agree with their sentiments but the age restriction was in the legislation, so we can't apply any discretion in this regard. However, I reassured Nicky that we could present this client as a case study at the end of the trial as evidence that the age criterion should be reconsidered. Perhaps we could recommend that a similar approach be taken as for methadone treatment, where people between the ages of sixteen and eighteen need to be assessed by two practitioners instead of just the one, and a case management approach be adopted, reviewing such under-age people's progress over time.

The only way I have been able to reconcile my own clinical dilemmas associated with the licence criteria has been to remind myself that this is still a trial, which is yet to be proven worthwhile, and that we are relegating people like Jane in this instance to the same situation drug users have been in until now. But as a clinician I understand why situations like this are professionally demoralising, so I also recommended to Nicky that this case be referred to our regular clinical supervision sessions.

Despite myself, at another level I cannot help marvelling at Jane's brazenness—at registration she didn't just try being eighteen, she gave her age as almost twenty. The registering practitioner didn't doubt this—and she got away with it for a whole 38 visits. She does look older than eighteen, let alone sixteen. She has now gone onto the methadone program; we hope she doesn't relapse to injecting drugs, which is not uncommon, as she has now been informed that she cannot attend the injecting centre again until she turns eighteen.

Saturday, 20 October

At Kirketon Road Centre yesterday I saw the client who overdosed at the injecting centre on Wednesday and was transferred to hospital by ambulance. I asked him exactly what he had taken on that day. He confirmed that, apart from receiving a dose of methadone at 10 o'clock in the morning, he hadn't used any other drugs until half an hour before he came to the injecting centre that night, when he had injected 25 temazepam gelcaps. While benzodiazepines are not as dangerous as opioids like heroin, because on their own they don't directly cause respiratory depression, if they are used along with heroin, they can potentiate its CNS depressant effects and lead to respiratory arrest and death. We counselled him about this, particularly given that this is not the first time he's overdosed on these drugs.

However, he was presenting to the injecting centre with a very different problem today. Apparently the script pad he had stolen from a doctor's surgery somewhere, which he was using to write himself prescriptions for temazepam, had run out and so he was experiencing drug withdrawal. One of the staff accompanied him to Kirketon Road for further assessment. The symptoms of withdrawal from benzodiazepines can be quite serious and include grand mal convulsions (generalised fitting). This prompted us to joke that script pads should be like chequebooks—when you get to the last five, there should be a warning so that clients are alerted to the need to start prescribing themselves reducing doses of benzodiazepines so as to prevent such acute withdrawal symptoms from occurring. This is an example of the kind of black humour that helps us maintain our ability to keep pressing on in this sometimes disturbing area.

eight

Reaching the six-month milestone

Thursday, 25 October 2001

I spent some time in the second stage this morning. Just as we were about to close, I looked across and saw that one of the clients, who was still sitting upright, had stopped breathing and was becoming blue after injecting heroin.

We laid him out flat and administered oxygen. He also ended up needing Narcan. It took a bit of time before the heroin was reversed, and he started breathing again. This was quite a serious overdose; we believe that, if this had occurred in an unsupervised situation, it may have led to death within a few minutes.

We noticed during the resuscitation that there was a faint whiff of alcohol about him so it seemed likely that he might have had a couple of drinks, although he certainly hadn't presented as being alcohol affected upon arrival at the injecting centre. When he regained consciousness, he admitted he hadn't used any heroin for a couple of weeks which would have lowered his tolerance to it. He had had a few beers and then had a $100 hit all in one go. He felt embarrassed, realising that this was not wise, but said he had been feeling greedy today. He's visited the injecting centre a number of times; certainly on this occasion being here paid off for him.

During such procedures it's our protocol, where possible, to move other clients through into the last stage and not to allow any new clients into the injecting room stage until we've completed the resuscitation. Those people who are moved out are, of course, well aware of what's happening, so we also use this as an opportunity to remind them about what the risks are. Witnessing such an event can have an important health educational role.

I attended a community meeting this afternoon. One of the people there said she'd been told that the Chamber of Commerce was confidently telling people that they were going to close the injecting centre down. (Again!) Apparently, they're now logging ambulance call-outs as it's their belief that we've had far too many of these. Also they claim that there aren't medical staff on the premises at all times.

At this stage we've only had two ambulance call-outs, both last week, one of which was to a client who had overdosed before he actually used the injecting centre and both of them involving benzodiazepines, requiring ongoing observation over a number of hours, which the injecting centre is not set up to accommodate.

According to the legislation, we are not required to have a doctor in attendance at all times; indeed, it would be a first in the world and unnecessarily expensive to employ doctors when registered nurses can be trained to resuscitate drug overdoses, just like ambulance officers are. This is the only injecting centre that I know of that has a designated medical director and nurses authorised to administer Narcan in heroin overdose situations, which much reduces the need for ambulance call-outs. It is only in complicated circumstances that medical advice may be required and this can usually happen over the phone. Even hospital intensive care units do not have doctors in attendance at all times.

While such rumours are clearly not a serious threat, it's nonetheless difficult not to become irritated when you hear these things, particularly on a day when you have managed an overdose which might well have been fatal in other circumstances.

Sunday, 28 October

In his campaign speech for the upcoming federal election in two weeks time, the prime minister, John Howard, has pledged additional money towards his government's Tough On Drugs strategy. He went on to also declare that, unlike the Labor Opposition, he continues to oppose supervised injecting centres, which he believes will only increase drug use in the community.

And, as night follows day, shortly afterwards Pat phoned to say he'd received calls from AAP and other media outlets seeking our response. We decided to direct them to federal Labor's health spokespeople. Given the political context, we don't feel it's appropriate to respond, but of course it is dismaying that the service should find itself continually dragged into partisan politics in this way.

Wednesday, 31 October

A fortnight ago, at the last clinical supervision session, staff expressed that perhaps our honeymoon period—as far as clients no longer being as compliant—was over. However, today Andy expressed the view that this has been turned back and that a certain calmness has returned. Some clients have caused difficulties because they are using benzodiazepines, but our approach to date has been not to ban them from using the service. Instead, we flag their registration number on the database after any incident and then, the next time they come, we discuss it with them before they're allowed to re-enter the facility. We explain that if an aggressive pattern were to emerge in their behaviour, that would result in us imposing service sanctions, such as having what we call a time-out period. But so far we haven't had to take this ultimate step. People have pulled up after a warning.

Monday, 5 November

Leigh McLaughlin from the premier's office called, informing me that, since tomorrow is the end of our first six months of operations, it is planned that Bob Carr will deliver a speech in parliament on Wednesday giving a progress report on how the service is going.

I'm a bit anxious about this, partly because all of the data are not yet available and fully analysed for the entire six months. We also don't understand why the premier would pre-empt the six-month evaluation report, which is to be launched at the Annual Symposium of the National Drug & Alcohol Research Centre, scheduled for 28 November.

In the last week, in the run-up to the federal election, the prime minister has been saying that, since all the states are under Labor control, our operation is a forerunner of injecting centres being established all over the place, in line with Labor's soft-on-drugs approach. So I'm also worried that the premier's plan to speak in parliament three days before the election risks stoking this fire, with very little to gain. However, when I suggested delaying it for at least a week, so it would be after the election and the data would all be fully analysed, I was informed that now is a good time, for reasons that weren't explained. So we are scrambling around to get the most recent service activity data ready for this speech.

Wednesday, 7 November

My reputation as a pedant and a red-penning terror is almost legendary among staff, so you can imagine that I felt I had reached Valhalla when earlier today I was sent a draft of the speech the premier was due to give. What's more, the various amendments I had suggested were taken on board. The speech was made to parliament at 2.30 in the afternoon, but only 2UE and ABC Radio followed up on it.

It was very reassuring to hear the premier cautiously support the project, especially given his original apparent ambivalence. By his own admission during the Drug Summit his position on illicit drugs seemed to shift somewhat and he showed great courage in being the state premier willing to trial Australia's first injecting centre.

During the premier's speech today he highlighted the fact that the majority of heroin overdoses at the MSIC have been managed using oxygen alone and did not require Narcan administration. There has been an extraordinary interest in this aspect of late, particularly by Piers Ackerman, who has suggested that we are exaggerating our overdose numbers and that it's not a real overdose unless Narcan is used. Apparently there has been previous dialogue on this matter between the premier's office and Mr Ackerman, which made me feel uneasy. I suggested that inquiries like this should be directed to me, rather than being fielded at a political level.

Clearly the premier has now attempted to lay this issue to rest. Of course, we could easily increase our use of Narcan by simply standing back when we detect the first signs of overdose and doing nothing during the time it would take for an ambulance to be called and arrive while we watched overdosing clients' consciousness further decrease. When they'd stopped breathing altogether, we could then use Narcan and it would be classified as a 'real overdose'. But, needless to say, this would be totally ludicrous, not to mention seriously unethical.

At our regular team meeting I congratulated staff on getting to the end of the six months. Our latest figures indicate we're seeing on average over 100 visits each day; the number of client referrals into treatment continues to be high and the number of overdoses managed has increased slightly. The number of people using benzodiazepines, while still relatively low, continues to increase and, for the first time in four months, heroin has exceeded cocaine as the drug most frequently used; but it's still neck and neck, with heroin representing 47 per cent and cocaine 45 per cent of the drugs injected at the MSIC.

We also discussed ways in which we might be able to raise some money to buy Christmas presents for clients who come to the injecting facility on Christmas Day. Although some clients manage to return to wherever their family home is if they still have one, for those who remain in the area it is often a time of emotional crisis. We feel it's important to try to create some sense of Christmas celebration at this time. Meanwhile staff have contacted The Body Shop, which is well known for being a socially aware organisation, and they have agreed to donate some toiletries as Christmas presents.

Thursday, 8 November

The NSW Leader of the Opposition, Kerry Chikarovski, issued a press release today along the lines that the premier's support for this facility will mean that regional and country areas can now expect injecting centres to be opened on a street near them. So now it's not only every state that will have injecting centres thrust upon them any day soon, but every country town in NSW too!

These are clearly scaremongering tactics, which sadly sometimes work. No one would suggest—least of all our premier—establishing such facilities in areas other than where there is a high prevalence of street-based injecting, which only tends to occur in urban situations. Apparently the media in Yass have picked this up, with the sitting Coalition MP featuring in a lead story in the local newspaper berating the premier for opening the door to the possibility of an injecting centre being established in the area of Yass. Yeah, right.

Tuesday, 13 November

A Mr Garry Taylor, who says he's from the UN's International Narcotics Control Board (INCB), and a colleague arrived to discuss some research they're interested in doing and also to be shown through the injecting centre and to ask a number of questions. This appointment was arranged with me over the phone last week. But I must say, on meeting both Garry and his colleague, I was somewhat surprised by their informality—they did not present as the sort of people you'd expect to be working for the UN. I asked them if they had a card or other documentation but they told me no, they didn't—they're just setting up their office at this stage so they don't have cards or stationery, but they'll send one to me later. Anyway I proceeded to show them through the facility and answer their questions, even though I continued to wonder whether they were in fact from some other organisation or have some other interest. This project, unlike others I've been involved in, does seem to attract incredibly wide and diverse interest so you have to keep in the back of your mind that occasionally people might even use bogus credentials to obtain information, which can then turn up in unexpected places.

Thursday, 15 November

I was at a community safety committee meeting of South Sydney Council when someone stuck their head in the doorway to tell us that there had just been a public announcement that the North Ward of South Sydney Council, which includes the Kings Cross/Darlinghurst area, is to be transferred to Sydney City Council.

Only yesterday afternoon the City of Sydney's lord mayor, Frank Sartor, dropped in to the injecting centre quite unexpectedly and asked if he could have a chat with me. I had met him before, soon after it was previously mooted that there might be a boundary change and this would bring the MSIC into his electorate. So he popped in again yesterday to discuss some of his ideas for the area if such a thing were to happen, and now, within twenty four hours, there's this announcement.

At this early stage at least, it does seem as though there is good support for the injecting centre in the Sydney City Council. Also the council's bureaucracy is quite sophisticated, with a unit specifically focused on illicit drug issues. Given the rather lukewarm support we've had from John Fowler, the current mayor of South Sydney Council, this may well be better for us.

Friday, 16 November

In the evening I headed off to Geneva for a two-day World Health Organization meeting focusing on the need to establish standard drug regimens to treat HIV/AIDS among people in resource-poor countries. I'm wearing my Kirketon Road hat at this meeting, which makes a nice change, but it's a long way to go just for a two-day meeting.

Tuesday, 20 November

In my absence Colette attended a forum organised by the 2011 Residents' Association. Despite the fact that this association originally opposed the MSIC's location, as part of the Kings Cross Community Coalition, Colette's feedback is that those in attendance at this meeting were mainly supportive. They noted that drug-related activity in the area has declined during the six months since we opened, which is more reassuring news.

Wednesday, 28 November

We presented the results of the first six months at NDARC's Annual Symposium. Jo Kimber detailed the evaluation methodology and I talked about our experience from a clinical perspective. Mark Robinson wrote a preview in the *Sydney Morning Herald*. He quoted me as being cautious in my interpretation of these results and urging everyone to wait until the end of the trial before assessing our overall success. I am glad this finally got on the record in the media.

After my presentation I was interviewed by Channel Nine News. The journalist seemed to be miffed by the revelation that cocaine had been the most injected drug at the facility over the six months and suggested that we had been promoting the place as a heroin injecting room—so wasn't this a case of false advertising? I told him that, right from the outset, we had been concerned that the media kept describing the facility as a heroin injecting trial, knowing that many different drugs would be injected there and that it would cause confusion with a heroin prescription trial, which is quite a different type of intervention. But, try as we have, we could not reverse the media's preference for this misnomer, so we ended up just ensuring that at least our press releases always used the correct terminology of 'Medically Supervised Injecting Centre'.

It seems the mere mention of cocaine conjures up pictures of stockbrokers and advertising executives snorting the drug in nightclubs on a recreational basis. Many are surprised that we would be hosting such activities at this facility, which of course we aren't. It is among long-term heroin injectors that we have seen an increasing level of cocaine injection, which has been directly related to the heroin shortage this year.

It is in fact a good thing that the centre also accommodates cocaine injecting because, at least in the United States, this has been associated with as many overdose deaths as heroin. It can be associated with a rapid increase in blood pressure causing cerebral haemorrhage, seizures and cardiac arrest, either from irregular heartbeat or from spasm of the coronary arteries, leading to a myocardial infarct. Cocaine-induced psychosis is also a serious problem as it increases the risk of traffic accidents and other sometimes fatal injuries. We have managed all of the manifestations of cocaine toxicity (overdose) at the facility, which shows just how robust and versatile this type of initiative is. Drug use is not a static phenomenon; it is very subject to local conditions— what drugs are being supplied and what their relative quality and price is, which changes from day to day.

During my presentation to the NDARC symposium, I also mentioned that we appear to be managing quite a high rate of overdoses in the facility, compared to anecdotal reports from European facilities where overdoses apparently only occur in about 1 in 500 visits. We don't quite know the full explanation yet; it needs to be investigated further. Perhaps it is due to fluctuations in purity and drug users' tolerance because of the current heroin shortage. Particularly during the heroin shortage, drug users have also turned to the benzodiazepines for their sedating properties, which help tide them over heroin withdrawal symptoms and enhance the effect of the lower quality heroin. Clients develop a very high tolerance to benzodiazepines quite quickly, so they have to use more and more to get the same sedating effect and this then increases the risk of heroin overdose, even when only a small amount of heroin is injected. Both our client base and we are learning a lot about what the relative risks really are.

As previously noted, every time somebody overdoses at the facility it provides an opportunity to educate them as to why this happened. The European facilities have been in place for considerably longer than we have, so perhaps their client base will have had more opportunity to integrate such ongoing education into their patterns of injecting, lowering their risk over time.

Thursday, 29 November

The *Sydney Morning Herald* ran a follow-up article about the NDARC symposium, which included a boxed piece in which I was quoted as saying that there had been positive feedback from the community. But opposed to this there was also a contrary quote from the manager of a nightclub two doors down from our back exit onto Kellett Street stating that we had made no difference— according to him, there were still people shooting up near the exit to the injecting centre. When we looked into this we discovered that they are usually patrons from his own establishment nipping out for a quick shot. Given that this nightclub doesn't open until well after we have closed each evening, there is little we can do about that. But again we see how any positive reports in the press are usually neutralised by negative reports the next day. The media say they are just ensuring balance!

Friday, 30 November

We had a visit from Major Brian Watters today. In mid-August Brian had criticised the injecting centre on a number of different counts, including that it was not cost-effective, that we were hosting cocaine injecting among middle-class yuppies and that he had had reports of increased drug use and drug dealing in association with the MSIC. I had subsequently written a letter to him correcting this misinformation and asking whether there had been a shift in the ANCD's until then neutral position during the MSIC trial. Rather than replying in writing, he decided it would be better to visit the facility and speak to me in person.

Brian ended up spending a total of three hours at the facility, including a lunch break in the middle. As we walked out for this, we passed a client who was sitting in the waiting room. She was a particularly shocking example of someone who had been a long-term heroin injector who was now obviously using a lot of cocaine. I could tell this just from looking at her—the skin on her face was excoriated, with scabby sores; she was incredibly gaunt and emaciated; her scant clothing was grimy and dishevelled. Apparently Brian had seen her earlier teetering about on her scuffed stilettos at Kings Cross train station, on his way here. Brian was clearly quite shocked by the state she was in and said to me when we got outside: 'Well, I suppose that's really what this is all about.' Given his previous statements, I took the opportunity to inform him that she was typical of cocaine injectors seen at the MSIC—not exactly a middle-class yuppie.

Brian commented that it would be better if such people were required to attend treatment on a compulsory basis. But I suggested to him that, if a law was passed that forced people like her into treatment, it would be most unlikely that she would be in our waiting room now being engaged by our staff specially trained to help people in her situation. That sort of legislation would probably have the effect of driving people like her underground and making it even more difficult for us to make contact with them. Surely we are better off assisting her to minimise the harms associated with her drug-using lifestyle, keeping her alive until she is motivated to enter a treatment program? Unfortunately, even then, the long-term success of treatment programs is modest. But it's even less so when people aren't yet interested in stopping their drug use.

During the course of our meeting, Brian indicated that he'd only spoken out to quell reports that the centre was already a great success. I made the point that we, as operators of the facility, had never and would never assert that the service was a success while the trial was still in progress. Therefore, Brian should not feel the need to counter such claims in the media from our perhaps sometimes too-enthusiastic supporters, over whom we have no control. I urged him to distinguish us from such reports. At the same time I stressed that, as the service director, I would continue to describe our work in public forums to ensure that the community has a realistic understanding of what the facility may achieve.

It was clear from Brian's attitude overall that he is uncomfortable with the whole idea of the facility at a deep visceral level. I suppose it is quite radical that a facility has been custom-made to accommodate what continues to be an illegal activity in all other situations in Australia. On the other hand, it isn't when viewed as an extension of the needle syringe program (NSP), which has been the cornerstone of HIV prevention among injecting drug users in Australia for the past 15 years. Now, as well as dispensing clean needle syringes, as has occurred for all this time, we are allowing people to stay to inject their drugs in a clinical setting instead of heading off to a less safe public place in the local environs.

In this sense we are accepting a duty of care both to drug users and the rest of the Kings Cross community, which is not a very radical step at all really. If anything was radical it was the NSP, which acknowledges that some people will continue to inject drugs, despite all the best efforts to discourage this. But perhaps the injecting centre has forced us to face the reality of this in a way that the NSP never has. Brian did acknowledge that the Kings Cross area is different and may well warrant such an extreme response, but I get the feeling he is nervous that it won't end here.

Saturday, 1 December

Inevitably the MSIC's detractors have chosen to interpret our results in their own way, suggesting that the injecting centre has actually created the overdose problem. A letter to the *Herald* today from Paul Haege, the president of the Chamber of Commerce, claims I admitted there had been a significant increase in overdoses since the injecting centre opened and that there are more of them in Kings Cross than in any other area in the rest of the country, which of course is not at all what I said. I have written a letter to the *Herald*, to correct the assertions ascribed to me, and hope it will be published.

Monday, 3 December

In the late afternoon I got a phone call from Andy, reporting that there had been a serious incident at the MSIC involving Carly, a girl well known to the service, who had been intending to inject a benzodiazepine. At 4.45 pm, with blood smeared around her booth and on the floor from her various attempts, she still hadn't found a vein despite having been in the injecting room section of the facility for over an hour. We actually close at four, expecting people admitted up to that time to move through by about four thirty, when staff take their break before re-opening at six.

Staff had already warned her that time was running out and that she needed to make a decision, either to inject it intramuscularly or to take it orally, but that she couldn't remain there indefinitely. When one of the nurses finally asked her to finish up, Carly became extremely aggressive and abusive. She then stood up and sprayed the contents of her syringe, which was blood-filled by this stage, all around the second stage of the facility so that everything, including the computer equipment, desk, chairs, walls was covered in blood.

She threw the needle syringe down onto the ground and, as she did so, it stabbed the shin of the nurse who had asked her to call it a day. Then Carly stomped out angrily, first stopping to wash the blood off herself.

The staff were in shock, particularly Liz, the nurse who had sustained the needlestick injury. I advised Andy to refer Liz to Sydney Hospital for assessment. Meanwhile the remaining staff spent quite a lot of time cleaning blood from various surfaces in Stage 2 as well as from the trail Carly had left on her way to the exit from Stage 3. The facility was described to me as looking like a crime scene. It's amazing how a small amount of blood can spread. Such abuse and aggression, particularly from a known client, is always very distressing to staff; also then having to clean up so much blood was additionally disturbing for them.

For me there was also some added poignancy in my recollection that Carly had been among the clients we showed through before we opened. She had been very impressed with the facility, but she said she wouldn't be using it because she was now 'clean' (drug free). But, alas, this was not to last and now look at what has happened with her.

Andy later advised me that in view of how upset all the staff were he decided not to reopen the facility for the second session, and to let them have the rest of the shift off. I agreed to this. After I left Kirketon Road Centre later that evening, I went past the injecting centre, just to check that a sign had been put up to notify clients the service wasn't open. Unfortunately the sign on the door read *This service is temporarily closed until further notice*. I went in and took that sign down, replacing it with one saying that the service would be closed tonight and would be open again in the morning.

A sign like the original one could have been very quickly drawn to the attention of those vocal few in the community who are forever looking for any sort of indication that things are not going well for us. It's especially irritating that, when we are managing a horrible incident like this—which, when put into perspective, is the first of any magnitude after 12 000 individual visits, which we think is pretty good going—we also have to try to stop our detractors hearing about it so that it doesn't end up being reported in the press the next day.

I also informed Colette of the incident so she would be prepared when she arrived the next morning, and rang Tracey. She described the staff's reaction as ranging from being stunned to being very angry, with some suggesting that Carly should be charged with assault.

Liz, the nurse involved, has been working with this client population for a very long time and is therefore likely to be able to put this incident into a professional perspective. Her long experience should help her cope. Some people in such situations feel a lot of anger towards the client, which can be healthy, but sometimes this anger can go on to be directed at the entire client population, and you end up questioning your whole career choice. This is one of the reasons why burn-out is so rife in this sector, with few people hanging in there for the long haul.

It's hard enough working in this area, where it's so often two steps forward and one step back, without staff feeling threatened by the very people they're attempting to assist. So it's incredibly important for us to try to get our response to incidents like this right, balancing both the clients' and the staff's needs, if we're to maintain a skilled workforce over time. Liz already has lasted quite a distance, which we hope will help get her through this.

Tuesday, 4 December

Prior to opening, Colette brought the staff together. Particularly for those people who had been there, she arranged individual debriefings. She also wanted to discuss how to proceed in the event that Carly turned up again. The decision was that Carly shouldn't be able to use the facility in the foreseeable future and that sometime down the track, once the incident had been digested and processed, we would decide how long that time-out would go on for.

We're always very hesitant to apply long-term or indefinite bans to service access and in fact we deliberately don't use the term 'ban', preferring 'time-out'. Some clients boast about how many services they've been banned from and wear this as a badge of honour, and we don't believe that's particularly helpful.

We also try to avoid the notion that clients just have to do the time for the crime, which they very readily identify with, given that this is how the criminal system works and they are all too familiar with that. Instead, I would prefer clients to know that they have to do more than just serve the time— they actually have to make an effort to understand themselves better, give undertakings that this will not occur again and accept that their continued use of the service is conditional on that. In that way we hope to provide a learning opportunity about how to get on in the real world and at the same time show that we do understand that sometimes, particularly when they are using drugs like cocaine, methamphetamine and benzodiazepines, clients may have less control over their behaviours.

What complicates this particular situation somewhat is that Carly is on the methadone program at Kirketon Road Centre. Liz, like quite a few of the other staff members at the injecting centre, also works at the Kirketon Road Centre. Even though the two services are separately administered, given how close they are, both geographically and in terms of the target population, there's considerable crossover of clients and staff. So we need to ensure that staff at both facilities feel safe in their contact with Carly, while maintaining clients' confidentiality between the two services.

Wednesday, 5 December

At ten thirty this morning, before the service opened, four people from the Health and Police Departments arrived without notice to carry out one of their random service audits, to monitor that the MSIC is operating according to its licence conditions etc. I'm in Brisbane presenting a paper to a two-day conference entitled 'Drugs: A National Problem, Local Solutions' organised by Brisbane's lord mayor, Jim Sorley, as part of the capital cities' lord mayors initiative. Luckily Colette and Tracey were in the building, but they both had appointments that needed to be cancelled then and there so they could answer the various questions about the service's operation during the next four hours.

This is now the second time we've had one of these random, unannounced audits. After the first one, Harry Herbert was of the view that they were overdoing it. I argued that perhaps, if we just went with the flow in the early stages, they would ease up and we would not end up being over-audited. But not yet it would seem.

They couldn't have come at a worse time, so close on the heels of the Carly incident. Also, they remained while the service was operating, during which a drug overdose was managed in Stage 2 and an ambulance transport had to be organised for another very sick client with suspected septicaemia. Both these events were apparently well managed and nothing untoward happened during the visit.

But I think we should be given some notice, even if it's only 24 hours, so that existing arrangements don't have to be cancelled at the very last minute and I can be there. Also, such inspections shouldn't occur while the service is operating—the presence of four inspectors in the room while a drug overdose is being managed is unsafe; they get in the way and it makes staff tense when they need to be calm and in control. There's also the issue of client privacy, especially given the otherwise illicit nature of the activity.

On the matter of Carly, we have now received a report from Kirketon Road Centre that not only is she unrepentant about what happened but she is still feeling very angry towards Liz, who is actually rostered to work at Kirketon Road this weekend dispensing methadone. The centre operates on low staff levels, just providing needle syringe and methadone services on weekends, so this is a time when staff are more vulnerable security-wise. In view of Carly's lack of contrition we have arranged for Liz to be rostered off both days. A decision has also been taken to transfer Carly to another methadone program after the weekend.

Friday, 7 December

As it's turned out, this has been our busiest week so far—we've broken three sets of records in the course of five days. We've had 92 visits in one four-hour session; across one eight-hour day we saw 145 people and then the very next day 156. Staff reported that they coped well with this high level of activity. At a difficult time like this, being very busy also provides a distraction and allows us to regain perspective.

Thankfully Carly didn't return to the facility, so we were given a bit of breathing space. It is our intention to inform her, when she next goes to Kirketon Road, that she is not to attend here until after the new year. Liz does not want to pursue assault charges with police. Of course this is always an option but it would involve Liz having to testify in court, which might involve more trauma for her, and there's not a lot of evidence that an assault charge would modify Carly's behaviour anyway.

We've also communicated to the rest of our clients what occurred, especially because some were angry that the service had been closed for the evening session on Monday. We use every opportunity to reiterate to clients what is unacceptable behaviour in the injecting centre. But the vast majority of clients support the service and the staff who work here, and they certainly wouldn't wish them to be harmed in any way.

The *Herald* never ran my letter correcting Paul Haege's misrepresentations of what I'd said, even though I sent them two more emails suggesting I should have a right of reply given that I was personally identified in his letter. These weren't responded to either, and I didn't pursue it further.

Everybody was very pleased to come to the end of this week. Christmas is nearing but there's no indication that things are settling down and we also know that, if anything, this is the season when illicit drug use, and all of the health and social problems that go with it, increase. Christmas is when family issues often come to the fore for drug users; it can be a very emotional time, which affects how people use their drugs and how many risks they're willing to take. Suicide rates and assault rates, in association with alcohol, also increase across this period. The festive spirit, with more parties and more people drinking more alcohol than usual, further adds to the risks. So, as part of our regular fortnightly health promotional activity, we are developing a poster to remind clients that alcohol and heroin don't mix. We put these up in all the injecting booths in Stage 2.

Sunday, 9 December

And just to top the week off, Piers Ackerman has devoted another of his columns to attacking the MSIC in the *Sunday Telegraph*.

Wednesday, 12 December

I'd been invited to attend a meeting of the NSW Expert Advisory Committee on Drugs, at 8.30 am in the city. This meeting reports to the Special Minister of State, John Della Bosca, who was present; Professor Ian Webster was in the chair. We reviewed our progress during the first six months; then discussion moved on to the issue of when the trial will finish and what will happen after that.

The current Act allows the injecting centre to operate as a trial for only 18 months. Having been proclaimed on 1 May this year, it means that, come 1 November 2002, the centre will have to close unless there is further legislation already in place to allow it to continue. But the results of the service evaluation will not be available by 1 November—in fact, it will take some months before those results are collated, interpreted and reported to government. So, unless we are granted an extension, we will already need to start winding down by early September at the latest. We will need to arrange for staff to terminate their therapeutic relationships with clients, and to make alternative arrangements for clients, while staff themselves seek alternative employment. It's also likely that we would have to reduce our level of activity as staff find new jobs. This might even necessitate closing the service before 1 November if staff got other jobs before then, which they'd be advised to take up given that very few jobs are advertised later in the year. If the evaluation and subsequent debate resulted in allowing us to continue, we would then have to start up again almost from scratch.

So it follows that either we need to have an extension of the current legislation beyond the 18-month mark, to allow us to continue to operate while parliament considers our future, or the evaluation report needs to be tabled well before the end of the 18 months so the decision can be made by early September, when we would otherwise be starting to wind down. The evaluation would then end up not actually covering a full 18-month period, but more like a 15-month period. This would be a great pity, particularly because 18 months is quite a short time as it is to demonstrate impacts; we are only just now after 6 months really getting into our stride as a service. Ideally service evaluations shouldn't start until utilisation is representative of future use, so we are already likely to see the impacts dampened by the early months of relatively low activity. These matters were discussed, but not resolved during this meeting.

There were also concerns expressed that the full value of the centre cannot be properly assessed during what is now being regarded as a prolonged heroin shortage. But I impressed upon the group that I do not believe this has impaired our ability to show the value of the injecting centre; it is a strategy that addresses injecting-related harms, not heroin-related harms per se. The move across to cocaine injecting is associated with many significant harms and the centre has shown its ability to address those while at the same time managing the heroin overdoses that continue to occur despite this heroin shortage.

Later in the day, at our fortnightly clinical supervision session, we discussed the Carly incident. Now is a more appropriate time to think about the operational aspects that may have contributed to the incident happening. We considered various strategies to reduce the risks at closing time—just as in pubs at last-drinks time, there are often people who take exception to this. We agreed to warn every client who enters during the last fifteen minutes that they will be required to leave by four thirty—not that this wasn't done before, but we've decided to make it more systematic and explicit. We also decided that the security guard would move into the second (injecting) section at four thirty and that, if staff have any reason to believe that a client might be reluctant to finish up, they should stay a safe distance away, behind the security guard.

In the event that the security guard is unable to handle the situation, we agree that it's appropriate for the police to be called. We also need to keep impressing upon clients that the injecting centre is not a police-free zone and that we will call them if our own safety is at risk. Particularly in this situation, where clients are all essentially armed with blood-filled needle syringes which can potentially be used as weapons, we perhaps need to consider calling police sooner than otherwise.

Friday, 14 December

We have received news that Carly expressed remorse for her behaviour last week but accepts that she needs to be transferred from Kirketon Road's methadone program. In fact she has decided that she wants to get out of Kings Cross altogether and is actually quite pleased at this transfer. So, in a way, this time-out, like limit-setting of behaviours in general, may end up being a therapeutic intervention in itself and—who knows?—may be the making of Carly. I hope so. She certainly has a long history of many ups and downs. When she's up, things go very well indeed for Carly, but it's almost as though she can't cope with that unfamiliar state and then sabotages herself, a not uncommon phenomenon among this client population who are most accustomed with failure.

Carly has also agreed to testing for HIV, hepatitis B and hepatitis C at Kirketon Road Centre. These results will be of assistance in reassuring Liz, who is undergoing testing herself as part of the post-needlestick testing protocol. We have also decided in future to obtain consent from clients at first registration for us to contact the agency where they've had their last blood test for HIV, hepatitis B and C in the event that they are involved in a needlestick injury at the injecting centre.

This week one of our clients reached new heights—or perhaps depths—in terms of drug storage. She came in with her little balloon of heroin in her vagina and sat on the toilet in the third stage of the facility, where she found to her increasing dismay that she was unable to remove, or even locate, it. Becoming fairly desperate, she was inviting all and sundry in to have a go, but staff discouraged this. Despite trying over and over again herself, she was totally unsuccessful and we ended up referring her to a nearby medical service. Another for the collection of odd places to store your drugs!

On an even lighter note, a client commented to us today that another good thing about the drug speed is that there's only two sleeps to Christmas—despite it still being 11 days away!

Meanwhile staff went out during the break to buy more presents for the clients, which they'll wrap over the weekend. The Christmas cheer is definitely upon us now. Tracey ended up mentioning to Harry in passing that we wanted to raise some money for these presents, and he immediately said that UnitingCare would provide this. We were impressed, but he just kept castigating himself for not having thought of it himself. I sometimes forget that Harry is a holy man.

But then just today we received a letter from a solicitor stating that she represented someone who lives overseas, who has anonymously donated $3000 to pay for client-related expenses not covered within our budget. We are all amazed and intrigued. No one ever donates money to services for this clientele. We are all putting our minds to what we could purchase with this generous donation.

Tuesday, 18 December

I have written a letter on Harry's behalf to the licensing authorities raising our concerns in regard to the recent four-hour visit from the Health and Police Departments. The letter also questioned the condition that prevents us providing needle syringe to non-clients, particularly when other services are closed. While Dr Andrew Wilson, the previous Chief Health Officer, had indicated that he thought this might be varied on public health grounds back at a meeting in June, he has since moved to a professorial position in Public Health at the University of Queensland and been replaced by Dr Greg Stewart, so this needs to be revisited.

Thursday, 20 December

This was the evening of our very first Christmas party, and we'd arranged to have it at the Exhibition Hotel on Devonshire Street, opposite Central Station. The $200 left over from the Christmas donation from Uniting*Care* paid for the finger food provided by this rather modest establishment. I felt it was important that this should not come from the MSIC's budget, in line with the government sector, where Christmas functions are not allowed to be paid by the taxpayers' dollars.

The staff who were on duty until 10 o'clock came shortly thereafter, along with Arthur, our security person. When they arrived they announced that they had broken yet another record—with 188 visits for the two four-hour sessions today, so this was our Christmas present. I think staff were particularly gleeful that this record had been broken in the absence of management. Bad luck Damian and Andy!

Harry Herbert was there. It's great that Harry comes to these functions— I think it's very important for staff to see his involvement with the service and he seems to enjoy it too for that matter, although he thinks we could have chosen a slightly more salubrious venue!

Friday, 21 December

The presents are all wrapped and the Christmas decorations hang in the injecting centre. On the one hand there's a sense of holiday spirit and on the other a need to keep a special eye out for how the clients are faring throughout this period.

With Harry's support we have a multi-denominational approach at the facility. Sister Noeline from the Good Shepherd Sisters order, Rev. Ray Richmond from the Wayside Chapel, Father Steve Sinn from St Canice's and Rev. Greg Thompson from St John's Anglican Church are amongst the chaplains who drop in on occasions to spend some time, mainly in the third stage of the facility to make contact with clients. This has not been intrusive and has worked well. We've really appreciated having the support of all of the parishes in the area for this controversial initiative.

Tuesday, 25 December

There were 88 visits during the two sessions over Christmas Day, less than usual. As planned, clients were given Christmas presents that had all been wrapped and signed beforehand, which they enjoyed. It was a festive day with no crises.

nine

A New Year, new challenges

January 2002

I had time off between Christmas and New Year, although I did end up dropping in a couple of times, just to catch up on a few things. I then took all of January off—the longest holiday break that I'd taken in years.

I've found that running two services this past year has really stretched me. Although it's been a very, very interesting experience, personally and professionally, and I certainly wouldn't want to be doing anything else, it has taken its toll and I feel quite exhausted.

During January things are usually quieter from an administrative point of view, with no scientific or community meetings to attend. Even IDUs tend to take breaks away from Sydney at this time, so it's a good time to be having off. In keeping with the core public health principle of needing to ensure the sustainability of all efforts in this regard, I'm a strong advocate of people also taking care of themselves over time. You should also never allow yourself to become indispensable or, even worse than that, to *think* that you are indispensable.

I'd arranged for Dr James Bell, the specialist physician in charge of the Langton Centre in Surry Hills, to act in my role while I was away. James has been on our Policy Advisory Committee from the start so was abreast of clinical operations at the MSIC. While the average number of visits each day was 126 in December, it dropped back to 115 for the month of January.

However, during this period there seemed to be a slight easing of the heroin shortage, at least in the Kings Cross area, and there were a total of 24 heroin overdoses managed with fourteen of those requiring the use of Narcan. It is the protocol that, when an overdose occurs, the medical director—myself usually—is informed so as to be able to advise on what further action needs to be taken. I had assured James that drug overdoses were fairly rare and usually uncomplicated, but during my absence this changed significantly and there were more, and quite a few of them were actually quite complicated, but still nothing he couldn't manage over the phone.

Tuesday, 29 January

We had our first community consultative committee meeting of the year, which was very well attended. We met Superintendent Dave Darcy for the first time. He is the new patrol commander for the Kings Cross Police, replacing Alan Baines, whom we'll miss. Dave was a beat policeman in Kings Cross back in 1997, under Mal Brammer's command, so he already knows the area quite well from a street policing perspective. He tells us how back then they would be called to at least two drug overdose deaths a week, and it was their job to make contact with the person's relatives to tell them the bad news, something they all used to dread. He said this was in stark contrast to now—there not having been a single overdose death for almost 5 months—which was a great relief to police.

I'd never stopped to think about what it would be like for police to have the role of informing the families of drug users that they had died like this and how that must affect them. Parents can react in a lot of different ways to such news—family relationships often having been under a lot of strain and pressure as a result of their child's drug use. On the other hand some parents have absolutely no idea their child has been injecting drugs.

Dave further reported that in the last couple of weeks since his appointment, he has spoken to almost all of his officers and they have reported that they have had no difficulty policing around the facility and that they are broadly supportive of the injecting centre. The police department's Drug Coordination Unit has also produced a card with a map showing where the injecting centre is and detailing the various services offered here and by other agencies in the area. Police will give these cards to drug users should they come across anyone still injecting on the streets.

Dave reported that the police also believe there has been an increase in the quality of heroin in the area in recent weeks and that the ambulance service has been called out to more overdoses, with Narcan needing to be used more frequently than for a very long time.

We have also been surprised to hear from people in the area that they were glad not to hear the sound of ambulances on the main street of Kings Cross as often since the MSIC opened. It wasn't the actual noise of the sirens, but the thoughts they conjured of someone lying unconscious or dead from an overdose somewhere nearby, which disturbed them. They are relieved that we are now here to look after people in this situation. It shows again that this is a very caring, humane community in the main.

Hotel owner Tom MacMahon said they've observed a slight increase in injecting around the Springfield Mall area. We agreed, as a group, to keep in communication on this and particularly to advise local services, including the police, of the need to inform drug users about the increased risk of drug overdose at this time.

We also discussed with Dave the use of drug sniffer dogs in the area. He said that recent new legislation has confirmed the legality of using dogs to conduct searches on people for drugs, and that this type of patrol will continue. It's his view that cannabis supply is an important problem in the Kings Cross area; there are more arrests for cannabis supply and possession here than in any other area in NSW. While this doesn't directly affect the injecting centre, I impress upon Dave that heroin users sometimes sell small amounts of cannabis to help fund their habit. Putting additional pressure on this type of activity may well see them move across to other cash-generating activities, such as break-and-enters, bag snatches and street prostitution to get money, which may have a more negative impact on the local community. He agreed to monitor this.

Friday, 1 February

We are now at the halfway mark for the trial—it's nine months since the enabling legislation was proclaimed and we have nine months to go. We congratulated the staff for at least getting to the halfway mark.

Carly has returned to both Kirketon Road and the injecting centre in recent weeks. Liz is coping very well with this, as we had hoped, and the other staff likewise are no longer as emotional about the situation.

We had previously made no definitive decision about Carly. It's very important not to make such decisions in the heat of the moment; it's inevitable, and understandable, that in those circumstances staff would feel a strong need to support the staff member most directly involved and want to punish the client, which at a certain level may be well deserved. But we've found that ultimately this doesn't necessarily lead to the best outcomes for all concerned.

By the time Carly came back, she was expressing great remorse about what had happened. In the interim she had gained a lot of insight and she undertook not to allow any situation like that to occur again. While of course we know this can never be guaranteed, we do try to give clients an opportunity to show they can change, if given a second chance, particularly when, as in Carly's case, it is the first such incident. So we asked Carly what she thought would be a reasonable condition to impose on her to prevent it happening again and she agreed that perhaps she should not be allowed to inject benzodiazepine drugs, which had been involved in this incident, at the MSIC. So we agreed to that.

The recent review of our budget performance to date shows we're operating well within budget. In fact it looks like we may be several hundred thousand dollars in the black by the end of the financial year so we have had anything but a 'budget blow-out' in this first year of operation.

We've also decided that in two weeks' time we will extend the afternoon session to 4.30 pm, instead of 4, as at the moment. We will then close and reopen at 6 pm. We have found that the time between the sessions isn't always that well utilised and that the afternoon session continues to be our busiest time so we can extend it to 4.30 pm at no additional cost and meet client needs a bit more than before.

I am scheduled to address the 12th International Conference on the Reduction of Drug-related Harm being held in Slovenia in March about the MSIC, so I will have some work to do for this between now and then. I also intend to visit some injecting centres in Frankfurt at that time. I have visited centres in the Netherlands and Switzerland before now, but have never seen any of the German injecting centres.

Tuesday, 26 February

I received a call today from AAP, informing me that the UN's International Narcotics Control Board (INCB) is tomorrow releasing its annual report together with a press release, currently embargoed, which, amongst other things, recommends the closure of the Sydney MSIC. It considers the MSIC to be in contravention of the UN's drug control treaties by condoning drug use. I was asked for my comments. I passed this inquiry to Pat Kennedy to pass on to Minister Della Bosca's press secretary. The INCB is, after all, being critical of the government's policy in allowing us to operate, so it seems most appropriate that the government should respond. From our end, if anybody responds to this, we decide it will be Harry Herbert as the licence holder.

This evening we had our monthly community consultative committee meeting and I alerted members to the likelihood that tomorrow there will be negative publicity from the INCB. I specifically briefed Clover Moore, a member of our committee, in case she is called upon to respond. Of course the injecting centre no more condones injecting drug use than does the needle syringe program, which has prevented a serious HIV epidemic among injecting drug users and therefore the rest of the population in Australia. The Kings Cross community has been very supportive of the NSP over the years; most people moved to the area knowing that it had a street-based drug problem and understanding the complexities of the illicit drugs issue in general. But for many years I have often been asked at local community meetings why Kirketon Road only gave out needle syringes and didn't also allow people to inject there rather than in residents' front yards, and the back lanes, public parks and toilets nearby. I could only respond that it wasn't legal to do so at that time. But now it is—at the MSIC—so how can this have made things worse?

Wednesday, 27 February

Dave Darcy rang me this morning to say that last night there'd been a death from heroin overdose at the Hampton Court Hotel, quite near the injecting centre. Apparently the person involved was a 37-year-old male who had just been released from prison. He was found dead in the hotel bar's toilets, with the injecting paraphernalia spread out on the floor. This overdose death was probably contributed to by the fact that he would have had a lower tolerance to heroin, having just come out of prison. Given where he was found, he may well have been alcohol-affected too.

When Dave told me about this, the first thing I wondered was whether he was a client of ours—being recently out of jail, probably not. The very next thing I asked is what time it occurred. It was apparently at 9.30 pm, which is the time we close our front doors. I suppose it's a sad indictment of myself that the first thing I thought of was what this meant for the injecting centre, knowing that this is the sort of event that can get into the press as proof that the MSIC has failed.

However, Dave was actually ringing me because he was wondering whether it would be worth putting additional manpower out to specifically bust heroin dealers, since they must be selling particularly strong heroin at this time.

I advised him that I didn't think that this would necessarily prevent overdoses occurring. In fact disrupting street-level dealing is, if anything, counterproductive from this perspective. Dr Lisa Maher's research in Cabramatta demonstrates that the more the street supply of drugs is disrupted, the riskier it is for drug users because they are forced to make contact with dealers whom they don't know. When there's no existing relationship, the quality and the quantity of heroin becomes less reliable. This is never particularly reliable, of course, given the unregulated nature of the illicit drug market, but being even more desperate to obtain drugs and then buying them from whoever is selling rather than their regular supplier seems to increase the variability. It would seem that it is a change in circumstances per se that increases the risk of drug overdose, more so than drug purity.

I was also able to emphasise to Dave that the relationship between a drug user and their dealer is probably more important to them than their own lives. Besides, taking out local dealers is usually only effective on a very short-term basis, i.e. until other dealers operating elsewhere hear about this new window of opportunity—often within hours—and waste no time in taking the place of the removed drug dealers. It is as though there is a waiting list to be a dealer in Kings Cross. Drug supply is subject to free market forces like no other market that I can think of, and it is extremely efficient as a result.

I suggested to Dave that instead it might be worthwhile for police to warn drug users they come across on the street of this extra risk and to use their cards to direct people to the injecting centre. If police can get involved at this level, it sends a very powerful message to drug users that police are concerned for their welfare. It is also good for police morale to feel part of the solution; this is the best protection against police corruption in my view.

Later on today we had two heroin overdoses at the injecting centre which, like the other overdoses in the last six weeks, required Narcan and were successfully managed on site. We've given staff additional training in resuscitation in the last six weeks because of the increase in the number and severity of overdoses. Even in situations where we've had up to three overdoses occur within a half-hour period, they have coped. Other clients have also been very cooperative in this situation, moving on and not causing any problems with the flow.

In our phone conversation Dave Darcy also mentioned that they had recently seized heroin in the area which was in 'rock' form and was extremely high quality, the sort of quality that they had not seen in the area for a very long time. So all the signs suggest that the easing of the heroin shortage is continuing.

The radio stations and newspapers have carried stories on the INCB's call for the injecting centre's closure. John Della Bosca's office has put out a press release in our support, pointing out that this is the third annual report in which the INCB has called for this initiative to be abandoned so this is nothing new. The NSW government sought their advice way back in 1999, specifically as to whether the proposed facility would constitute a contravention of the relevant UN covenants, and members of the INCB subsequently visited

Sydney. Harry Herbert, along with Minister Della Bosca, met with them on that occasion and explained the nature of the trial. At that stage the INCB indicated that it was at least pleased that the service would be thoroughly evaluated and was oriented towards health outcomes for drug users, rather than just reducing the public nuisance associated with street-based drug use.

So it does seem very odd that the INCB has singled us out, particularly given that it is based in Vienna, within spitting distance of about fifty other injecting centres in Europe, none of which is run on such a controlled clinical service model as this is. But perhaps this explains the INCB's strident opposition to us—if a more formal operation like this proves to be effective, it may be the thin end of the wedge. Their report does also criticise the heroin prescription programs in Switzerland and the Netherlands and the Dutch drug policy in general, so at least we are in some good company!

As planned, I refrained from making any public comments and Harry Herbert spoke on our behalf to some of the radio journalists. The story was already losing its legs by the afternoon when Kerry Chikarovski weighed in by holding a press conference to raise the issue of our budget 'blow-out', which had first been raised in the media last June. We dealt with this very proactively back then, explaining about the unexpected costs from the delays and legal challenges and what comparable services cost, but it seems we didn't undo the damage these allegations caused even though we are in fact running well under budget. Many people, even our supporters, still remember this being aired in the press and what they took away from it was that we are indeed an expensive service, although interestingly they didn't necessarily see it as a major problem on the basis that it's hard to put a dollar value on lives saved. Hearing it all regurgitated yet again is disappointing and irritating, to say the least.

We had a team meeting late in the afternoon and reassured staff that we are operating well within the budget and that the government will not be closing the injecting centre in response to the INCB.

Brian Watters appeared on Channel Ten's News that night. Identified again, as the chair of the ANCD, he agreed with the INCB's directives for the injecting centre to be closed. He said that the injecting centre initiative gave voice to those people promoting the legalisation of drugs, confirming his nervousness that the MSIC may be the thin end of that wedge.

This evening I was told that apparently it is standard protocol for the INCB to give advance notice to the relevant national government when they are going to make any adverse comments about activities in that country. It would seem that the federal government received notification of this some weeks ago, but apparently didn't pass this on to the NSW government, which as a result was caught on the back foot today. There is a suggestion that the difference in political colour between the two levels of government may have had something to do with this.

It is unfortunate that this initiative is continuing to get caught up in such politics; we've already long given up hope that we will be spared becoming an election issue in the run-up to the state election next year and events today have confirmed that. It's such a pity that the drugs issue hasn't been approached in the same non-partisan way that Australia approached the serious threat of HIV in the mid 1980s. This has been widely recognised as having been crucial to getting our response right.

Oh, and we have never heard again from Garry Taylor and his colleague—the pair who had purported to be from the INCB.

European 'drug consumption centres'

Saturday, 2 March 2002

I flew to Frankfurt and then on to Ljubljana in Slovenia, where I am presenting a paper on the injecting centre, in tandem with Jo Kimber from the evaluation team at the 12th International Conference on the Reduction of Drug-related Harm. On the plane I read a letter in the *Herald* from Tony Trimingham calling on Brian Watters to clarify yet again what the ANCD's position towards the injecting centre is, given that it had previously been its position to refrain from comment until the end of the trial when the results could be assessed. Tony, whose son Damien had died of a heroin overdose at the bottom of a stairwell of Surry Hills' St Margaret's Hospital, has been a member of the ANCD himself in the past, and a vocal advocate of the harm reduction approach. As always his was a good letter.

Monday, 4 March

I made my presentation about the rationale for having developed a clinical service model for the Australian MSIC on this, the second day of the conference. At this symposium, which was dedicated to presentations on supervised injecting centres, Jo and I, along with the Canadians, who are planning a trial facility in the near future, occupied four of the six spots. The other two were taken up by speakers from Switzerland and the Netherlands.

Other very interesting presentations at this conference related to the heroin prescription trials being conducted in Switzerland and the Netherlands. They're soon to commence in Germany too. Switzerland has been trialling heroin prescription among IDUs since 1994. At the end of this session someone moved that in view of their excellent results, they hoped that by next year's conference these would no longer be referred to as trials. I had a sudden flash that maybe, rather than making a definitive decision as far as to continuing the MSIC on a permanent basis after the evaluation results are reported, the NSW government might be similarly tempted to just extend the trial, as has happened with these heroin trials.

Another member of the audience noted that Switzerland, unlike, say, the Netherlands, is perceived to be a very conservative country, so it was surprising that it had initiated the first heroin trials (and also injecting centres for that matter). The Swiss panellist retorted: 'No, we are not progressive but, as a country, we do listen to reason.' In those few words I think he really summed up what I would hope to be the approach in Australia.

Sometimes these harm reduction conferences can have a slightly evangelical tone about them, which, because I am very science-based myself, I find disconcerting. At times, you get the feeling that, if you were to criticise any of the harm-reduction strategies, you might be lynched! But, particularly since Gerry Stimson has taken over as program director, the presentations are becoming less polemical and harder in terms of being evidence-based. On the other hand, it is always reassuring to come together with colleagues from other countries who run similar programs for a bit of solidarity, encouragement and support. Quite a number of them emailed during the course of last week, following the INCB's international press release, urging us to keep our chins up and press on.

Wednesday, 13 March

I arrived back in Frankfurt on Monday and arranged to visit the four different 'drug consumption rooms', as they call their injecting centres, over the next few days. These rooms have now been operating in Frankfurt for up to eight years—so they are by no means new initiatives. I lamented to a female staff member in one of the facilities there that we had been inundated with visitors wanting to see the MSIC which we found hard to cope with, but figured this would drop away when we ceased to be seen as such a new and radical thing. But she was quick to say that they continue to host many, many visitors (like me) from many different countries around the world, despite operating for years.

I was allowed to see the injecting rooms while they were operational.

Compared to these centres, and others I have seen before in Switzerland and the Netherlands, the MSIC—with its very contemporary stainless-steel walls, bold colours and high-tech equipment—looks very state-of-the-art. A Swiss colleague once described it as the Rolls Royce of the series!

The drug users here in Frankfurt generally looked a lot more ragged—their clothing and general appearance are far more unkempt; they are a lot less healthy-looking than drug users in Kings Cross. This perhaps stems in part from it being much colder and wetter in this part of the world, making homelessness more gruelling. The HIV situation is also much worse among IDUs in Europe. The prevalence of HIV in this street-based population in Frankfurt is up around 50 per cent, which is very, very much higher than what we see in Kings Cross, where it is only 2–3 per cent. About 80 per cent of the injecting episodes hosted in these facilities are to inject crack cocaine. Crack use has apparently become much more prevalent in Europe since the mid-nineties, and has well and truly taken over from heroin injection as the main drug used. This would be another important reason they have a lower rate of heroin overdose compared to us.

I told the operators at these facilities that I wake up every morning and thank our lucky stars that we don't have crack cocaine in Australia (touch wood). Crack is usually smoked, which is less of a barrier compared to injecting, so more people try it. It is also very cheap, which means it's affordable to young people and those of lower socioeconomic status, who are the most drug-price sensitive. The feeling it induces is apparently intensely pleasurable, but only very short-lived, so it quickly leads to compulsive use to regain this intense pleasure over and over again. It has also been shown to be a gateway to the transition to injecting as a mode of drug administration and increases risky sexual behaviour. Then, to top it off, just about all the treatment interventions that have been attempted—particularly in the United States, over more than a decade now, and in Europe for at least five years—have had very limited success, if any at all. Let it never reach our shores.

These injecting centres are often staffed by university students on clinical placement as part of their social work or other related degrees. It is considered good experience early on in your career in the human services field, while still bright-eyed; high turnover of staff is assumed. They don't employ current or recently ex-injecting drug users in the injecting room section of their facilities, which is in keeping with the professional model that we operate under too.

I have had a concern that witnessing so many injecting episodes might demystify the procedure among staff, so that they might be at risk of contemplating injecting drug use. But when I've checked on this among our staff there has been the resounding response that, if anything, since working at the MSIC they are much less likely to, given just how messy and desperate the whole thing seems to be at times. From my own personal perspective, I agree. So maybe we should consider allowing school kids to visit the MSIC after all, just as I facetiously suggested when addressing the issue of what message an injecting centre might send to young people in my speech to second the resolution at the Drug Summit!

These drug consumption rooms do not employ registered nurses but the counsellors are all trained in basic life support measures. They resuscitate using air (which has 21 per cent oxygen) and not 100 per cent oxygen as we do, and it is only in two of the centres that there are doctors nearby who can administer Narcan in opioid overdose situations, so their ambulance call-out rate is much higher than ours. The overdoses that occur tend to be associated with heroin or pill and barbiturate use. Since the restrictions were imposed on barbiturate prescribing in Australia in the eighties, it's extremely rarely used by IDUs here. Before then, when I was a junior doctor at St Vincent's, barb overdose cases were admitted to hospital almost daily.

All the centres here have mirrors on the walls to help clients to inject in their necks, which makes them look a bit like hairdressing salons. As previously noted, neck injecting is not allowed at the injecting centre in Sydney. We even ended up removing the mirror in the bathroom to discourage this. Injectors can remain in the injecting room section of these facilities for up to half an hour, and inject as many times as they please. In Sydney we only allow people to inject the once but don't have a time restriction.

They are very busy, often creating quite a chaotic atmosphere, with a lot of blood around. Clients clean up their own areas afterwards. We started out with this policy but found that it was rarely done to infection control standards, so our staff now clean the booth area between clients.

Smoking is also allowed in all the injecting centres, in some even the areas where actual injecting takes place. Staff are also allowed to smoke while on duty, which adds to the overall atmosphere of informality. But in Europe generally, smoking is still very prevalent and more socially acceptable everywhere. It was of course not that long ago that it was the same here; it's amazing how quickly you adapt to having smoke-free environments—so you really notice it when somewhere isn't smoke-free.

Staff say that, because of the high prevalence of crack cocaine injecting, they have almost daily incidents in which clients are abusive. There is verbal aggression on an almost hourly basis, which they say is highly stressful for staff. In one instance recently, a knife was drawn on a staff member. They showed me their list of clients who were timed out for aggression, and it had at least fifty names on it. We have about five clients timed out at any one time.

At least three of the four facilities are integrated with programs that provide drug treatment, including methadone. There is also integration with employment and training programs, and even accommodation, which seems very worthwhile given the higher level of homelessness among these drug users. They rotate their staff around through those programs to reduce the stress on them. I wish we could do that with KRC and the MSIC. As well as reduce stress, it would improve continuity of care and increase staff job satisfaction too.

A great initiative here, on the accommodation side, is providing what they call day beds or what we are now starting to term 'crash beds' for people who have been on crack cocaine binges. We're currently recommending that this be considered in the Kings Cross area for people who have been on cocaine injecting binges, sometimes not sleeping for several days at a time.

Three of the facilities in Frankfurt are centrally located, in the red light district near the railway station where drug supply has been concentrated for many years. The area is very similar in character to that of Kings Cross. These are all shopfront, ground floor services, like the MSIC. Apparently the local chamber of commerce there actually contributes to their funding because they consider it good for business and tourism that drug-related activities occur there instead of in public on the streets. Good idea!

The fourth service is located in an industrial area five or six kilometres from Frankfurt's CBD. It was interesting to discuss the issues involved in locating services like these, particularly speaking to the person who ran the facility in the industrial area, because it's been suggested that drug facilities in Australia should be located in industrial areas too. Unlike the others, this particular facility has had a lot of complaints from neighbouring industrial premises. Because there is no reason for people to be in this area other than as clients of the facility, when break-and-enters occur—and of course some of these industries have things worth taking—then the finger is immediately pointed at this service.

There is a shuttle bus that goes to this consumption centre on the hour every hour while it is open, picking up drug users from the part of Frankfurt where the other facilities are located. It's mainly drug users who are no longer allowed to go to those other rooms, because of crack- or pill-related violence, that make this round trip. (I don't envy that bus driver's job!) As a result, dealers have now established themselves in the industrial area around the facility as well. The authorities try to control this as much as possible but they know they're fighting a losing battle, which further raises the ire of the industrial operations nearby. So they've had more difficulties with this location, even though originally, back in 1994, it was decided by the police and the city to locate this first injecting centre specifically in this area because it was assumed that this would minimise any impact IDUs' presence may have nearby. This experience confirms to me that you need to locate such facilities in areas where the drug-using population already resides, which is where drug supply already occurs. This doesn't solve the drug supply problem, of course, but at least it doesn't increase or expand the problem out to an area where it doesn't already exist.

In Frankfurt a trial heroin prescription program has been proposed and a site, away from the red light area and quite deliberately in a more suburban part of the city, has been identified. But it's currently being held up by protests from quite a few different sectors of the local community near the proposed site. This may mean Frankfurt won't become one of the seven sites in Germany where they're commencing a heroin prescription trial in July.

It seems that the problems of service location are currently also being experienced in other parts of Europe, including Switzerland. In Bern the heroin prescription program which has operated for six or so years is now being threatened in the courts with closure by local businesses. So there is clearly an urgent need to gather evidence on the effect of the location of facilities on local communities and on this basis decide where it's best to locate them. It's all very well demonstrating that needle syringe programs and the like save massive economic and social costs through the prevention of HIV and other blood-borne infections, but if communities aren't willing to host them then we're no further ahead and at risk of going out backwards. Our injecting centre trial will provide evidence on this impact and hopefully make a contribution towards the body of knowledge we need to develop in this regard around the world to sustain public health programs for drug users.

The Frankfurt drug consumption centres are also set up as what they call 'contact cafés'—the injecting room is off to one side and is only one of a number of facilities offered, which may also include subsidised meals, showers and laundry. So they are more extended service models, which are less clinical and more social-welfare focused than ours. In one contact café they have a pillar on which they have various stickers bearing the names and dates of people who have died, either from AIDS or from drug overdoses or other mishaps, including murders. It's a very sobering sight.

In fact I've found the whole experience of visiting these facilities quite sobering. The drug users here look much older and more hopelessly entrenched in their habits compared to the majority of the people we see in Kings Cross, who are among the most marginalised drug users in Australia. It's very challenging to inspire the MSIC's core client population towards drug treatment and rehabilitation; they've usually seen it all before and lack much-needed motivation. But as a clinician I wouldn't know where to start with this IDU population in Frankfurt. I take my hat off to the staff here who work here.

I continue to be concerned that these more extended social welfare models potentially normalise injecting—people often stay there for the best part of the day, having a bite to eat, then popping in to the side room for a shot before doing their laundry and so on. In sharp contrast, I very deliberately designed the MSIC like a hospital emergency centre. I hoped to send the message that every time IDUs put a needle in their arm and inject a drug they are taking their life into their hands, such that a high-tech, clinical set-up with staff equipped to resuscitate medical emergencies is required to keep them alive. By doing this, I hope that over time other unsupervised injecting environments will become increasingly less acceptable to the client base and meanwhile we will continue to look for opportunities to encourage contemplation of other ways forward in their lives. But given where this IDU population is at, in Frankfurt anyway, perhaps a more social-welfare focused approach is more appropriate; they also have few other places offering these services compared to Kings Cross, where a range organisations provide such assistance. Horses for courses, I suppose.

But sometimes I do wish that the people who criticise the social welfare and drug treatment systems in Australia could see how it happens elsewhere and realise how well we are doing. We have a relatively well-funded, comprehensive and equitable health and social welfare system, which we should be proud of.

I also can only hope that we never have to cope with the scourge of crack cocaine; that we manage to contain the current cocaine injecting epidemic that we've seen in the Kings Cross area for the last year and that our HIV prevention efforts continue to be effective in this population.

eleven

Celebrating our first birthday

Monday, 18 March 2002

I'm back and everything at the injecting centre has gone well during my two weeks away. However, there has been another heroin overdose death in the neighbourhood; it occurred early one morning at Maxim's, one of the 'private' hotels on the main street in Kings Cross. This second death, quite soon after the recent one, which was the first in many months, suggests that the heroin shortage is continuing to ease in Kings Cross.

Wednesday 20 March

This evening I drove out to a motel near Westmead Hospital, where I'm being put up for the night in preparation for a breakfast forum talk I'm to give at 7.30 am tomorrow morning. I always feel nostalgic driving to this part of the western suburbs. I grew up only a mile away, in the suburb of Wentworthville, and went to the state high school at Greystanes, further west towards Blacktown. Of course it's all changed a lot since then. The Westmead Hospital complex didn't exist when I lived here, before moving closer to the University of NSW where I undertook my medical degree, all those years ago. Concerned that I might get lost, the organisers went to the trouble of sending me a map to help me get to Westmead. They hardly needed to—my father taught me to drive in Parramatta Park, just one block from here!

My parents migrated to Australia from the Netherlands with my two older brothers in 1950 when Australia was actively seeking to expand its labour force, recruiting from various European countries. My family spent their first ten years at Warragamba near the Nepean River, further west of Sydney. My father worked on the dam construction; he was a fitter, turner and welder.

My parents were married and had my two brothers during the Second World War, when they lived in Amsterdam, which was under German occupation for most of those years. My father had been part of the youth socialist movement in the 1930s, which became the Dutch resistance movement during the war. Like most migrants, they took a step backwards socially and economically, joining the working class when they arrived here in Australia. But also like most migrants, they invested heavily in their children's education, believing that this was the only playing field on which we would have a chance of successfully competing. Despite having little money and no job security—my father was often out on strike, unpaid for weeks at a time during the industrially unstable 1970s—nothing was too expensive when it came to our education. I only narrowly escaped being sent to the Methodist Ladies College in Burwood for my high school years, preferring instead to go to a state school where I feared for my personal safety on a daily basis. Greystanes High had a lot of 'tough kids' then, who weren't exactly enchanted with some of my apparently uppity ways despite all my efforts not to seem different to them. Attending ballet classes and performing on stage in pantomimes during my earlier years probably didn't help much either!

The careers adviser at Greystanes said it would take a computer error for me to get into medicine anywhere—our school rated well below average in terms of getting its HSC students into the top percentiles necessary to study medicine. And perhaps that was what happened—I was by no means the brightest in my class. But what probably gave me an edge was my parents' support and that I had role models; my older brother Jurriaan was already studying medicine at the University of NSW throughout my high school years, having completed a Master of Science majoring in physics before that. He now has a rural general practice and sub-specialises in obstetrics in northern NSW. My other brother, Hajo, was a marine engineer and worked on BHP's ships freighting iron ore. He died in a car accident in 1985.

People often ask me why I chose to work in this particular field of medicine. I think this evolved from a deep concern for social justice, which originated from my parents' involvement with the Dutch resistance during the war; they would say that personal integrity was about having the courage of your convictions, even when these were contrary to prevailing beliefs of the day.

This was later reinforced by my appreciation of social inequity—my 'success', if indeed becoming a doctor is an indicator of success, had come about largely because I had more opportunities than most of my peers in the west.

The clients I now look after as a doctor have likewise usually had very few opportunities in life. I consider myself lucky to be able to address this social inequity in my professional life by promoting health and well-being among this marginalised population.

Thursday, 21 March

There was an excellent turn-up to my breakfast forum presentation, especially for such an early meeting. It was videotaped and copies were sent to all of the drug and alcohol coordinators in the seventeen area health services in NSW.

I returned to Kings Cross by 10 am to be interviewed by a team from ABC-TV's *Four Corners*, who are doing a story on the heroin prescription trial that was proposed for the Australian Capital Territory some years ago and was eventually scuttled, largely for political reasons.

I agreed with the interviewer that a heroin prescription trial might have some benefits for the more long-term, entrenched and homeless injecting drug users, who have tried all types of treatments, without success, and who are often heavily engaged in criminal activity to support their heroin habits. At the Slovenia conference, the Swiss and the Dutch both presented very compelling data to suggest that this small but important sub-population of drug users do better on all parameters when introduced into the drug treatment system through a heroin prescription program.

While I endorsed this, I also suggested that we should avoid being nihilistic in our views—we mustn't succumb to the idea that, because we don't have a heroin program in Australia, our entire broad-based drug program is of no worth. But while it shouldn't necessarily be the litmus test to assess all progress to date, I do appreciate that, like this injecting centre trial, the abandoned heroin trial is symbolic in terms of the federal government's willingness to embrace evidence-based drug policy-making.

However, you always know that, in such situations, television program makers have usually developed their themes long before they talk to you, particularly in a situation like this, when I was the last person interviewed for this program, which is going to air in a week or two. So, even though I was interviewed for a full hour on wide-ranging aspects of drug use, I was also always aware that 99 per cent of my words would end up on the cutting room floor and the only grabs used would be those that fitted in with the overall theme already developed and decided upon.

Friday, 22 March

We had our Policy Advisory Committee meeting in the morning, which Harry Herbert chairs. I informed the committee that we are currently reviewing our operating hours. Being well within budget at this stage, we think it's time to consider extending our hours so as to further maximise the impact that this service can have.

Operating eight hours a day, as we presently do, we don't enjoy any economies of scale. The large-ticket items, such as the rent for the facility, are fixed costs so they wouldn't increase with an extension of hours, particularly if those hours were in the morning, which wouldn't attract salary penalty rates. The staff are also keen for longer sessions—being able to work 12-hour shifts would make it more attractive for them as they could get their work over and done with in a few days and then have a block of days off in a row. To prevent burn-out this actually works better—having a good break in between a run of shifts, rather than having multiple shorter shifts, can be beneficial.

Originally I had anticipated that staff might find the work so stressful that they would not want to work long shifts and this was part of the reason for deciding to operate in two four-hour sessions. The other reason was to try to straddle as much of the day as we could. However, staff would now like to be able to work longer continuous shifts, which may also enhance our ability to recruit staff. Recruitment is an important consideration, particularly as the nursing shortage across the country has made this harder.

We have still not heard back about the licence condition being amended to allow us to provide needle syringes from the front counter of the service when other NSP services in the area are closed. Apparently a letter has been drafted and is currently with the NSW Police Commissioner, the other licensing authority. However, the Health Department's representative on the Policy Advisory Committee indicated to us that it's unlikely that the licence condition will be changed. Up to now, when there were no NSP services open in the area and staff judged that refusing to give needle syringes would be a public health risk or an occupational health and safety risk, they have used their discretion. Thankfully, this has only occurred very rarely.

I will now also explore with KRC whether its weekend hours can be adjusted so that the MSIC overlaps with these. Luckily I am on good terms with the director there! And I will also write to NSW Health letting them know that MSIC staff will continue to apply their discretion in situations where they judge their safety to be at risk.

At times like this, it concerns me that the bureaucracy sometimes seems to avoid changes in policy merely because this might indicate that they got it wrong in the first place, which may then lay them open to criticism and risk upsetting their political masters. Not accepting the need for a policy change may reduce the bureaucracy's political risk, but in this case it increases the safety risk for the people at the front line, who are my responsibility. This is where being a non-government organisation is very different and I find this decision hard to swallow.

Tuesday, 26 March

I was interviewed by Mike Carlton in the studio at 2UE. He's been a supporter of this initiative from the start. I underlined the fact that this is not a heroin injecting trial, but a Medically Supervised Injecting Centre, where the full range of drugs can be injected. Having said that, in the last month or two heroin has again become the most commonly injected drug at the centre, superseding cocaine. About two-thirds of client visits are to inject heroin. The heroin also continues to be of higher quality than before Christmas, although the supply is still not back to pre-shortage levels.

Thursday, 28 March

This morning John Brogden challenged Kerry Chikarovski for the leadership of the NSW Liberal Party and won. We are pleased by this news. John Brogden was one of six members of the Coalition who voted in favour of the resolution supporting the injecting centre trial at the Drug Summit back in 1999. We hope that Mr Brogden's appointment will herald a more bipartisan approach to this trial in the run-up to the state election due this time next year.

This evening I boarded a plane to Geneva, where I'm involved in the final meeting of the editors of the book soon to be published by the World Health Organization which will outline the most up-to-date guidelines on anti-retroviral treatment for people with HIV/AIDS in resource-poor countries. I wrote the chapter on injecting drug users, who represent a significant and increasing proportion of those people with HIV infection globally, particularly across Asia. WHO aims to increase access to effective treatment for all the millions of people with HIV in these countries as soon as possible, which will be a huge task. But better late than never I suppose.

Easter Monday, 1 April

Pat Kennedy emails me that the *Four Corners* program has run and that it was good. I look forward to seeing it when I get back.

Friday, 5 April

I'm back this morning to find an invitation from a person in the UK who is editing a book looking at all aspects of injecting drug use internationally. He has asked Dr Robert Haemmig, who established the first Swiss injecting centre in Bern, and me to co-write a chapter on supervised injecting facilities, which we have agreed to do. I've also been asked to contribute a paper about the development of the MSIC's clinical model to a special edition of the *International Journal on Drug Issues* specifically focused on what they are calling safer injecting facilities around the world.

These are quite important contributions to the ongoing international debate, and I feel they are part of my role as the medical director of this facility. However, finding the time they require is of course always a big challenge. It is this type of 'big picture' work that I am increasingly involved in, but it takes me away from the front line, which I miss a lot. However the staff who are working at the front line are certainly proving to be more than capable of managing most situations themselves now.

Thursday, 11 April

This evening I attended a reception at Government House to recognise the twenty-five years of service provided by the Adolescent Unit of what is now called the New Children's Hospital at Westmead. During this I received a phone call from Dave Darcy, who informed me that a woman had died from a drug overdose near Springfield Mall. Then I received a call from Nicki, one of our registered nurses at the injecting centre, informing me that the person who had died was Jenny, a well-known client of the MSIC, KRC and K2. She was thirty-six years old, from a middle-class background, and had a long history of drug dependence and an even longer history of anorexia nervosa.

After the reception I rang Colette at home to inform her. She was very upset, having worked with Jenny from before she started working at KRC six years ago, in her previous capacity as a clinical nurse consultant at a private psychiatric clinic where Jenny's anorexia was being treated at the time. We find it's not unusual for people who suffer the distorted self-image and self-loathing that seems to come with anorexia to develop problematic drug use as well. For many years now, Jenny has been engaging in what we call oblivion-seeking drug-using patterns—from the moment she woke up until she slumped at the end of the day, she seemed to be on a mission to use as many mind-altering drugs as was physically possible. She seemed to have very little interest in being lucid and sober, ever.

Friday, 12 April

I am thinking more about Jenny; she was a great favourite of staff even though they realised that they could do little to assist her despite many, many attempts using many, many different approaches. In recent months staff at the injecting centre had major concerns about her presenting on numerous occasions so very intoxicated, which is an exclusion criterion for using the centre. In line with the responsible serving of liquor laws, it is considered inappropriate to condone further drug use knowing that there would be a high risk that the person would overdose. Even in clinically supervised situations, like the MSIC and hospital emergency centres, overdoses cannot always be successfully resuscitated.

Jenny visited the injecting centre no fewer than fifty times in recent months and on eleven occasions she was treated for overdoses, usually because of her concurrent use of benzodiazepines. At least once she was brought to the centre for resuscitation after having been found semiconscious in a back lane, after injecting there. We also treat unregistered clients brought in having overdosed elsewhere. Depending on staffing levels at the time, the nurses can also take portable resuscitation equipment to manage drug overdose cases when they occur elsewhere nearby, always ringing the ambulance service first in such instances.

Jenny's last visit was yesterday, when she was again assessed to be intoxicated and again refused entry. She had arrived with her partner, Peter, who was allowed to use the facility. She remained in the waiting room quite peacefully while he used the facility and then later on he came round and picked her up. Peter is older than Jenny, in his late forties, and is also a well-known client to services in the area. His partner of quite some long standing has now died and we are worried about the effect this will have on him.

As well, we've also just heard that Peter has recently inherited a significant amount of money from a long-lost relative. The combination of receiving a large lump sum of money and having a major personal loss like this can lead to heavy, high-risk drug use, placing him in danger of overdose too. You often see this with IDUs who have received large victim's compensation and other lump-sum payouts. What ought to be an opportunity for people to break the drugs cycle so often just goes straight up the arm, not just their own but also their friends'. Clients are often very generous in these situations and sharing the spoils is very much part of the drug user culture. So you see thousands of dollars squandered in this way, sometimes in a matter of weeks, particularly if cocaine is involved.

Staff will try to speak to Peter about this and to offer him support. And not just to him, but also to other clients in the area. Jenny was well known and well liked by the other clients so they too will be at higher risk at this time; we often see a run of overdoses occurring after an event like this.

Jenny had been a subject of clinical supervision sessions at the injecting centre because staff had felt quite impotent in their ability to assist her. They had identified that she had significant problems and that while the centre provided a short-term solution in terms of keeping her alive, it wasn't having much success addressing the underlying issues. Of course these issues had been addressed by various other services previously and on an ongoing basis, but to no avail either. Ultimately we had warned our staff that, of all the clients, she was the most at risk of dying of a drug overdose at some stage. And now it has happened.

We knew that a time would come when a well-known client of the centre would die elsewhere in this way and we have tried to prepare staff for this inevitability, attempting to minimise that sense of uselessness you feel as a clinician when something like this happens despite your best efforts. But, on the other hand, having specifically identified Jenny as being highly vulnerable in this regard some months ago, her death seems like even more of a failure on our part. You can't help thinking that surely there must have been something we could have done that could have made a difference. I'll bet her parents would think so. But then again, they too are probably asking themselves the same question.

Tragic as it is, with somebody like Jenny you do get the sense that at last she has found some peace; she will no longer need to spend her waking moments in endless pursuit of oblivion. Why a 36-year-old would need to find peace in this way at this early stage of her life is something I can't answer. But those of us involved in this field somehow have to accept this kind of event in order to be able to continue the work. At least it seems to happen a lot less now than before the MSIC was here.

Monday, 15 April

I received a phone call from Minister Della Bosca's office informing me that Cabinet has agreed to draft legislation to extend the licence of the injecting centre beyond the 18-month mark, which we'll reach at the end of October this year. Assuming that the Uniting Church agrees, this will allow us to continue until the evaluation results have been collated, analysed, interpreted and tabled in parliament. So this comes as particularly good news and a public announcement is planned for this Friday.

Tuesday, 16 April

This was the day of Jenny's funeral. Her parents had decided to hold a requiem mass at St Canice's Catholic Church in Kings Cross by the parish priest there, Father Steve Sinn. Steve, a Jesuit, always has his church door open for people like Jenny and the other clients that we see.

The funeral was attended by over one hundred people. Quite a number of the staff of the injecting centre were able to go as it was in the morning, before we opened. Kirketon Road Centre hosted a wake for clients afterwards and I attended that. It was one of the most moving occasions I can remember in my work with these clients. There was a subdued atmosphere, as you would expect at a wake. Our clients were all dressed to the nines in their very own way, hair combed, wearing ties and mostly matching suits, probably bought second-hand at the Wayside Chapel, but nonetheless looking very dapper indeed. Peter seemed okay. He is a very sensible person and at this stage has a reasonable outlook on what has happened, all things considered. He is of course terribly upset, but he also feels that for Jenny there was really no helping hand that could have saved her and that in some ways she has indeed at last found the peace that she was obviously searching for.

Peter talked to me about the money that he has recently inherited and I expressed my concern about what the risks are for him in this regard. He said that he'd like to speak to Tony Trimingham of the Family Drug Support Organisation. He has seen Tony speaking in the media over the years, and is very supportive of what Tony does. He asked me to mention to Tony next time I see him that he would maybe like to have a role in supporting the establishment of a heroin prescription program with this money. He plans to buy a fax machine and a telephone to assist with this. So I agree to discuss those things with Tony.

The clients were particularly grateful to KRC for hosting the wake. They told staff that very few of them had ever attended a wake before, surprising in a way, given how many of their peers they lose to overdose death over time. So, strangely enough, it was quite an uplifting morning for both staff and clients, despite its sad origins.

I then hurried across to the injecting centre. I spend much of my day running backwards and forwards between these two services, surely good for my fitness! In the 12–4.30 session, the injecting centre accommodated a record number of visits—130—which is about one person every two minutes. This large number of people seen today was undoubtedly an aftermath of Jenny's funeral this morning. I guess this was in some ways a second wake, of a somewhat different nature to the one held at Kirketon Road Centre earlier, which was drug free.

Friday, 19 April

Yesterday evening the Uniting*Care* board passed a motion agreeing to hold the licence for a further twelve months and this morning Minister Della Bosca, accompanied by Professor Ian Webster in his capacity as the Chair of the Expert Advisory Committee on Drugs, announced that the state government will be seeking to pass legislation to extend the licence.

In recommending this legislation to the government, the Expert Advisory Committee indicated that it was mindful of the logistical issues involved in closing the facility and then later possibly having to open it again. The committee believes that, while it is too early to make a definitive judgment, preliminary figures also suggest that the injecting centre has had some success (their words, not ours!), or at least is not a failure.

Harry and I followed this with a press conference in the city at 11.30 am and in the evening all the news channels carried the story. Channel Ten's report, in particular, stated that we've been 'a great success'. As always, we see this as a double-edged sword because, of course, any mention of that 'S' word tends to smoke out Brian Watters, who then seems to feel duty-bound to hit it on the head, often with a sledgehammer! I just wish he felt similarly inclined when people say we've been an abject failure—but then there is only dignified silence.

Most of the channels used the file tape of the facility in action which we originally distributed. Andy, especially, has come to regret his participation in this tape, which has been aired as far away as the UK, where he started his working life as a nurse in the drugs field. Even though he is not readily recognisable, looking rather shady with a dark hat covering much of his face, former colleagues from there have contacted Andy and expressed concern that he has started injecting drugs since coming to Australia. This of course amuses us a lot more than it does Andy.

Tuesday, 23 April

A letter from NSW Health was faxed to Harry's office, responding to his letter regarding our concerns about the periodic random visits to the injecting centre by representatives of the licensing authorities. Their response is unsatisfactory as far as we are concerned, so we sought a meeting with the relevant parties, which is scheduled for next week. The existing inspection protocol is an all-purpose one but it is of limited applicability to the injecting centre's situation, which is very different to all other health services. Identifying what exactly needs to be looked at and monitored during such visits will be the subject of the meeting. We do, of course, accept the need for such visits, embracing the need for accountability, so we don't want the licensing authorities to think that we are unhappy about being inspected per se. After all, we have nothing to hide and have in fact passed previous inspections with flying colours.

Monday, 6 May

Today the meeting was held to review the issue of inspection visits to the centre. It was held at the Cabinet Office in Governor Macquarie Towers and both the Health and Police licensing authorities were represented.

There was agreement that they needed to develop a checklist of items that can only be monitored when the service is operational, which will be kept to a minimum so that it doesn't take hours to get through each visit. It was also agreed that only one person from Health and one person from Police will conduct the spot checks, rather than the four that went through last time. However, it was also decided that the duty officer from Kings Cross station—that is, a sworn police officer instead of a civilian from the Police Department—will represent Police on the inspection team in future.

I expressed my concern that, even though this officer will be in plain clothes, it's likely that clients at the centre will recognise him or her straight-away. Even though clients injecting at the centre aren't doing anything illegal, I suspect that they still won't want to be identified by police engaging in a behaviour that is illegal everywhere else in Kings Cross. But this was the decision, so we'll have to wait and see how that works out. We also now intend to let clients who are in the facility at the time know when the licensing authorities have arrived, partly for privacy reasons but also to impress upon them why we do need to operate according to our licence conditions at all times and need their cooperation with those. At the same time we will assure them that they are within their rights to be in the facility while also giving them the opportunity to scarper, which is what I predict will happen.

There was some debate about whether the visits should continue to be random. Dave Darcy asserted that he'd actually had businessmen come to the Kings Cross police station to report that staff at the injecting centre are dealing in heroin. I find it quite bizarre that unsubstantiated vexatious nonsense like this would be considered a valid reason for random visits. Besides, surely these 'businessmen' would realise that if we were actually dealing in heroin on the premises we could easily cease when the inspectors turned up, however unannounced. On the other hand, it would take us much longer than 24 hours notice to transform our operations, particularly client behaviours, if we were operating outside the internal management protocols. Although I pointed out that no other health facility in the land is routinely inspected by licensing authorities without notice, it was argued that some in the community might expect this and we must be seen to be absolutely squeaky clean in all respects. Perhaps I am being a little precious that there is no presumption of innocence in terms of being an ethical service operating with professional integrity.

The Health and Police representatives agreed to consult with us about their checklist before this is signed off. We have now reached the end of our first twelve months of operation. Somehow I now recall that we have never had any further diabetics wanting to use the centre to inject insulin. This makes me think that, as I'd suspected, perhaps we were being tested in those first few weeks when two attended in quick succession.

Wednesday, 22 May

A couple of weeks ago we decided we would have a bit of a celebration among the staff on reaching the one-year mark of this controversial initiative. We asked Michelle, who is a graphic designer at KRC, to do up an invitation to be sent out and late last week I was shown a proof of the invitation. It depicted a boater hat, looking like a birthday cake, with a needle syringe on top as a candle. But the needle syringe was pointing down into the cake and was half filled with blood.

My first reaction was that this was altogether too risqué. But I couldn't help being amused by the design so, in a moment of boldness, I just suggested that the needle syringe be upright—so that the candle's flame would be coming from the needle, rather than having the needle pointing down into the cake—and also that the blood be removed from the syringe. Otherwise, I said, it was okay to be used.

Originally, it was just going to be a very small group of people celebrating our first year of operation (also knowing full well that such celebrations can bring bad luck as well!), but since then our plans have expanded somewhat. Also, because time was marching on and the party was now to be on 31 May, Tracey faxed out the invitations. Of course the rather colourful invitation, once faxed, not only lost some of its prettiness but the candle's yellow flame on the top of the needle also disappeared.

This series of events resulted in a phone call from Minister Della Bosca's office today. Having been amongst those on the mailing list, they suggested to me that the invitation might, if it got into the hands of the media, cause some problems. I gather that this phone call was reluctantly made, basically to put on record that they had some concerns and didn't endorse the invitation. I reassured them that, even though it was no longer just our staff who were receiving the invitation, it wasn't going out too widely—not beyond our inner circle of supporters. But I did appreciate that one can never be sure, particularly when faxing to general offices.

Friday, 24 May

The twelve-month evaluation report, also referred to as the Interim Report, was tabled in parliament today. The Opposition has previously stated that it would make its decision regarding the 12-month trial extension on the results in this report. I was informed yesterday that the evaluation team's press release would be embargoed until 11 am today. However, upon making coffee and opening the *Sydney Morning Herald* this morning, I saw on page three that Paola Totaro had written an article with the headline 'Injecting Centre Gets Clean Bill of Health'. Beneath this was quite a lengthy article including everything in the embargoed media release and also being quite positive about the results in the Interim Report.

Later the evaluation team circulated an email saying that clearly their press release had been passed on to Paola Totaro ahead of time. They seemed peeved about this but, given that it was such a positive article, we weren't too concerned. The main risk in these situations is that, if only one of the papers gets the inside run like this, the temptation is for the other papers either not to run the story the following day, because it's no longer news, or to put another spin on it. Because Paola's story was positive, this increases the likelihood that the other papers will opt for negative spins, and of course the Chamber of Commerce continues to be ever willing and able to provide the 'balance' for such stories.

Throughout the morning radio ran the story quite positively and this evening television ran brief news items using the file tape yet again.

During the day I also let Minister Della Bosca's office know that we were taking all possible steps to limit any damage that might result from the invitation to our celebration. I even enlisted a friend of mine at the *Australian* to remove the one left on journalist Sian Powell's desk while she is away on leave in case someone else saw it. I do appreciate that by approving the invitation I have placed the service at some risk. Julie Sibraa was reassuring but she added that they had all been amazed, particularly given how carefully I've shepherded the project to date, paying attention to even the most minute details—and wondered whether I'd had a minor 'brain explosion'.

I hadn't, but I did go away and think hard about what it was that allowed me to approve this, particularly, as Julie said, when it was in contrast to my very, very careful approach on all matters to date. I suspect that part of it was that for over two years now I've constantly been looking to the right, to the left and behind me, always conjuring up in my mind what conceivable negative consequences might flow from any of our actions. Then I've put in place whatever measures were required to forestall such adversities, to date with some success in that no really bad things have happened—touch wood again!

On this occasion, when I first saw this one-year birthday invitation, particularly because it was a staff event, perhaps I thought most of all about our staff. I suppose they have been the ones most affected by my approach of pouring cold water over anything that could be seen to be flippant or jovial. On this one and only occasion I thought to myself, no, I'm not going to be the school ma'am this time, always taking all of the fun out of things. I'll let this go ahead with only minor amendments and we will have a bit of a frivolous laugh and allow our black humour to hold sway. After all, at the end of the day this is what gets us through emotionally demanding work like this.

But it certainly didn't occur to me that, if I ever wanted to take one decision that might be widely regarded by posterity as ill-considered, then faxing it to every single Power That Be, including all the various ministerial offices and departments, was certainly an extraordinarily fast and efficient way of doing it. You wouldn't want to take yourself too seriously at times like this, I suppose.

Tuesday, 28 May

Colette rang me to let me know that we'd had another random spot check. The Kings Cross Police Crime Manager out of uniform and Deborah from the Private Health Branch of NSW Health came through, arriving unannounced as they had indicated they would. Colette showed them through and it took no more than half an hour, as they had promised, which we were pleased about.

Apparently earlier there had been a completely full waiting room and a particularly large number of people injecting benzodiazepines, which can create a pretty electric atmosphere. But by the time the spot check occurred half an hour later, all had returned to calm.

As it turned out, the police officer was new to the area so nobody actually recognised him. He also indicated that he didn't recognise clients either so our concerns about a sworn officer being part of the inspection team have not been borne out, or at least not on this occasion.

Thursday, 30 May

The *Daily Telegraph* columnist Piers Ackerman this morning let fly with his most blistering attack to date on the injecting centre. It was headed 'Lies,

Damned Lies' and referred to the various statistics in the Interim Report, in numerous instances not letting the truth get in his way—thus making his column's headline very apt indeed. He concluded his attack in a particularly mean way, by suggesting that the report is all based on what drug users—or rather 'junkies', as he prefers to call them—have said and that of course he couldn't believe a word they said. Apart from this not being the case—most of the reported data are verifiable—studies have actually shown that self-report by drug users is just as reliable as it is for the rest of the population involved in research. But it has been over six months since Piers last launched a broadside against us, so at least for this we feel grateful.

Friday, 31 May

I was contacted by ABC-TV's *Media Watch*, who sought clarification on Piers Ackerman's statement that 'serious medical intervention' had occurred when seven people required ambulance transport to hospital, the implication being that we couldn't handle these cases. I told *Media Watch* that, as stated very clearly in the report, these seven cases were already successfully treated and stabilised in-house at the injecting centre—they were merely transported for further observation at the local hospital as the injecting centre was never set up to accommodate ongoing observation when required. We close at 10 pm, for a start.

Piers had also referred to 'so-called overdoses'. It does seem a sad day when there is a public suggestion that we, as health professionals, would in some way be beating up drug overdose figures. But I have come to appreciate during the course of my work here that nothing is sacred and to put to one side my medical preciousness about aspersions on our ethical behaviour. Harry reassures me that people project onto you what they themselves would do in the same circumstances, which I find reassuring.

In the evening we hosted our one-year birthday party at the Lord Roberts Hotel in East Sydney, in a private room upstairs. We were able to put some money on the bar and provide some food, funded in fact from the advance for this book.

Harry kicked off with a speech thanking me and the rest of the staff for having operated the service in the last twelve months. He claimed that the two best decisions he'd made had been choosing the site location and appointing me as medical director, which was generous of him. He went on to say that, because we're managing things as well as we are, he's really not had to do very much himself. I do remember some early discussions with Harry in which he indicated that his management style was non-interventionist and I remember thinking yes, well, I'll wait and see about that. I've heard controlling, interventionist managers describe themselves as non-interventionist before. But he has been true to his word.

During the last few days I have developed quite severe laryngitis, which means I'm only able to whisper. I had asked Tracey to make sure that the venue had a microphone because I wanted to make a speech on this auspicious occasion, and my laryngitis wasn't going to get in the way. I followed Harry with a raspy speech in which I took the opportunity to thank him and the management team. I conceded that if the service needed a father then he was indeed the best dad for the job. (Mind you, I still think I could have managed it okay as part of KRC!)

After the speeches I circulated among our guests and ended up speaking (read *whispering*) to someone who had apparently been a consultant to the Cabinet Office three years ago. He congratulated me for getting to the one-year mark and for having guided the project through (very competently, he said) but he did have one criticism. I braced myself. He then told me with great earnest that he had come across the invitation to this party and he did think that this was a 'grave mistake'. My heart sank.

This conversation came at the end of a long and tiring day. I had spent the last two weeks on tenterhooks, anxious indeed that this matter might emerge in the press before tonight and burst the bubble of our first celebration. I looked him straight in the eyes and said: 'You know, there are times, particularly when you've been so very cautious overall for so long, that you reach a point where you just think to yourself "fuck it".' I smiled politely and then moved on to speak to others there.

It's curious, when I think back, that I was also very careful about the wording on the invitation. I avoided saying that we were celebrating our first birthday because I thought that might imply that we would be having a second and, quelle horreur, we can't be seen to be making assumptions like that! So instead it was worded that we were celebrating 'turning one', which didn't seem to assume that we would turn two. Right now I have this exasperating sense that you can do many things right and then, yes, okay, you have one minor brain explosion and that is what you are remembered for, forever more. We shall see. Maybe I need another holiday.

twelve

Managing drug overdoses

Monday, 3 June 2002

Colette and I attended the Australian Needle Exchange Conference in Melbourne today. I was giving a keynote speech about the injecting centre's first twelve months. Colette spoke on a panel later in the afternoon about the lessons learned at the MSIC and their implications for needle syringe program workers, particularly referring to the high-risk injecting behaviours that we've observed at the centre.

Later that evening *Media Watch* ran their piece on the Piers Ackerman article and criticised various aspects of it. They also made the point that the seven 'whisked' to the hospital by ambulance were not being whisked away for 'major medical intervention', but in fact for further observation. I was quoted during this segment, by showing a still photo of me with a female voice-over saying exactly what I had said over the phone some days ago although a lot clearer than my still hoarse voice! This is another new media experience for me.

Tuesday, 4 June

We met with the licensing authority representatives for a review of last week's spot check. A number of small issues were raised—like not being able to lay our hands on the documentation from the plumber certifying that the thermostatic mixing valves on the taps had been checked (more things I've learnt about!), but not much else. So we await our next round of inspections, presumably in three to six months' time as heralded.

Thursday, 6 June

Parliament has passed the legislation to extend our operating licence. This involved a minor change to the original Act so that the trial is now for thirty months instead of eighteen months. The debate took a fortnight and I followed it by reading Hansard on the Internet. It proved quite painful to read so much misinformation, all stated as fact with great authority. Hansard is the public record and I'm sure most people assume that what is stated there is true, but on this occasion we knew that this was definitely not the case. Part of me would have liked to be in Parliament House for the debate but I would have had to restrain myself from leaping from the gallery to throttle the offending MP, which of course isn't allowed.

John Brogden allowed a conscience vote for the Liberals, as did George Souris for the Nationals. More was heard in opposition than in support, but the government knew it had the numbers in both houses so it was a case of just sitting out the various speeches in opposition, and then being able to proceed to the vote. Five members of the Opposition ended up crossing the floor, John Brogden being one.

Friday, 14 June

There's been a further needlestick injury at the injecting centre. One of the nurses, 'Paula', was involved. The female client had injected temazepam and then proceeded to walk towards the third stage of the facility without her cloth bag. People who are drug-affected often leave things behind so Paula quickly picked up the bag from under the booth table to chase after the client. However, in so doing she was stuck with a needle that poked through from inside the bag. She then proceeded to follow the needlestick injury protocol.

The client was very upset that this had happened but quickly reassured Paula that it was just a loose needle in her bag that had been used to hold the temazepam gelcap, in order to aspirate its contents to inject. It was not a needle used for injecting, which might have been contaminated with the client's or someone else's blood. We encouraged the client to attend the Kirketon Road Centre nearby to undergo testing, which she did.

Monday, 17 June

This is now the fourth needlestick injury that has occurred at the injecting centre in just over a year and each one has had policy implications. After the first incident we developed a vein care advice policy—when we are asked to give advice about veins we now require that the client remove all sharp implements from the area first before the staff member comes into close proximity to the client. The client is also instructed not to resume trying to inject until the staff member is well clear of the booth.

The second needlestick injury was last December with Carly. She's no longer allowed to inject benzodiazepines on the premises. She continues to comply with this and has resumed using the injecting centre on a regular basis with no further problems.

The third incident occurred in January this year when a nurse recapped a needle syringe after administering Narcan. The old procedure was to put the needle's plastic sheath back on after use and then discard it but there was always the risk that the needle would miss the sheath and instead go into your finger (particularly if your hand was unsteady, as it can be during a resuscitation procedure). However, since HIV/AIDS became a risk, this practice has been totally abandoned and now, after use, you don't resheath, but simply throw all uncapped needle syringes and other sharps straight into the bright yellow sharps safes, which are distributed throughout all health facilities. This simple change in policy has been shown to have significantly reduced needlestick injuries among health care workers over these past years.

The nurse involved on this occasion admitted that recapping was not something she had done for over a decade, when this practice changed. It is amazing how simple, routine things can come unstuck in stressful situations. So we just reminded all staff of this. Further training in resuscitation and gaining more experience on the job has also reduced the stressfulness of overdose management, it being almost a mechanical routine these days, which is what we aim for.

On all these occasions the staff member was tested and nobody was infected with HIV or hepatitis B (health care workers are all vaccinated for that anyway) or C.

Wednesday, 3 July

I left for Vienna this afternoon to attend a two-day meeting of the just-formed UN Global Reference Group into the Prevention and Care of HIV among Injecting Drug Users to which I have been appointed. This group focuses on those IDUs in resource-poor settings, in particular. Vienna is also home to the International Narcotics Control Board (INCB), and our meeting was held in the United Nations building where the INCB is located. I had an opportunity to talk to the person who represented the UN Drug Control Programme (UNDCP) which is connected to the INCB. I asked him why the INCB continues to single out the injecting centre in Australia when there are more than fifty injecting centres much closer in Europe.

While sympathetic to our plight, he said that many of the UNDCP staff were rather pleased with the attention we are getting because until recently the INCB had been focusing on needle syringe and methadone programs as being the root of all evil. As far as they were concerned, the need to establish needle syringe and methadone programs, particularly in the developing world, is of primary importance from a public health perspective. So they rather welcome the INCB's obsession with our project in Australia for its diversionary value. Wearing a more global public health hat, I can empathise with that view.

Monday, 8 July

I'm back from Vienna and meanwhile we've been asked to respond to a request from Minister Della Bosca's office. The minister was questioned for over an hour by the Cost Estimates Committee, which scrutinises government expenditure. Despite the fact that he has responsibility for over a hundred drug programs as part of the Drug Summit rollout, apparently 90 per cent of these questions focused on the injecting centre and, interestingly, not so much on our expenditure this time, but more about what we define as a drug overdose.

All along I've been uncomfortable that in the media the tally of drug overdoses managed at the injecting centre has been equated with lives saved and is widely perceived to be the chief indicator of our success or otherwise. Of course, as a result of that, various people who don't support this facility have questioned these numbers and also our definitions. A suggestion actually made by one of the politicians seeking information from the minister was that perhaps we 'wanted to please the minister' and therefore maybe we counted 'patting somebody on the back of the hand' as an overdose. Needless to say, this is very offensive to us. The minister deferred his answers to most of the questions and these were forwarded to us to provide a written response to his office through the Health Department.

As distasteful as I find such discourse, I am at least pleased that this has been referred to us this time. It is a good opportunity to provide accurate information to both the government and the Opposition for the record. Unfortunately we do seem to need to verify that we are using definitions and diagnostic tools widely recognised within the medical world.

I have come to realise that the lay public often defines an overdose as being when someone loses consciousness and stops breathing altogether. Some even think it necessarily implies death (from drug overdose) whereas an overdose actually occurs when a person receives a dose of a drug which is 'over' that required for the intended effect. In the case of heroin, symptoms of overdose include constriction of the pupils, a slowing of the respiratory and heart rate along with decreasing responses to external stimuli. It is already well established that these symptoms of heroin overdose do not usually occur instantaneously upon injecting, but develop over time as the heroin reaches the brain, not peaking until up to about 20 minutes after intravenous injection. When the person's respiration slows down and becomes shallower, this will result in a decrease in the amount of oxygen transferred to the lungs and then into the person's bloodstream (hypoxia). If hypoxia is not treated with oxygen, it is likely to progress and may result in a respiratory arrest (complete cessation of breathing), followed by cardiac arrest (the heart stops) and eventually death.

Increasingly I appreciate that the injecting centre provides a unique setting in which health care workers actually see the overdose occurring from the very outset, identifying symptoms of heroin (or whatever drug) overdose and administering appropriate treatment very soon thereafter. This can't and doesn't occur in any other circumstance. By treating an overdose so early in its course, the damage already done and its natural progression is reversed so that Narcan (used to start breathing) will no longer be needed in most cases. This is how injecting centres potentially reduce the morbidity (damage to vital organs, especially the brain) and the mortality otherwise associated with overdose in unattended situations, even when there is a very prompt and efficient ambulance service on hand.

Appreciating that we have time on our side at this facility, we have modified our resuscitation procedures from those used by the NSW Ambulance Service and instead manage heroin overdoses initially, even when people have stopped breathing altogether, by performing what's called EAR (Expired Air Resuscitation) for five minutes. This involves what we call 'bagging' the client, which refers to the 'bag' which is filled with oxygen from an oxygen gas cylinder. This bag is squeezed so as to push the oxygen into the person's lungs via a mask held over the face. We assist this process by extending the neck and inserting what's called an airway in the back of the person's mouth, which ensures that the oxygen can pass without obstruction into the lungs. This oxygen is then delivered from the lungs to the rest of the body, especially to the brain, where it is most needed to reverse the CNS depressant effects of heroin.

It's only when the person doesn't start breathing again after receiving 100 per cent oxygen in this way for a full five minutes that we then administer Narcan, which takes the heroin right out of the equation for a time, thereby causing the person to start breathing again. So our use of naloxone is much less than the ambulance service, which doesn't do EAR first, because many people do begin to regain consciousness during this five minutes of assisted respiration.

Minimising the use of naloxone has important advantages. Because it temporarily reverses the effects of heroin, naloxone causes the heroin-dependent drug user to go into what is called an acute withdrawal state (the same symptoms as are experienced by people who go 'cold turkey' from heroin, including an intense dysphoria, sweatiness, nausea and stomach cramps). Unsurprisingly drug users don't usually thank you for producing this effect, often not realising just how unconscious and dangerously hypoxic they were before you intervened. They are often subsequently tempted to go out and inject more heroin, to overcome these acute withdrawal symptoms and feel normal again, but there are serious risks involved in doing this. Naloxone is only a short-acting medication—its effects wear off after only about 30 minutes and then the original heroin's CNS depressant action kicks back in again. Especially if the drug user has meanwhile injected more heroin, there's a risk that they will lose consciousness again.

Increasingly, hospital emergency departments are shifting across to just using oxygen to resuscitate people with a heroin overdose, providing they have the manpower—somebody has to continue to 'bag' the client with oxygen for however long it takes. But, providing the oxygen is being delivered to the lungs, there is no harm that the person can come to while this is happening. Bringing overdose cases back to a state of consciousness more gently this way provides a greater opportunity to observe the person afterwards, since they're a lot less likely to abscond in an unhappy state of acute withdrawal. This is considered a much better outcome overall.

Fred Nile has also put questions to Minister Della Bosca as part of these Cost Estimates Committee hearings, asking whether or not we also seek to 'rehabilitate prostitutes', rather than just addressing their drug-using. We have assured Fred in our reply that we encourage sex workers to consider alternative means of income, appreciating the dangers that can be associated with this type of work, particularly when they are based on the streets and are drug-affected. However, given that street-based sex work is predominantly undertaken to obtain funds for drugs, acquisitive crime would be the most likely alternative and therefore we believe that addressing the underlying drug dependence should be the mainstay of our approach.

Friday, 19 July

Yesterday Dave Darcy informed me that he has received a vague report of a TV station having the injecting centre under surveillance as part of a story that there is systematic drug dealing occurring there with police knowledge. So this time the Kings Cross police are also implicated along with the nurses and counsellors at the MSIC—of course they do have more of a history of this sort of thing!

Dave agrees that it seems unlikely that a TV station would waste its time and money on something like this. However, we are concerned about this apparent perception somewhere out there so we have decided to initiate a campaign at the injecting centre for the next two weeks to actively discourage the purchase of drugs anywhere near the MSIC. This will involve putting up signs in all the injecting booths and in the other two stages of the facility. These will have the familiar police blue-and-white checked pattern across the top and the bottom with a statement that buying or selling drugs in the vicinity of the injecting centre attracts community and police attention.

We try to develop messages that are a little subtle rather than commanding 'Don't deal or buy drugs near the injecting centre'. We find that this approach prompts more meaningful dialogue between clients and staff, giving us a greater opportunity to convey to clients some of the political realities of the injecting centre, which of course we can't expect people to be mindful of at all times. It's surprising, however, just how aware drug users are of such realities, and the extent to which they are keen to cooperate in these matters is heartening. There is a real sense of ownership and pride in the service developing among clients, which we think is a good thing. Being the subject of controversy may have enhanced their appreciation of the need for some solidarity, so we try to work with this as much as possible.

Meanwhile we also convey to clients that we would have absolutely no hesitation in reporting any drug dealing that we saw near the facility because, from our perspective, the need to protect the service is a priority. However, sometimes our clients can't understand our position on this. As far as they are concerned, we must be aware that every person who attends the injecting centre by definition has bought drugs from a drug dealer—so why does it matter to us exactly where that transaction occurs?

Only the other day, Colette and I were in her office upstairs at the MSIC, overlooking the entrance to the Kings Cross train station, when we noticed a guy in a wheelchair appearing to buy drugs from someone there. He then crossed the road and entered the facility. This of course is the very scenario that we are accused of encouraging, so I called up Jake, one of the counsellors, and asked him to confront the client in Stage 2 about what we just saw.

I asked Jake to explain to him that this sort of thing could see the centre closed down, and that we would not hesitate to report any dealer to police.

There is no question that drug dealing disturbs the local community, even though it doesn't actually cause public nuisance in the way that discarded needle syringes or antisocial behaviour on the streets do. The actual drug and money transaction itself usually takes place very quickly and discreetly, not interfering with anybody else; for obvious reasons the dealers are trying not to attract anybody's attention, least of all the police's. When you examine more closely exactly what it is about drug dealing that upsets people, it's more the fact that it is an illegal activity and, especially when it occurs in broad daylight, it is seen as a public flouting of the law. When it occurs out of sight, in the strip clubs and 'private' hotels on the main street it seems to bother the community a lot less.

So, in some ways, where clients actually buy their drugs should be neither here nor there. After all, what difference does it make whether they buy it across the road as opposed to 50 metres further down Darlinghurst Road? The law is being flouted in both locations. But when it occurs near the MSIC (which it has done for decades) the perception among some is that the MSIC has actually caused this transaction to occur and that without the centre these dealers would not be in Kings Cross so the drug users wouldn't be there either and the area then wouldn't have a drug problem anymore. So we have a pragmatic approach, and proactively run regular campaigns to discourage this.

When Jake confronted the particular client seen buying drugs across the road, he was very unnerved and promised never to do it again. The view from that particular window upstairs lets us in on many of the stories of the streets of Kings Cross, some happy, others sad.

Wednesday, 24 July

I flew down to Canberra this evening to be an after-dinner speaker for a group called Faith and Work, a coalition of Christians who get together to consider the spiritual aspects of people in workplace situations. I was asked a wide range of questions after my talk, particularly concerning my views about the underlying causes of problematic drug use.

Many of our clients have a background of sexual, emotional and physical abuse; they frequently have parents who still are, or have been, heavy users of alcohol and drugs, and are also engaged in other addictive behaviours such as gambling. They have rarely grown up with two parents, let alone both biological parents; many have been wards of the state. Often they didn't complete schooling, have reading and writing difficulties and have never entered the formal workforce; they are largely unemployable, especially in a tight, competitive youth employment market, and end up reliant on social security from a young age. Many have been involved in school truancy, various sorts of petty crime and spent time in juvenile custodial situations long before drugs even entered the picture. All this is associated with very low self-esteem, which may be temporarily raised through the use of drugs such as heroin, which clients describe as filling the void, giving them a sense of being whole and in control.

I talked about the need, at all points along the way, to prevent such problems arising in the first place. But when drug addiction occurs, we must try to keep people alive so that there remains an opportunity for people to address and ultimately overcome the issues they need to confront, a long and arduous journey for most. I actually titled my talk 'Where There Is Life, There Is Hope—Stories From The Medically Supervised Injecting Drug Centre'. In some ways this cliché underpins the injecting centre's philosophical approach and makes it hard for us to understand the often rabid opposition to it.

Following this discussion a woman stood up and identified herself as the mother of a heroin-using son who had died of an overdose. She thanked me for my talk but said that, unlike the picture I drew of the typical drug user, her son had been a university graduate with much to look forward to and no apparent psycho-social issues as far as his background went. He didn't start injecting heroin until he was well into his twenties, which is unusual but does of course happen. Her contribution reminded me that, while there is a typical background we associate with the more problematic drug users, at least in the Kings Cross area, it's important not to generalise. Anyone, regardless of their background, can become addicted to this drug and anyone who uses heroin can die of an overdose.

Meeting parents of drug users, especially those who have lost a child to overdose, is always a big reality check for me; it gets right under my professional veneer, which, despite the discomfort it causes me, is a good thing I think.

Monday, 29 July

Dave Darcy rang me this morning to let me know that there's been another heroin overdose death in Kings Cross. Dave and I have an arrangement in place whereby when this happens he lets me know, both when and where it occurred, so we can then assess whether the injecting centre may have prevented such a death in other circumstances. On this occasion it is a male backpacker who has died at a Macleay Street hostel.

Wednesday, 31 July

At our team meeting today we discussed the significant number of backpackers we see, particularly from Britain and Ireland. We had not anticipated this. They are particularly at risk because being on holidays they often also consume more alcohol than usual and, as tourists to the area, they may not be aware of what services are available.

Backpackers have told us that being on an extended world adventure like this, they're able to adopt different personas and do risky things they wouldn't normally do at home. Trying drugs is seen as being equivalent to getting a tattoo or a piercing in an unusual part of your body. Some people decide that since they're in Kings Cross, where there is a ready supply of heroin, they might try some as part of the local experience of the place as a tourist. Frightening thought. And of course there's nothing quite like Dutch courage, readily available at no less than 200 licensed premises in the environs, to increase people's willingness to take such risks.

There are also some backpackers who have already developed a drug habit at home in Europe but, because of the (basic) chemical form of heroin sold there, they often only smoke it. Then they travel through Thailand on their way here, where the quality of heroin is much higher and the price much lower than in Europe, so they develop a greater level of heroin dependence. It is also in the acid form, which is more suitable for injection. When they travel on to Australia, because the heroin sold here is likewise in acid form, but more expensive they start injecting it to maintain their now higher level of dependence. Injecting as opposed to smoking heroin increases the risk of overdose.

We agreed to make contact with the publishers of a newspaper that circulates among backpacker hostels with a view to writing an article about the risks of heroin use in Kings Cross. I have also asked the Outreach Team at KRC to visit some of the local backpacker hostels to see if they have had any problems with discarded needle syringes on the premises. If so, they could then discuss with the hostel management ways to inform drug-using backpackers of the relevant services, including the needle syringe program, the injecting centre and drug treatment programs, as well as assisting with safe sharps disposal.

Just now it has also been drawn to my attention that the injecting centre is mentioned in the latest Lonely Planet Guide for Sydney; it appears as a boxed article in the section on Kings Cross. When I told other staff, everyone agreed that we must have really made it, now that we're in Lonely Planet! Humour aside, we actually think it's also a very good thing and decide to make contact with their researchers so that the next edition can contain more information about our exact location and the hours that we operate.

We think Lonely Planet, particularly because it is so well-read by this population of travellers, would do well to include a section about the risks of drug use, particularly emphasising that the combination of drugs and alcohol is not a good thing and that, if people are injecting in the area, their risk could be reduced by attending the injecting centre.

It must be a shocking, shocking thing for parents back at home to receive a phone call from the NSW Police about their child, who they thought was on their fun holiday of a lifetime, informing them that their child's life has ended from a drug overdose.

thirteen

The 18-month trial ends quietly

Tuesday, 13 August 2002

While I was at the injecting centre today Andy asked me to come down and see a client who seemed to be suffering a more complicated heroin overdose. She was an American woman in her mid-fifties who has been injecting heroin for many, many years and had used it on this occasion and lost consciousness. She then proceeded to have what looked like a grand mal seizure (a generalised fit). This is unusual after heroin usage because heroin is a sedative, which usually dampens down cerebral activity, unlike cocaine or methamphetamine or other stimulants, which can actually cause fitting. But then again, hypoxia, which can occur after using heroin, can be a cerebral irritant and cause fitting.

Her fit lasted for about five minutes and afterwards her level of consciousness remained quite low. We observed her for some time and found that her blood pressure was extremely high, again unusual with heroin on board. We continued to observe her and gradually her blood pressure returned to within the normal range and her level of consciousness increased. When she was more alert and able to speak again, I discovered she had been prescribed various other medications by a Sydney psychiatrist, who by coincidence Andy had worked with in the UK some years ago, and who has a special interest in matters related to drugs and alcohol.

So I wrote a letter of referral for her to see him to be reassessed with regard to her various medications in light of today's fitting, particularly since one of these medications is specifically contraindicated in the event of seizures. I told her she would probably be at risk of having further fits if she kept injecting heroin, which in unsupervised circumstances could be fatal, so suggested she should consider giving it away altogether. But I also advised that if she did intend to inject further heroin, she should inject a smaller quantity to avoid another seizure, even though this is the first time this has occurred. She assured me that she wasn't going to inject heroin any more. She was also so impressed with our service that she promised to write a letter to Minister Della Bosca in support of the injecting centre, particularly noting that nothing of this sort would ever be allowed to occur in her home country, which she's absolutely right about!

Afterwards I worried over the fact that I'd written in the referral letter to a doctor that she should only use small quantities of heroin, wondering whether or not this might be interpreted as actually recommending the use of small quantities, rather than complete cessation. The first message when operating within a harm reduction framework is of course always cessation (be 'good'). But we are realistic and know that, even though someone will have very good intentions, especially after an event such as this, they often do use again. In that case the next message—that she should use less, less often (. . . if you can't be good, be careful)—might then still be of some salience and benefit her. But again, given the controversial nature of this project, I did have cause to wonder afterwards about the possibility of this letter being misinterpreted. Andy reassured me though that the psychiatrist involved has a good understanding of harm reduction and most certainly would agree with giving this advice.

Monday, 26 August

Some weeks ago we submitted our projected budget for this new financial year, which incorporated an extension of our operating hours. We now intend to operate for an additional 20 hours during the week from Monday to Friday, i.e. for 12 hours continuously each day instead of the current two four-hour sessions across 10 hours. We've consulted the Nurses' Association and the Health and Research Employees' Association about the possibility of 12-hour continuous shifts for nurses and counsellors and they have approved our plan to offer these shifts. However, after some initial interest, increasingly staff feel that these longer shifts may be too taxing after all, especially since the MSIC has become so busy. This is of particular concern for the nursing staff who supervise the emergency resuscitation of drug overdoses and other clinical incidents, and therefore need to be especially on the ball at all times, even when it's quieter. So we expect that we'll be offering combinations of four-hour, six-hour and eight-hour shifts, but it's good to have the added flexibility in this regard.

Tuesday, 27 August

We received a phone call today from Waverley Police that they have had a report of a missing person and that they had found among this person's possessions at home a letter of referral to a psychiatrist following a fit at the injecting centre. It now turns out that the American female client who used the facility recently has not been seen since being at the Bourbon and Beefsteak Bar and Restaurant in Kings Cross in the early hours of the morning five days ago. Waverley Police have asked that we notify them in the event of her returning to the facility, but she has not been seen here since that first visit two weeks ago. It does seem that my original anxiety about this letter has been borne out, although not for the reasons I was concerned about.

I have found in my clinical practice that for no apparent reason you get a sense of foreboding that something is going to happen to certain patients, and I had a strong sense of that with this particular client. I hope something bad hasn't happened.

We have been getting reports recently from some of the clients that they believe there's an undercover police person attending the centre. Staff have felt that this particular young male, 'Mike', seems to have a slightly different air about him to most of the other clients. They've also noticed that he seems to use a large quantity of drugs but nonetheless he doesn't appear very drug-affected afterwards, so there's been speculation about whether he was injecting glucose or other powders used to cut drugs, rather than any mind altering drugs. He also seems to stare at some of the other drug users around him so, if he really is an undercover police person, he's not doing a very good job of being discreet to maintain his cover.

So, when Mike visited today, one of our staff pulled him to one side and explained to him that some of the other clients believe that he is an undercover police officer. While we wouldn't have a problem with that, we suggested to him that his own safety may be compromised, particularly after leaving the centre, should that be the case. But he assured us that he is too young to be in the undercover police.

Wednesday, 28 August

At six-thirty this evening another random spot check occurred with representatives from the Private Health Branch and Kings Cross police attending, to inspect the premises. None of the management team were still in attendance at this time and it was extremely busy, with staff run off their feet. Seeing this, the inspection team offered to come back at another time; however, staff agreed to allow them through, but indicated that they may need to wait at times if they were called away to attend to whatever might demand their attention.

Before too long some of the clients recognised the policeman, even though he was in plain clothes, and staff reported that this definitely added a certain tension to the atmosphere. Staff, however, used this as an opportunity to again emphasise to clients why the various licence conditions at the injecting centre need to be policed by us at all times—and that's what these inspections are about.

Jink, the nurse in charge on this shift, rang both Colette and me at home afterwards to let us know how it all went. According to her, apart from some concern about access to the hand basin in the storage room, and the fact that two mops were on the ground instead of hanging, the rest all seemed to go pretty smoothly. She said that, as well as being very busy, they also had some of the more difficult clients in, confirming Murphy's Law. Some of these clients were injecting temazepam, which continue to be associated with more problems than other drugs in terms of client behaviour and how long they spend trying to inject in already blocked-up veins. But nothing untoward happened.

It was probably good that they got to see the place operating in top gear. But I continue to be concerned that we do not have the staff capacity needed, especially after hours, to host such visits and that having strangers, particularly a sworn police officer from the local command, in Stage 2 could be enough to tip the delicate balance, risking a critical incident.

Thursday, 29 August

Now there's a rumour that a female undercover police person has been attending the injecting centre. We looked up the file of this person and discovered that this particular client had previously overdosed, in which case we feel that the police might be going a bit too far in wanting to seem realistic! But I decided to check with the Police Department anyway and learnt that under no circumstances would an undercover police person inject anything—drugs or glucose, let alone overdose—so neither of these people could be undercover police. They do, however, sometimes employ quite young people for undercover work.

So perhaps there's a sense of anxiety among the clients at this particular point in time. Despite various clients occasionally claiming that there are police stationed at the front and the back of the centre to apprehend people, clients continue to use the centre in droves, so this bit of paranoia obviously hasn't been a deterrent in any way and we continue to be fine with the way the local police are operating around the facility.

Friday, 30 August

Another record has been broken; we've finally cracked the 200 visits mark with 202 visits accommodated today. Throughout August the average number of visits was 152 per day. This would appear to coincide with a continuing increase in the proportion of visits in which heroin is injected, as opposed to cocaine—in August 80 per cent of the injecting episodes were for heroin and only 10 per cent were for cocaine.

Among almost 5000 visits during the month, only 112 were for benzo-diazepines, (almost always temazepam), however those felt more like 112 000 to our staff, in terms of both physical and behaviourial problems. We do question whether, for this very small population of injectors, the injecting centre provides an environment that is conducive to what can become very close to self-mutilating behaviour, in a way that perhaps a back street isn't. Given all the fiddling about and time involved in aspirating the gel from multiple temazepam gelcaps, it would surely be hard to do in a less controlled, more public setting. Mind you, judging from the number of empty temazepam bottles KRC's Needle Clean-up Service retrieves from the back streets, it obviously can and does occur in those settings too.

We also notice that there are far fewer visits on the weekends to inject these drugs compared to during the week and we suspect that this is because prescriptions from doctors are harder to obtain on the weekend than during the week.

When clients tell us about doctors or pharmacists who overprescribe or oversupply this medication, we report this to the Pharmaceutical Services Branch of NSW Health, which investigates such matters. But drug users are usually very protective of their prescribers, knowing full well that they are operating outside of the law. So we also make an effort to look for their names on the bottles that clients bring into the MSIC. These suppliers have probably not realised that now the injection of this drug is supervised in a health facility, other health professionals have access to their details in this way. I have also asked the Clean-Up Service to forward to me the bottles discarded on the streets. I have no sympathy for drug dealers, but I have even less for health professionals who profit from drug users in this way, knowing the impact it will have on their health and well being. The staff at the MSIC are so convinced that temazepam injecting is harmful when injected, they strongly support this effort to control supply.

I got an email from Dr Andrew Byrne today, asking whether the Division of General Practice of the Area Health Service should develop a policy on prescribing benzodiazepines to drug users—whether this should be limited or whether arrangements might be entered into whereby clients are dispensed this medication on a daily basis, similar to what occurs with methadone. Andrew has a general practice in Redfern, which sub-specialises in managing patients with drug-related health issues, also prescribing and dispensing methadone from the site. Living in Kings Cross for many years and having been involved in a local residents' association which has always supported the MSIC, Andrew is also a member of our community consultation committee and we liaise on a regular basis about all sorts of matters to do with drugs.

I actually responded quite emphatically, saying that I don't think there are any indications for the prescription of such medication to drug users. I'm aware that drug users often try to convince general practitioners that if they cease prescribing these medications the users will be at risk of what's called withdrawal fitting, which can indeed be dangerous. However, I said to Andrew that, while being aware of this theoretical risk, in my entire clinical experience I've never come across this as a phenomenon in this heavy drug-using population. I suspect that this is because they very rarely allow themselves to withdraw sufficiently from drugs for that to happen. I'm sure that many doctors prescribing may do so with the best of naïve intentions, but the reality is there is no control over how many doctors are prescribing in these circumstances. This may mean that some people receive very large quantities, which inevitably they sell on to others.

Curiously, drug users themselves, perhaps because such medication is prescribed by a doctor, often don't perceive these drugs as being in the same category as heroin and cocaine in terms of the harm associated with them, which of course is not the case at all. Perhaps for similar reasons, users also don't see selling on such drugs as drug dealing and, particularly at Kirketon Road Centre, which has a drop-in area where anyone can hang out, we've had to police this very heavily.

I suggested to Andrew that I think it would be an excellent idea for the Area's Division of General Practice to develop a policy and implement it across the board, but I strongly urged that the policy should be not to prescribe any psychoactives to IDUs at all. Where there might be a genuine need, such people should be referred to a more specialised agency, where the person's drug and alcohol issues can be assessed in a more comprehensive, holistic way.

Meanwhile, the American female client has returned to the injecting centre. She has obviously been found and we have informed the Waverley Police. She has also attended her appointment with the psychiatrist following her seizure on her last visit to the injecting centre and he has ceased the other medications that she was taking. We are very glad that nothing bad had happened to her.

It is sometimes easy to forget in Kings Cross—given how some of the people we see do survive, against all the odds—that, on the other hand, many don't. We've known many clients over the years to die as a result of drug overdose and quite a few to die of AIDS. We've also lost people to serious physical assault and others have been murdered in hideous circumstances. This is always very shocking when it occurs, especially as the victims are usually the younger, most vulnerable females in street sex-work situations.

Friday, 6 September

I got a call from Dave Darcy at ten-thirty informing me that there's been another drug overdose death this morning. Apparently the body of a boy called Danny was found on the steps of St Canice's in Roslyn Gardens, Kings Cross. He is someone who was known to the injecting centre although he was not as regular a client as Jenny was. But he was also known to be a heavy drinker and we wonder whether alcohol has been involved on this occasion.

Later in the day we also heard from clients that another well-known client in the area called Garry has apparently died of an overdose. He is no less than 6 foot 6 tall, and is a very, very long-term drug user. He was on high-dose methadone for many years, but came off a while back and has been very problematic behaviour-wise since resuming an active drug habit. His huge size and often erratic, threatening behaviour can be quite intimidating, especially as he seems to direct his aggression mainly towards females; he has had more than one AVO taken out by staff of health services in the area in recent times. I found it hard to imagine that Garry would have died of an overdose; so I rang Dave Darcy to confirm whether this was true, and he indicated that there've been no other overdose deaths in the area.

Using Mark Twain's famous words, perhaps reports of Garry's death have been greatly exaggerated. But events like this do remind me what happens whenever the client grapevine brings us such a rumour. We usually seek to confirm it one way or the other because overdose deaths wreak such havoc among clients, causing them to sink into an even greater sense of the futility and inevitability about the lives that they lead. We also want to know for our own personal and professional reasons.

Tuesday, 10 September

We had the review meeting today following the random spot check of two weeks ago. The inspectors indicated that they had gained a lot from seeing the place as hectic and busy as it was, and they extended compliments to all the staff, who they said were working very well and very hard throughout.

It's nice to get some positive feedback. I suppose the relationship with this body has always been, by design, an adversarial one, because they are the regulators of our practice after all. This spot check did come exactly three months after the previous one, so they continue to occur at the lower end of the three to six months range in visit frequency agreed upon at our recent meeting with the licensing authorities about the inspection protocol. Especially when you consider that these also involve subsequent review meetings and then written correspondence to confirm what actions we have taken as a result, it is too often. Other public health facilities are inspected on a three-yearly basis and only if they seek to become accredited. But then again, we appreciate that this initiative is new and different and there's a lot of anxiety from many different quarters that seems to require managing.

We'll most certainly be recommending that, if we get to continue this service beyond the trial or others are established, they should reconsider this level of scrutiny. Their argument—that the community probably expects it— I continue to find surprising because, when I mention it to members in the Kings Cross community, they are quite surprised that it's occurring at all, let alone on a three-monthly basis.

Wednesday, 11 September

We had another training day at Coogee and this time invited Paul Bacon, a social worker from the emergency centre at St Vincent's Hospital, to talk about the assessment of suicidality (the likelihood that someone will act upon suicidal thoughts). Paul was also an outreach counsellor at KRC for many years, so he understands the population we are working with.

We have found that some people feel quite acutely suicidal straight after injecting. Perhaps, immediately prior to this, they were completely absorbed in the efforts involved in obtaining and injecting the drug. But once they've achieved those two things, some of the more existential concerns about their life seem to surface and it comes home to some just how crazy and desperate a life they're living. The MSIC staff naturally find it very disconcerting when people express a desire to kill themselves, and need additional training in how to assess which of these clients are at serious risk and need further assistance from the mental health service sector. This is another thing that we in the field had no idea happened among IDUs post-injecting until the MSIC existed.

Wednesday, 23 October

I have just arrived back this morning having been in Lisbon, where Jo Kimber from the evaluation team and I had attended a two-day meeting organised by the European Union's European Monitoring Committee on Drugs and Drug Addiction. The objective of the meeting was to consider which data should be collected by the injecting centres in Europe to help assess and monitor their effectiveness.

The first part of this meeting was taken up with presentations from people operating centres in Switzerland, Germany, the Netherlands and Spain, describing the history of their establishment and presenting what service activity data they've collected over time. Jo Kimber and I then performed what's becoming our regular horse and pony show with me describing the MSIC model and Jo presenting some of the data collected to date. Being a more clinical service model and having to accommodate a formal service evaluation, we of course collect far more information in almost every respect compared to the others, so we were held up to this meeting as the best practice model for the future.

Some of the others had doubts about the feasibility of increasing their efforts in this way, concerned that they didn't have the manpower or technology, and that such data collection might reduce the acceptability of their services to their target populations, which is crucial. As far as some were concerned, they'd been operating successfully for up to 16 years, so they questioned the need to change arrangements now.

Especially as the most recent newcomer to the block, this all made Jo and me feel a bit uncomfortable at times, but there were no hard feelings expressed towards us. As a service provider myself, I know what it's like when the bureaucracy has a great new idea about what you should be doing this week, so I felt a little like a traitor to the cause. But the reality is that the data we collect provide us with very useful information to help evaluate and improve our service for our client base. Mind you, I think we are at the upper limit in data collection and I would resist any more measures being added.

I spent the remainder of my first week away working—finishing off various projects, and staying in daily contact with both the injecting centre and Kirketon Road Centre by email and occasionally by telephone, as required.

Upon my return I learnt that Dr Margaret Tobin, the Director of Mental Health Services in South Australia, had been murdered. She was apparently shot four times in the back after leaving the lift on the floor where she worked in the South Australian Health Department. Before 2000, when she accepted the position in Adelaide, Dr Tobin had been the Director of Mental Health Services in the South East Sydney Area Health Service, which KRC and now the MSIC are part of.

Apart from being shocked that such a terrible thing had happened to someone I'd known professionally, I must admit to also having a sense of personal vulnerability at the thought that someone in the health bureaucracy may have been murdered because of something related to their professional role. Since I have been associated with the injecting centre as its medical director, I have received quite a number of anonymous phone calls at work, some of them very angry personalised attacks. I've also received correspondence suggesting that I'm cooperating with the devil and, at least in one instance, reassuring me that they would pray for me, although they doubted that this would prevent me from being harshly judged by God when my judgment day came.

Health care workers in the drugs sector sometimes end up feeling a bit marginalised, like their clients, because a vocal few in the community do sometimes project their general antipathy towards drug users onto the people who look after them. In this instance it's almost as though they think that by keeping IDUs alive we are perpetuating the drug problem—as though not doing so would get rid of it. An extreme, analogous, example to this occurred after the Port Arthur tragedy, during which the mass murderer Martin Bryant sustained third degree burns to much of his body. The nurses who dressed these wounds at Hobart hospital afterwards received hate mail and death threats from some people in the community who were outraged that he was receiving any treatment in hospital at all, given the shocking crime he had perpetrated. Of course we have a criminal justice system to deal with criminal behaviour; denying access to health shouldn't be used to punish people.

While I was away, things operated very smoothly. Dr James Bell from the Langton Centre and Dr Craig Rodgers from KRC shared the on-call for me. There were quite a number of heroin overdoses but all were successfully resuscitated.

We also received written notification from Dr Greg Stewart, the Chief Health Officer, following the recent random spot check by representatives of the licensing authorities indicating that, apart from some storage issues at the injecting centre, there were no other problems identified. This letter also complimented the staff working on the night of the visit and the cooperation they had provided, so we circulated it to everyone at the MSIC.

We completed our third community newsletter, renaming it *Face Up*, with the cover showing pictures of all the nursing and counselling staff who work at the injecting centre—an attempt to increase the human face of this initiative at the community level. We had 4000 of these newsletters distributed into letterboxes in Kings Cross, Darlinghurst and Woolloomooloo. This is an important way we keep the community informed about our activities at the MSIC.

We have also hand-delivered 140 surveys to residents in Kellett Street, which is the street into which clients exit from the injecting centre. We felt it was time we surveyed those residents and businesses which are in the immediate vicinity of the injecting centre, to get feedback about any concerns they might have. So we asked whether or not they had seen an increase, a decrease or no change in the amount of visible injecting, in the amount of injecting paraphernalia discarded on the streets, and in the amount of drug dealing in the area. We also invited them to meet with us to discuss any other issues and asked them to drop these surveys back in through the door or send them in the post. In our experience surveying residents systematically is a more objective and reliable way of gleaning what the views of the community are, rather than relying purely on what is reported by individuals at community meetings, who are not always representative of the broader community.

Friday, 1 November

Yesterday was the last day of the 18-month trial period. We will continue on now until the government makes a decision about our future. Only one journalist (from the *Australian*) seemed to be aware of yesterday's significance. She rang Harry for a comment and was referred on to Pat, but he was unable to take her call immediately and she never rang back. So, while we had opened the injecting centre with a very big bang, followed by more big bangs for some time, we seem to have finished the trial period with not even a little bang.

Of heroin and nursing shortages

fourteen

Wednesday, 13 November 2002

Staff at the injecting centre were keen to report to me that Garry, the IDU who was rumoured to have died of a heroin overdose recently, had arrived wearing a white satin dress. Earlier I had received reports from Kirketon Road Centre staff that they had seen Garry walking up the main street dressed as a woman. Apparently he had dashed into K2 to tell staff there that yes, indeed, he was now a woman and that everything henceforth would be okay.

As previously mentioned, Garry is a physically intimidating person who is deliberately menacing, particularly towards smaller female staff; your classic gutless bully. Six months ago, after numerous aggressive incidents involving Garry, one of the frontline reception staff at KRC decided to take out an Apprehended Violence Order (AVO), which is still in place. Given that she works at both KRC and K2, this effectively prevents Garry from attending either of those services. Naturally staff only ever take this type of action as a very last resort; in fact, this is only the third time in fifteen years that KRC has had to take this step.

It would be far better in these instances if AVOs could be taken out on behalf of organisations, rather than individual staff, as it is rarely just one staff member affected, and this increases the likelihood that the client will further personalise their attacks to this individual. Having myself taken out one of the three AVOs at Kirketon Road Centre, after being punched in the jaw by a female client, I know just how traumatising the whole process is. As in a rape case, the person who takes out the AVO becomes a prosecution witness subject to cross-examination by the defence team with the person you want to avoid being right there with you in the court room. Particularly when you have been personally threatened, that's not a good situation to find yourself in, even when you are supported by the local police, which on all of these occasions we have been.

It's a great disappointment to reach the stage of having to deny people access to what we do believe is essential care but of course we cannot have a situation where staff's health and safety are threatened by a client. All things considered, this is a pretty good record, especially given that we specifically target some of the most potentially violent and frequently incarcerated people in the Australian community.

This AVO does not apply to the MSIC, so Garry had been allowed to attend the centre, but I did let the managers know that we needed to monitor his behaviour carefully. However, my early feedback was that the more controlled environment of the injecting centre, with the presence of a uniformed security guard, seemed to constrain him.

Of all the clients I've seen over the years, Garry was someone I would not have thought would ever have a gender issue—his female side has been extremely well hidden to date. So it was a great surprise to our clinical staff to see him arrive in a white satin dress, explaining to staff that he has always wanted to portray a virginal female image, that this has been his problem all along and that, now he has faced up to this issue, all will be well. We shall see.

Thursday, 14 November

Pam Walker has written an article in the *Wentworth Courier* highlighting the planned extension of our operating hours, and also alluding to the national nursing shortage and its impact on our recruitment. We recently advertised for nurses without any success and the proposed extension of hours continues to be delayed because of this. I encouraged her to write this piece in the hope that perhaps there may be nurses in the eastern suburbs who support the initiative and could be encouraged to apply. An article in the Sunday papers last year which mentioned the challenges of recruitment resulted in at least thirty calls from health care workers all over the state offering to fill shifts to ensure that the project went ahead.

It is a very good article; however, in the final paragraph she quotes Malcolm Duncan saying he's surprised to hear about the extension of hours and regards it as typical of the arrogance of the NSW government that the Chamber of Commerce was not consulted about this.

I emailed Pam to tell her I was pleased with the article, if not with the photo of me looking yet again very poker-faced! However, I was less than happy with Malcolm's comments. In the past the Chamber of Commerce has criticised the MSIC for not being open for long enough hours. As far as consultation goes, we gained unanimous support from all members of the community consultation committee, which includes local business and resident representatives. I have also continued to write to the Chamber offering to attend one of its meetings to keep them up to date with our progress and address any ongoing concerns they may have. But so far these offers have not been taken up. I get the impression they'd rather not have their concerns addressed because being in support of the MSIC would not be newsworthy.

It was becoming clearer that the Chamber was going to maintain its opposition regardless of how hard we tried to appease it; so we stopped hoping for a change of heart and focused on minimising the harm they could wreak against us.

Malcolm has recently been elected as president of the Chamber of Commerce and Tourism, taking over from Paul Haege, and has also announced he will again stand as an Independent for the seat of Bligh. One of our staff who lives nearby brought in a leaflet which had recently been dropped in his letterbox advertising Malcolm's candidacy for the seat of Bligh. The leaflet asserts that he has 'disabilities not shared by other candidates'—he is 'male, heterosexual, rational, doesn't like injecting rooms, can take the Premier on at his own game and win and has an IQ above 115'. He also describes himself as a trained killer. Scary stuff!

This all causes us to smile but his leaflet confirms that he intends to identify the injecting centre as an explicit point of difference between him and all the other candidates. Bligh's current Independent member, Clover Moore, plus the candidates for the Liberal Party (Shayne Mallard), the Labor Party (Barri Phatarfod), and the Greens are all supportive of our work.

So this means that the next few months are unlikely to be as low profile as we had hoped. We have enjoyed not being in the media spotlight over the last few months. It allows to us to actually get on with our real work.

Friday, 15 November

I attended a meeting organised by Dr Barri Phatarfod, the recently endorsed ALP candidate for Bligh, who works in the area as a GP. I began by stating my slight discomfort at speaking at a political meeting but said I also appreciated that they were important stakeholders in this community. As an employee of a government organisation (KRC), I have always needed approval to speak at political meetings, regardless of colour. But the MSIC is non-government, so this isn't required. I informed them that I'd previously spoken at a Liberal Party branch meeting for Shayne Mallard, a Greens meeting organised by South Sydney Councillor Amanda Lennon and have briefed Clover Moore about illicit drugs matters in the area many times. I said that I thought it was very important that we strive for a non-partisan approach to complex issues like this at a local level too.

There seemed to be general agreement on this and they were interested to hear the 18-month clinical activity statistics, which I was presenting for the first time. They were surprised to learn that we've registered a total of 3818 individual injecting drug-users in the first 18 months, that we have accommodated over 50 000 injecting episodes on the premises, that we have referred people into treatment and care in other relevant services on almost 1400 occasions, and that we've managed 429 drug overdoses without fatality. This certainly gives a sense of the magnitude of the illicit drug use issue in the area.

Sunday, 17 November

Garry apparently rang me several times leaving messages at Kirketon Road Centre variously as 'Silvia' and 'Samantha'. However, staff recognised his voice.

Monday, 18 November

Garry has turned up at the injecting centre dressed once again as a male, saying that he only wore a dress to stir people up because Kings Cross was such a boring place and it needed a shake-up. I suppose the fact that he never shaved his beard whilst getting around in the white satin dress did suggest that his commitment to living as a female may have been limited.

Wednesday, 20 November

At our team meeting staff expressed their concern that since becoming a male again, Garry has been attending frequently and engaging in more menacing behaviour. He has refused to abide by some of our policies; in particular he has been having increasing difficulty injecting himself and has been trying to recruit other clients to do this. Clients are also intimidated by Garry's size and this has created anxiety, which can translate into aggression between them. It can also discourage other clients from using the facility; understandably they want to feel safe at the MSIC too.

Garry has also been threatening towards staff and has already been spoken to on a number of occasions. So we decided to time him out indefinitely. Normally we set a specific time, a week or a month, subject to review, but, given the chronic nature of this behaviour and his complete lack of insight on any previous occasion, we decided to apply an indefinite time-out period for him. Andy is the person designated to inform Garry. Andy has known him through KRC for many years and is quite comfortable about taking on this role.

We have also put the Kings Cross police on alert—our security guard spoke to them so that, should the situation escalate and he become violent when he's informed about the time-out, we can be assured of a rapid police response. They have previously been called to K2 and Kirketon Road Centre regarding Garry, as well as to other establishments locally, so they were quite quick to assure us that they will be ready should the situation start to get out of control.

I have had a discussion in the past with Garry's long-time methadone prescriber, who assured me that Garry, while challenging in his behaviour at times, has never been violent. Nonetheless, I am always hesitant to rely on that sort of information as there is always a first time for violent people. Now being off methadone for the first time in many years may have also increased Garry's propensity towards violence.

Regrettable as it is, I feel confident this is the right decision; at least for some months Garry has been able to access the service, which is better than never having used it at all. I hope that we don't need to go to the next step of an AVO, which ensures an even more rapid police response and a likely custodial sentence in the event of a breach.

As important as each and every individual client's health is, I've always taken the view that you shouldn't compromise the health of the whole client base for the sake of one individual client.

Monday, 25 November

The evaluation team has released its 18-month evaluation report to the government and sent out a press release to major media organisations. The *Australian* carried an article focusing on the shift in heroin use over the duration of the trial, particularly since December last year, when cocaine represented 51 per cent of injecting episodes compared to heroin's 41 per cent. In October, the last month of the evaluation period, that had swung right around so that heroin was now injected on 80 per cent of occasions and cocaine on only 8 per cent. Taking a national perspective, the *Australian* suggested that perhaps the so-called heroin drought is now lifting right across the country. I think it is still too early to be drawing that conclusion, but it has certainly eased in the Kings Cross area since early this year and, interestingly, been replaced by a cocaine shortage.

Wednesday, 4 December

At KRC this morning I was informed by staff that Garry breached his AVO at K2 last night. He apparently entered the facility and was abusive towards staff and the police came and took him into custody. Meanwhile Andy reported that he'd seen Garry walking up and down the street outside carrying a bottle of beer, loping along and looking very pumped up.

Today was a particularly hot day, with the temperature reaching 37 degrees and very hot winds smelling of the numerous bushfires burning on the fringes of Sydney. In Kings Cross the atmosphere seemed electric; some days it just does for no apparent reason. Suddenly our management meeting was interrupted by loud shouting from below. We went downstairs and, sure enough, there was Garry, shirtless, striding around in the front reception area. He'd pushed his way in past the security guard and was waving his arms around shouting that he was Australian, he was the police, and that we couldn't stop him from coming in. Andy and I took the place of the reception staff who had been involved up to now while Colette spoke to them to check that they were okay. Meanwhile an overdose was taking place in Stage 2, confirming Murphy's Law again!

Andy told Garry that if he didn't leave the premises he would call the police, at which he ranted back that he was the police. Andy then tried to talk him down but nothing would settle him so Colette proceeded to call them. They seemed to take an inordinate amount of time to arrive, even allowing for the fact that in such situations things always seem to go into slow motion and one minute seems like an hour. I was actually quite keen for Garry to still be there when the police arrived so we tried to continue to engage him without escalating the situation any further. When Andy put his hand out in Garry's vicinity, he slapped it away; he'd already shoved Branko, the security guard, to the side. Garry normally confines himself to verbal rather than physical abuse, so things seemed to be worsening.

Then he turned on me, saying that he knew exactly who I was. Calling me 'van Beek', he surmised I was a product of post-war Amsterdam, and a medical student in 1947. Trying to lighten things up, I pointed out that that would put me in my late seventies, but he was undeterred and accused me

of being one of those rich doctors who earns all this money. As he bore
down on me, hissing and spitting, the thought went through my head that
I did not earn enough money to have to be subjected to this!

His pupils were dilated so I wondered whether he'd been taking a psycho-
stimulant, which can increase aggression. Although I knew from Andy that
he'd been seen drinking earlier on, he didn't actually smell of alcohol. Garry
then turned on the security guard again, calling him a Serb. Branko is from
Croatia. He then started calling Colette an 'English bitch' so race seemed to
feature strongly in this persona although he wasn't getting things quite right.
(Colette resisted pointing out that she is originally from Ireland.)

After what seemed like an absolute eternity, three police finally arrived—
two females and a male, all of them slightly built and barely 5 foot 8 inches
tall. To us they hardly seemed a match for Garry. (It's at times like these that
you curse those equal employment opportunity policies.) But the police have
weapons, which of course invokes a certain respect in these situations. They
didn't seem at all taken aback by the prospect of confronting the raging
Gary; it was hardly the first time for them.

They explained to him that they were the police and he had to leave.
But keeping to his script, he told them he was the police and refused to
leave. This exchange was repeated a couple of times before the police finally
said they would have to physically remove him. At this point, one of the
female officers looked across to us and quietly asked if we had some gloves,
which made me wonder exactly how they were planning to remove him.
One sees humour every step of the way in all of this, which I suspect is just
a coping mechanism to help you stay calm in such stressful circumstances.

Then Garry decided to walk out himself and the police quickly followed
after him, locking him in their paddy wagon which was parked out the front.
They returned to obtain statements from us and decided to charge Garry
with assault on behalf of our security guard, who would also apply to the
courts for an AVO against Garry.

While all this was going on, two clients came in wanting to use the
injecting centre. Having just seen Garry being put into the paddy wagon,
they asked us what had happened and we told them we had called the police
to assist us. Interestingly, I noticed that these clients didn't seem at all put
off by the presence of the uniformed police in our reception area, which is
a good sign that they now feel confident that their attendance at the injecting
centre is legitimate.

After hearing what had happened, the two clients headed back out the
front door to the paddy wagon, which was being rocked from side to side
by Garry from within. Pressing themselves up against the slats on the back

door, they were saying: 'Hey, Garry, just drop your cap out here for us; we'll get you some more . . . Come on, Garry, give us your drugs.'

It was certainly a very comical sight, seeing a paddy wagon rocking from side to side with two drug users outside trying to urge Garry to relinquish his drugs with all sorts of reassurances that they'd get him some more. It demonstrated yet again the resourcefulness of this client base, always thinking, thinking, thinking about where their next hit is coming from, although at another level it is quite poignant to see such predictable acts of desperation. But Garry was hanging on to his booty—drug users do not trust each other when it comes to money and drugs, having learnt that much from bitter experience.

The police indicated that Garry would be kept in custody overnight. I was relieved to hear that we would have this respite until an interim AVO is in place.

Tuesday, 10 December

Branko went before the Chamber Magistrate at the District Court at the Downing Centre and obtained an interim AVO. Now it has to be served on Garry in person by the Kings Cross police. This is of course more difficult when people are of no fixed address as Garry is.

Jo Kimber told me that there's been a death at the supervised injecting centre in Munster in Germany. He was a 35-year-old male who had attended the injecting centre in the morning to inject heroin and pills and returned later the same day to inject methadone. Following the methadone injection he apparently had a cardiac arrest. A doctor attended him within six minutes and performed cardio-pulmonary resuscitation for the next hour, but he could not be brought back to life and he was eventually declared dead. It's unusual to have a cardiac arrest following methadone injection. While this opioid, like the others, may cause a respiratory arrest, the heart usually keeps going, at least for a while. (We found out later that the post-mortem autopsy apparently concluded that the cause of death was severe acute anaphylactic [allergic] reaction, presumably to the methadone—which is very rare indeed.)

This is apparently the first documented case of a death in an injecting room ever. I must say I am surprised that it hasn't happened before now, given that there are so many injecting centres and they have been operating for so long. There is no ability to control what substances or how much people inject in such facilities. While people are presumably better off in a supervised situation, even the best-conducted resuscitation procedures aren't always successful, so it really is surprising that this is the first such death.

Having an overdose death occur at the MSIC has always been our worst nightmare. Even though I have emphasised that we could never guarantee it wouldn't happen, people continue to applaud the fact that we haven't had any fatalities. So I appreciate that, should there be a fatality, we could be judged harshly for it.

The injecting centre in Munster opened at about the same time as we did and has therefore been compared to us, especially at the very beginning. I hope this death doesn't result in the closure of their service.

Wednesday, 11 December

Colette informed me at our management meeting today that the recent advertisements for registered nurses have resulted in applications from three well-qualified nurses who have now all been appointed. So this means we should be able to extend the injecting centre's hours by the middle of January.

This evening I got a call from Geoff Barnden, from the NSW Cabinet Office of Drug Policy, to inform me that tomorrow the Australian Bureau of Statistics is releasing their overdose statistics through to the end of 2001. While overdose deaths fell quite dramatically in NSW in the year 2001 compared to 2000, this fall was not as dramatic as that in Victoria. I gather there is some concern—because there has been a greater reduction in overdose deaths in a state where there isn't an injecting centre, our critics may be tempted to accuse the MSIC of somehow causing the higher levels of drug overdose deaths in NSW, which of course couldn't be further from the truth.

I told Geoff that this difference between states is due to the fact that the heroin supply, as for all imported drugs, comes in through the eastern seaboard via Sydney and therefore any shortage in supply is experienced much more severely the further you go from this initial source, and vice versa. While Sydney experienced a heroin shortage during 2001, Victoria experienced much more of a real drought in that drug users were unable to buy any heroin at all for weeks at a time. By contrast, in Kings Cross the quality and availability of heroin certainly decreased significantly, but a day never went by when heroin could not be obtained right throughout this period.

We see the same thing with cocaine. Likewise it comes in through Sydney— but so little of it arrives in comparison to heroin, because it has much further to come (from South America), that there is hardly any left over after meeting Sydney's demand for it to get to anywhere else to any extent. This is why Sydney, and Kings Cross in particular, has always had the only real cocaine market in Australia.

Meanwhile, Victoria has seen much more evidence of drug users moving across to injecting temazepam gelcaps because the heroin shortage there has been much more severe than in NSW. Being a prescribed substance produced locally, temazepam's availability is unaffected by geography; the dramatic drop in heroin availability has led to much greater abuse of temazepam by heroin users all over Australia. Unfortunately this has continued despite the easing of the heroin shortage here this year.

Thursday, 12 December

The media carried the story of reduced heroin overdoses and generally the line seems to be that the significant reduction in overdose deaths has been due to the heroin shortage and the Kings Cross injecting centre. Despite the undoubtedly good work of the MSIC we could never affect national drug overdose death statistics. But, apart from Harry being requested to give one interview on 2KY, no other media made contact with us, so we were unable to influence the line being taken in this regard.

We registered our 4000th client today; the registration rate of new clients remains higher than I'd expected. These 4000 drug users are of course not all in Kings Cross at any one time; probably more like a thousand at the most might be in the vicinity. So the ongoing registration of new clients shows just how highly transient the population of drug users in Kings Cross is, with new people with new problems turning up and then moving on, often to the correctional system, all the time. There are times when we think surely there could be no more drug users left in Australia who are not already registered here, but it would seem that there are.

Friday, 13 December

Colette sighted Garry walking through Kings Cross accompanied by police, heading in the direction of the police station. She phoned them to find out whether or not they'd served the AVO yet but, despite Garry being in their custody, it would appear that, no, they hadn't. They were somewhat embarrassed and undertook to do so by close of business today, which will be a relief for all of us.

We've received another donation of $3000 towards hosting Christmas activities for the clients, from the same anonymous donor who last year gave money for this purpose. We have also just received a package with two Christmas cakes and $200 cash in an envelope with nothing to indicate whom it was from apart from a Rockdale postmark. A little while back I was asked to come down to the reception area to see an elderly gentleman who lived on the north shore and said he wanted to leave part of his estate to the centre. He explained that he had no family and wanted to leave his estate to worthy causes. I provided him with information about the service, thanked him for thinking of us and wished him well, worrying a bit that that may seem disingenuous in this circumstance!

In all my time at KRC we have never been on the receiving end of gestures like this. I suppose the injecting centre's higher profile exposes it to both good and bad things.

Tuesday, 17 December

Branko attended the Downing Centre for the AVO hearing against Gary but the case was adjourned until February because the paperwork from Kings Cross police station had not been received by the relevant court. Judging by the chaos at the Downing Centre—with numerous courts going all the time, various dismayed shrieks and shouts emanating from them (it must be the legal equivalent of KRC)—it is amazing that anything gets to where it's supposed to be at all.

Wednesday, 25 December

Eighty-four visits were accommodated at the injecting centre today—a relatively quiet day with no major problems. Christmas presents that had been bought with the money from the anonymous donor were distributed to clients, who were very appreciative.

fifteen

A serious investigation

Tuesday, 21 January 2003

I received an email today while away on annual leave from Colette to say that she had been phoned by the Premier's Department, which had just received a written complaint from a male alleging that he has personally witnessed four breaches of licence conditions and protocols at the injecting centre, to do with an under-age person injecting and overdosing; a pregnant person injecting; people injecting each other and drug dealing at the injecting centre. While the Premier's Department would not disclose to Colette who actually wrote the letter, they said that it had also been copied to the NSW Health Care Complaints Commission and to the Kings Cross Chamber of Commerce and Tourism.

Harry Herbert has recently been notified by the Health Care Complaints Commission that they are pursuing our report regarding a registered nurse whose employment we terminated for professional misconduct in May last year on behalf of the NSW Nurses' Registration Board. This particular ex-employee 'Jason' had threatened, on numerous occasions during the disciplinary process leading to his dismissal, to go public with allegations about breaches of policy if we also reported his misconduct to the Nurses' Registration Board, as we had indicated we would.

148   In the Eye of the Needle

Colette immediately made the connection between the letter of complaint to the Premier's Department and these previous threats to publicly reveal alleged policy breaches.

After considering all this, I advised Colette to recommend that the Premier's Department refer the matter to the office of Drug Policy at the Cabinet Office. I also advised her to let Pat Kennedy know, in case these allegations are leaked to the media. I already briefed Pat Kennedy about this in May last year, when this particular employee initially threatened to go public with his allegations. Harry is away on holidays so we can't yet brief him on this matter but, like Pat, he was aware of these threats at the time, and agreed that we had to proceed in reporting this employee to the Nurses' Registration Board regardless.

Tuesday, 28 January

The hours of the injecting centre have been extended so we now operate from 9.30 in the morning until 10 at night, Monday to Friday, and on the weekends from 11 am until 7 pm. One of our clients is especially chuffed about this—he recommended longer hours in the Client Comments book only last week and is now convinced he should therefore get the credit for our decision to extend the hours, which we don't dispel!

Wednesday, 29 January

The injecting centre has had another random inspection by the local police and the Private Health Care Branch. We assume that this particular inspection has been prompted by the complaint that's been received.

Monday 3 February

I returned today and have been informed that the licensing authorities will be investigating the complaint and that indeed the complainant is Jason. They appreciate that it is likely to be vexatious, but the reality is that, particularly with a state election impending and Malcolm standing for the seat of Bligh, the investigation needs to be meticulous.

I accept this and also appreciate that, even though Jason has his own reasons for making such a complaint, the licensing authorities can't assume that there is no substance to it. Disgruntled ex-employees are probably a significant font of all sorts of important information at times, I'm sure. However, I am confident that our systems are comprehensive and that there have been no breaches of this nature, so we will move forward confident that this investigation will further demonstrate that our service is tightly run and squeaky clean.

Harry is now back from holidays and I have brought him up to date. He is very relaxed and assures me that he will lose no sleep over this matter. I wish I could say the same.

Friday, 7 February

I was attending a Kings Cross Community Forum meeting when I received a phone call from Tracey to say that a new team from police and the Private Health Care Branch had arrived to inspect the premises. This is only nine days after the previous inspection, which in retrospect obviously didn't have anything to do with the investigation after all.

It was Colette's day off today so Tracey and Jake, the new Counselling Unit Manager, showed the inspectors through. They were asked to describe our drug overdose protocols and provide the definitions used for drug overdose, spending about 1½ hours there all up. This must surely be the only service in Sydney where administrative and counselling staff can describe such medical conditions and their clinical management so accurately.

Later in the day I received a phone call from Mark, the representative from the Kings Cross Police Service who had been involved in this morning's inspection. He introduced himself as the new Crime Coordinator for Kings Cross and asked to meet me so he could hand-deliver a letter formally requesting a written response to the allegations against the MSIC. I'm glad to be back in Australia in time to deal with this rapidly escalating investigation. The Private Health Care Branch has decided that their licensing authority partner, the Police, will lead this investigation at the local Kings Cross level.

Staff have seen Jason around the area this week, on one occasion sitting in front of the service smoking a cigarette with clients. He even sent one client in with a message to say 'hello' to Andy, Adam and Jake. It is very unsettling seeing him around and his fraternisation with clients is particularly irksome for the staff, who are all feeling very angry towards him. At a certain level we understand his desire to seek retribution for our having reported him to the Nurses' Registration Board. Mind you, the months of grief he caused us leading up to his dismissal should have been enough. But involving the Chamber of Commerce and Tourism is an act of heresy from our perspective. It not only shows that he wants to cause grief to those involved in reporting his misconduct, but that he clearly has complete disregard for the service's survival overall and therefore the needs of the client base, something all staff rightly feel very protective about.

The reality is that, regardless of the outcome of this investigation, some of the mud will stick, particularly in regard to drug dealing. We predict that the community will not necessarily be all that concerned about under-age or pregnant clients injecting at the MSIC. Malcolm is in fact on the public record as stating that he thought it most uncaring of us to deny access to under-age and pregnant drug users, which I actually agree with, but of course we have no choice in this matter. The community may not be all that surprised to hear of clients injecting one another either, but the drug dealing allegation is the one with the potential to gain traction, regardless of what evidence there is to show that this does not take place.

However, we are surprised that this story hasn't already broken. The original letter of complaint from Jason was written on 8 January. We hope against hope that it won't get into the press until after the investigation is completed and we can report a good result, which we remain sure of.

I was interviewed this afternoon by Steve Dow, a freelance journalist writing a story about the injecting centre for the *Age*. Because Malcolm had already been interviewed for this story, I took the opportunity to ask what he had said. Apparently it was all the usual criticisms of the injecting centre but no mention of licence conditions being breached.

We have not heard back from Malcolm since I wrote late last year to congratulate him on becoming president of the Chamber and also again to offer to speak at a meeting of the Chamber to brief it about our progress. Particularly in view of the new extended hours, I would like to do this so I have sent another letter to him today. I acknowledged that, while the Chamber hasn't supported the MSIC, it is an important community stakeholder in Kings Cross and so they should have an opportunity to raise any ongoing concerns they may have with the centre.

Monday, 10 February

By this Friday I have to provide a 'comprehensive response in writing' to the licensing authorities outlining our policies and compliance systems in regard to the four policies allegedly breached. However, at a meeting with the Private Health Care Branch this morning, a new procedure is already being suggested. At present, all women registering at the MSIC must sign a form declaring they are not pregnant and undertaking to inform staff should they become pregnant subsequently. It is now being proposed that the registration numbers of all female clients of reproductive age should be routinely flagged every six weeks so that they can be asked whether they might now be pregnant.

I am concerned that, despite no actual problem having been identified as yet, already these allegations are being seen as an opportunity to review and introduce a range of new policies. Given the number of policies in place, staff already feel that they operate more as police than as clinicians at times. I fear that clients will find these new procedures unacceptable, and that this may result in them not wanting to use the facility anymore. As clinicians we believe there are no medical and public health grounds to justify exclusion of pregnant women from the MSIC anyway. So staff compliance with a proposal like this would also be an issue in these circumstances.

Pregnancy is also, of course, a fairly sensitive and confidential matter to be routinely asking people about over the reception counter, so presumably this would have to occur somewhere more private, which would then also have space and staffing implications. Particularly for women whose children are in the care of the Department of Community Services, there are valid concerns that this may also be an inflammatory question, which could provoke aggression towards our staff.

It seems to me that there is absolutely no incentive to stop the licensing authorities devising more and more policies and regulations, all of which will then need to be policed over and over again. At times like this, as the service's director, I feel quite impotent and very much at the mercy of the regulatory body, which of course has a very different commitment to the health needs of this particular drug-using population in Kings Cross. At times, when I'm trying to impress upon them the importance of service acceptability to ensure access by this otherwise hard-to-reach target population, their eyes seem to glaze over and I get a sense that they are thinking that I should tell someone who cares. An under-utilised injecting centre would clearly not be a major issue of concern for them; what seems to be of concern to them is the occurrence of an event that could be tracked back to a regulation not being in place. So the more regulations the better; there is no downside in this from their perspective.

Such discussions eventually seem to end with 'Well, Ingrid, we're sorry you don't like it, but this is what will be happening'. I keep asking myself how much pragmatism is reasonable—at what point should your professional integrity overrule? How much are you willing to compromise to see this service through? I am always being counselled by others in the field that I just need to bide my time, put my various concerns to the side and get the project over the line—and then maybe some normality will be able to assert itself. I hope they are right.

Thursday, 13 February

In the last fortnight there has been another nasty incident, this time involving a long-term client known as Eve, who injects temazepam gelcaps. This was a very serious incident, culminating in her threatening the security guard with a blood-filled needle syringe. Staff evacuated other clients from the centre and called police, who removed Eve from the premises. It was their opinion that she most certainly would have carried through this threat had the security guard and staff not handled it as well as they did. We decided to sanction Eve indefinitely for such a serious incident. Threatening staff with a weapon is stepping way over the line, regardless of any mitigating circumstances.

Because of the disproportionate increase in aggressive incidents involving temazepam, we have decided to try to restrict the number of people injecting this drug at any one time in Stage 2. We appreciate the limitations involved in such a policy—it is impossible for us to police what drugs people bring in, so we rely on self-reporting. Clearly when a person intending to inject temazepam is told that they will have to wait, because there are already two people injecting it in Stage 2, next time they may just say that they're injecting something else. Once the client is in Stage 2, we have very limited ability to stop them from proceeding to inject whatever substance it is that they've brought in. But the staff need some respite, so we'll give it a go anyway and see. If it doesn't work we'll have to think of something else.

Meanwhile, Peter seems to be escalating out of control. His use of drugs has been very erratic recently and he is in grave danger of drug overdose. Peter was the partner of Jenny, who died of an overdose almost a year ago, and his behaviour appears to be connected to the first anniversary of her death, which is coming up shortly. He never did get round to pursuing his plan to lobby for a heroin prescription trial, but at least he's still alive one year down the track. Apparently he ended up dividing most of his inheritance money between his children, who are in their 20s and don't use drugs. Good move.

Friday, 14 February

Tracey hand-delivered my very lengthy response to the investigation team, which has based itself at the Kings Cross police station for the duration. I spent a lot of time ensuring that all aspects of our policies and compliance systems were fully described and I must say I was impressed myself to realise just how comprehensive they are. I hope that investing the effort into this will expedite the investigation. We are informed that the investigation may take a further two weeks.

I have discussed this matter with some of our supporters so they are not caught by surprise when it is reported in the press. Clover Moore thinks we should tell the media ourselves that there is an investigation taking place now, to avoid it being broken by Malcolm Duncan in the last week before the election. I am inclined to agree, although it would be so much better if we could report a good outcome at the same time. For the moment we have decided to wait.

Sunday, 16 February

I attended the peace march against the imminent war on Iraq. I saw two of the MSIC's most ardent critics marching too, which I find reassuring in a peculiar way. While pressed like a sardine among 200 000 other Sydneysiders in Hyde Park, I received a call about an overdose at the injecting centre. Drug use doesn't stop for events like this. The only silver lining to this dark cloud of war that looms is that the media have been very focused on this global issue of Iraq. There has hardly been any press even relating to national issues, let alone the upcoming state election, and in particular there has been virtually no media focus on the drugs issue for quite some time.

Monday, 17 February

I walked into the MSIC this morning and the first thing I saw was one client injecting another in one of the booths in the second stage. I stomped over to speak to the staff present, particularly concerned because this is one of the very allegations that has been levelled at us. The staff quickly reassured me that they had the matter in hand. They had already informed the clients that this was a breach of centre rules but, in keeping with our policy, for occupational health and safety reasons they had avoided coming in too close, given that the needle was actually already in the skin of the person being injected. So I quickly backed off; they were indeed doing the right thing according to our policies.

Andy told me later that the staff are worried about me being very stressed, afraid that I may be becoming a bit paranoid. Indeed they could be right, so I apologised for this too.

Meanwhile our new policy at the centre regarding temazepam does seem to be reducing the level of aggravation. However, in the drop-in area of Kirketon Road we have recently had the problem of two clients suspected of selling temazepam gelcaps on to other clients. Despite numerous warnings, they continue to deny that they are doing this, so I have asked Dave Darcy to deploy some uniformed beat police to the drop-in area to discourage any dealing from taking place there. The irony is not lost on Dave that, while I'm defending the injecting centre against an allegation of drug dealing, I am admitting that this may have occurred at KRC.

Contrary to what people imagine, drug dealing is much easier to control at the injecting centre than anywhere else. This is achieved through the presence of a security guard and the locked system we have at Stage 1, whereby we can control exactly who is admitted to Stage 2. At Kirketon Road Centre, the drop-in area has unrestricted access to anyone from the street, not just clients; there is no security guard and clinic staff have a limited ability to remove someone once they are inside.

Dave seems a bit taken aback by the request, checking that I'd said I actually *wanted* police to visit KRC and what's more *in* uniform. He suggests undercover police instead, but I said that the whole point was to send the message far and wide among all the clients that drug dealing is a crime for which we will summon police if necessary. Dave worries for a moment about police being seen chatting with drug users (now it is starting to seem like when you actually want police to inspect your premises you can't have 'em— maybe we should try this with the MSIC!) but ends up agreeing to this.

The two beat police who arrived the next morning ended up surrounded by quite a gaggle of clients asking them all about drug laws. (That's another thing I like about this client base: they make the best of all situations!) One of the police was apparently expressing his support for drug law reform, which the clients thought was just great. Meanwhile the two culprits had headed out of KRC in a hurry and the word spread as we'd hoped, that the place was no good for drug dealing. So I told Dave that the visit had been a success, but to send mean, old, hard-line cops next time!

One of the strategies we are putting in place for both the injecting centre and KRC to discourage temazepam injecting is the development of a comprehensive information pack including quite graphic clinical photos taken of the various kinds of harms caused by the injection of temazepam. This will accompany advice on how to diagnose these problems and what to do about them. We then intend to send these packages to health care workers in needle syringe programs, and to pharmacists and GPs in the area.

KRC has also produced a pamphlet with information about this for drug users, which will be distributed to other services who see temazepam injectors. We are preparing a submission to the Therapeutic Goods Administration in Canberra as well to recommend the removal of the gelcap formulation of temazepam from the pharmaceutical market altogether, which will include these case studies and photographs depicting the harms.

It is particularly this gelcap formulation which is injected because it can be heated and the liquid contents easily aspirated using a needle syringe, whereas tablet formulations have to be ground up and filtered, which is much more of a palaver. The problem is that the temazepam in the gelcap is an oil-based substance, which is not water-soluble. So, particularly when it cools down post-injection, it doesn't fully dissolve in the blood but instead congeals in and around the veins where it is injected, causing them to block and thereby increasing the risk of abscesses and ulcers. The chemical itself is also corrosive to veins. These cutaneous infections can lead to more generalised infection of the blood (septicaemia) and the heart valves, causing heart failure—both of these being potentially fatal complications. If the temazepam is mistakenly injected into an artery instead of a vein (which is not uncommon, especially when the person's veins start running out) the blood supplying the distal limb can be obstructed, resulting in gangrene and amputation of fingers and toes.

The gelcap formulation was removed from the NHS pharmaceutical listing of government-subsidised medications in response to these concerns, which were first reported from Victoria, most hard hit by the heroin shortage. It is now only available on what is called a private script, but because this medication is cheap anyway, this means that 25 gelcaps can still be obtained for about $15. This change has really only caused a reduction in gelcap prescriptions among pension card holders, who can no longer receive this formulation at the government-subsidised price of $3.50. They can still be prescribed the tablet form on NHS which is just as effective. Of course, dependent drug users who spend hundreds of dollars a day on drugs do not find $15 to be prohibitive, particularly in an environment where there is a heroin shortage making heroin more expensive than usual. Especially when these gelcaps can be sold on for upwards of $5 per cap, the $15 price of a private prescription of 25 gelcaps is quickly recouped.

It was the experience in the UK that the adverse effects among drug users were not resolved until the gelcap formulation was completely withdrawn from the market in the mid-nineties. While prohibition strategies tend not to stop people using drugs, they have the capacity to alter the range of drugs used, particularly when supply can indeed be stopped—as it can with temazepam—since the legal pharmaceutical market is the only source. Given just how harmful this drug is, a shift away from temazepam, even if it were only across to another drug, would have to be a good thing.

Meanwhile, the Apprehended Violence Order hearing against Garry has finally taken place and an AVO was granted to Branko for two years. The Kirketon Road Centre's one-year AVO against Garry has now also been extended for a further two years. We hope this works.

Thursday, 20 February

The licensing authorities have had a second letter hand-delivered to the injecting centre this afternoon seeking sixteen additional items of information by next Monday. They also want to interview Andy and a previous member of the nursing staff, Sorcha, at the Kings Cross police station.

Meanwhile Colette has been contacted by the NSW Nurses' Association to discuss the implications of their members' being interviewed as part of this investigation. They informed her that the standard practice with complaints is for all questions to be provided to the member in writing, which are then responded to in writing after legal advice from the Association. Peter Zahra, our legal adviser, believes Andy and Sorcha should have legal representation at any interview and a solicitor from United Medical Protection, the indemnity organisation which represents doctors in the event of complaints against them, has confirmed to me that that is their approach too.

I later phoned Mark to inform him of this advice and to say that I appreciate that this may slow down the investigation, which of course I am also keen to speed up, but that it is important not to deny staff their rights in these situations.

Friday, 21 February

Dave Darcy phoned. He was unhappy with the request for the questions to be sent in writing to the nurses involved. He said that the allegations against Sorcha and Andy are so non-specific that they have nothing to fear but that, if they are informed of the questions ahead of time and can prepare their answers with legal advice, this will reduce the integrity of their responses. He assured me that anybody, including a legal representative or a support person like myself, could be present at the interviews. He also agreed that these did not need to be held at the police station, but could be conducted at the injecting centre. I undertook to discuss this further with Sorcha and Andy.

The injecting centre had a record 296 visits today; it's been a long and busy day. Colette worked from home on her day off, collating information for the latest request. Meanwhile Tim, Tracey, Jake and myself worked all day at the injecting centre bringing together the response for Monday, drinking coffee and eating Monte Carlo biscuits for lunch yet again. But I will still have to come in over the weekend to complete the written response to this latest request for information.

Monday, 24 February

At 10 am today Colette and I sat down for what became a 3½ hour meeting with Cheryl from the Private Health Branch and Mark from Police, going through my responses to the sixteen pieces of additional information and discussing the allegations more generally. Various client files were examined along with other service records. In the interim we have also obtained agreement from both the nurses wanted for questioning that they are prepared to be interviewed (instead of requiring it all to be in writing) providing they receive some general information about the nature of the questions beforehand. They have both asked me to be present as their support person during those interviews, which of course I've agreed to.

Cheryl and Mark returned later to interview Andy, who was on duty today. Mark set his computer up at Colette's desk so he could type Andy's responses word-for-word. We were assured that this was not a police statement, but it certainly felt very much like one. After he'd spent quite some time providing details about his date of birth, his address, his position, the various roles he performs and so on, Andy was finally asked just two questions. Firstly, did Jason ever report any incidents to Andy in his capacity as Nursing Unit Manager, to which Andy replied that he could not recall any of significance. Secondly, did Jason ever report drug dealing in the centre to Andy? To this he was able to reply more categorically—*No, at no time did Jason ever report such a thing.* The interview was then concluded.

I cannot help wondering why these two questions needed to be asked in person, necessitating all the advice and discussion about how that would occur. But at least one of the interviews is now complete. The interview with Sorcha is scheduled for this Wednesday at 10 am, when she will take time off from her new job in community health in the Southern Highlands to travel up to Sydney.

This evening at about 8 o'clock, I got a phone call from Penny, the nurse in charge at the injecting centre, to say that Jim, a well-known client, came into the second stage and then proceeded to allow another client to inject him with methadone. What made this more complicated was that Jim had a central venous line in place, which had been hidden under his shirt. He must have absconded from St Vincent's Hospital, where presumably he was receiving intravenous antibiotics through this central line for something, but he was now using it to inject methadone.

Methadone can clog up veins because, like temazepam, it's an oral formulation not designed for intravenous administration. Central lines, which are only inserted to treat serious illnesses when there is no other venous access, should definitely not be clogged up. When the staff in Stage 2 became aware that Jim was injecting into a central line, particularly with another client injecting him, they strongly advised both of them to stop right there and then. But neither of them paid any attention and proceeded until it blocked. Jim then became quite drowsy—he had injected 80 mg of methadone, which is a fairly high dose to be injecting, even though he is apparently on the methadone program and so would have some tolerance to this drug. So I was presented with an overdose situation, plus a blocked central line and a policy breach (one client injecting another) by someone who was supposed to be an inpatient at St Vincent's Hospital. Particularly after a day like today, it was a challenge to think through all the implications of this.

I advised that the ambulance service should be called, to take Jim back to St Vincent's and that the emergency centre staff there be notified in advance that someone—presumably an abscondee from their hospital—was being returned to them with a blocked central line suffering an overdose. Methadone is a longer-acting drug compared to heroin, so in overdose situations the CNS depressant effects are also long-lasting and thus require longer monitoring and observation.

I also told Penny to emphasise in her referral letter to St Vincent's that Jim had been strongly discouraged from injecting the methadone, as I suddenly felt defensive about all of our policies in this regard. Putting the current investigation to one side, we realise that mainstream health care workers in other facilities may not yet have considered the range of circumstances that can arise from the existence of the injecting centre. We expected that some staff at St Vincent's might be disturbed to learn that someone could abscond from their hospital with a central line still in situ, then proceed to a Medically Supervised Injecting Centre down the road, inject a highly regulated pharmaceutical drug—presumably diverted from a methadone clinic or pharmacy—into the central line, thereby blocking it, overdose in the process and then be returned by ambulance.

We have not previously had a policy about injecting into central lines; this is the first time the issue has arisen, but we've now added it to the growing 'What's not allowed' list for clients. Penny also flagged the registration numbers of Jim and the person who injected him, so that they can both be spoken to at their next visit about having injected another person despite being told to stop.

Today the injecting centre reached yet another new record of 329 visits. A very big day for us all, both upstairs and downstairs. It sure is a case of never a dull moment here!

Tuesday 25 February

I got an urgent call during the day from Professor Richard Mattick, a member of the evaluation team for the injecting centre. He rang to ask if I'd heard of a Mark, who has just called him requesting information about the client database at the injecting centre. I confirmed that Mark is indeed a bona fide

Kings Cross police officer and that he is involved in an investigation of the service with regard to four alleged breaches of protocol. Richard expressed his concern about this and agreed that it would be inappropriate for the evaluation team to be providing information to the investigation, this being well outside their role.

I have already informed the investigators that data collected at the injecting centre by our staff belongs to the service and that the information they are seeking—which people we have excluded in the past as a result of them becoming pregnant—while recorded in the client's medical file is not specifically entered into our database and therefore could not be extracted. It would appear that Mark was verifying my information with the evaluation team, demonstrating again just how much more like a police investigation this has become. I am also somewhat peeved that someone from the evaluation team was informed of this investigation as it may influence the evaluation. But I also realise that, as each day passes, more and more people are becoming aware of the investigation and that it is likely to be in the public arena sooner or later, so there's not much point in getting precious about this breach of confidentiality.

At four-thirty in the afternoon I attended a Community Drug Action Team (CDAT) meeting at the Crest Hotel in Kings Cross. I am a member of this team, as is Dave Darcy. This was the first of three back-to-back community meetings going through until nine-thirty in the evening that we both attended. I informed the CDAT that the injecting centre is under investigation. I didn't detail the specifics but I assured everybody that I am certain that the investigation will find that none of these allegations has substance.

At 6 pm I headed back to the community consultation committee meeting at the injecting centre, of which Dave Darcy is also a member. However, before it began, Andy drew me aside and told me that Sorcha had now been informed by Mark that she is no longer allowed to have me as the support person in her interview scheduled for tomorrow morning. She was most distressed because it is now too late to make contact with the Nurses' Association to arrange legal representation instead. She had already informed her new manager that she would be taking the next day off in order to come to Sydney for this interview so she did not want to postpone it. She is also very supportive of the injecting centre and was keen to cooperate in order to expedite the investigation.

Sorcha does not understand why I can't be in attendance. Apparently she had been told that the previous decision to allow me to be present has been reversed at a more senior level because it's felt that the integrity of the investigation would be adversely affected as I might exert undue influence over her. They had explained to her that, because Andy is still a staff member, it was not a problem that I was in attendance during his interview but, because she is no longer a staff member, there is a potential conflict. I would have thought quite the reverse—Sorcha is now a free agent independent of me, whereas Andy currently works under my direction.

I was extremely angry to hear this, particularly because I had been reassuring both these staff that their cooperation would be in all of our interests. Sorcha has only recently graduated from university as a nurse and has always been one of the most diligent upholders of MSIC policy and an excellent documenter in client files. She was also one of the five people who had formally filed reports on Jason's misconduct leading to his dismissal, which may explain why he has named her in relation to this. I asked Andy to ring her back and advise her to come in tomorrow anyway to be personally debriefed by me about the whole episode.

Leaving Colette to chair the meeting, I asked Dave to come into the next room to speak to me. He admitted that he had been involved in making this decision, reneging on his own previous suggestion that I be present. We both returned to the meeting, but I remained very distracted by this for the duration.

I then proceeded to the third meeting, at the Millennium Hotel—a Police Accountability Community Team panel chaired by Dave, on which I sit, which is held every three months. If ever there was a night when you could have cut the air between Dave and me with a knife, this would have been it; but thankfully no one picked up on it.

Malcolm Duncan, in his role as president of the Chamber, was also on this panel. Dave had earlier speculated that Malcolm might reveal the allegations at this forum but when I arrived I was relieved to see that there were barely more people in the audience than on the panel, which made it less likely that such a disclosure would occur tonight. In fact Malcolm said nothing about the injecting centre and afterwards we even managed to exchange a few pleasantries. He said he hadn't received my previous letters so I now got to offer to address the Chamber at a meeting in person.

At the end of this meeting marathon Colette and I retreated to my place to lament our situation. But after tonight both of us now suspect that Malcolm doesn't actually know about the allegations at all—he's not acting a bit like the cat who's got the cream. I am beginning to wonder whether Jason actually sent the letter to the Chamber just to put an edge on the proceedings, or perhaps he's had as little success getting letters through to Malcolm as I have in recent times!

Wednesday, 26 February

At 10 am Sorcha arrived. She was very upset and angry, but I urged her to ring Mark again and offer to go ahead with the interview as originally planned. Mark said that he was now under direction not to proceed with this interview at all at this time. We had a good debrief, both feeling better for it.

Mark then turned up at the injecting centre unannounced, accompanied by Cheryl, and asked Colette whether it would be okay for them to audit more client files. She asked why and he replied that, although they had looked at quite a number of files during our Monday meeting, these would not be considered a statistically representative sample. It transpired that a decision had been made to audit 10 per cent of all the client files, randomly selected, i.e. 450 individual files.

This was an activity that would need to be accommodated in an office in the injecting centre and at this juncture we already had Sorcha and me in Colette's office upstairs, and there really was nowhere else. We then realised that the investigation was obviously going to be further prolonged so there ought to be no urgency for this file audit to take place right at this moment. So Colette suggested that they make contact with us later in the day and Cheryl replied that they would document that we had refused entry to the service. This was yet another slap in the face in what had now become a very unpleasant adversarial investigation.

At four-thirty this afternoon we had a team meeting and I brought staff up to date with the latest events. Staff morale has been badly affected by all this, particularly with the prospect of an extensive file audit now. Some casual staff have already indicated that they no longer want to work at the centre— it's simply not worth the extra hassle. Sorcha had also been planning to come back to do some casual shifts, but not now and I can't blame her.

Thursday, 27 February

I received a call this morning from the head of the Private Health Care Branch. She was clearly irate about my unwillingness to allow the file audit to proceed yesterday. She said it is standard procedure that file audits occur at the end of investigations, when all the information has been gleaned and it is known exactly what further information is required from the files. I stated that that may well be the case but that surely it did not have to occur without notice. A formal request in writing would have reassured us that they had the authority to audit these files, particularly given that there are laws to protect the confidentiality of medical information, which I am responsible for upholding.

I also pointed out that I thought it inappropriate from a privacy and confidentiality perspective that the Kings Cross Crime Coordinator be one of the two people auditing the client files, given his role in policing local crime involving these same clients. I also questioned the need to audit so many files, which will take at least two full days.

I was assured that it is quite standard to audit 10 per cent of all of the medical files in such an investigation. However, it was conceded that notification could have been given in advance and that it was perhaps inappropriate for Mark to be involved. I agreed to the audit beginning this afternoon without Mark being present.

As it turned out, Mark was quite relieved not to have to undertake this task, as frankly anyone would be; file auditing is very tedious work. Instead, he and Cheryl drove down to the Southern Highlands to interview Sorcha. The Nurses' Association sent a representative to be in attendance during the interview. The only question they had for Sorcha was whether she was present when an under-age person, not known to be under-age, had overdosed at the facility? Sorcha said that she had no recollection of such an event ever occurring. The odd thing about this question is that if the person was not known to be under-age, this would not have been a breach of policy anyway. When I pointed this out to the investigators, it seemed to be news to them. This would seem like a good reason not to involve people who have no prior knowledge of this facility. But apparently, to ensure that the investigation was bullet-proof, the licensing authorities didn't want to involve our usual inspectors because of concern about their independence too. Following the advice of the Nurses' Association, Sorcha also placed on record her objection to being questioned in this way.

Friday, 28 February

The two new staff from the Private Health Care Branch returned today to continue wading through the files. Their presence in the building, carrying files up and down the stairs, weighed heavily on the staff on duty. Unlike the rest of the investigation, this is having a more direct effect on frontline staff—each of them realising that among these 450 files they all will have made some entries and that these are currently being assessed. I suspect that the need to be diligent when documenting in medical files will never need to be impressed upon them again!

It being the end of another interminable week, I left for home early today and spent the rest of the afternoon in a pensive mood. Looking back over all the time that I've been involved with this injecting centre I cannot help feeling that it's been very arduous. Whenever things could have been either hard or easy, they always seem to have turned out to be hard. That has continued right through to today.

I remembered back to almost exactly four years ago when, similarly, it was six weeks before the last state election. I was co-opted to be the independent observer on an investigation following the front-page *Sun-Herald* allegations about an under-age person being provided with a needle syringe from the outreach service in The Block area in Redfern. That investigation was certainly conducted very differently to this one, despite the fact that it had been created by a media outcry at exactly the same critical stage in the electoral cycle as now—it took three days and was conducted by the Area Health Service which oversaw the facility, which I thought was perfectly adequate. Perhaps this is another instance of how being in the non-government sector is a disadvantage. It was actually that incident which led on to the Drug Summit and ultimately to the establishment of this service.

Should this service continue, I think the method of investigation needs to be reviewed. Having the police as one of the licensing authorities had advantages early in the piece in terms of bringing them on board, but being investigated by police like this makes us feel as though we are under criminal investigation even if we're not. The police themselves admit they have never investigated a complaint against a health service before—they are trained to investigate crime.

A while back, when we questioned the alarming frequency of the random periodic audits of the MSIC, we were told that this way the licensing authorities would be able to readily demonstrate that the service was squeaky clean in every respect. But that doesn't seem to have helped at all in this instance; this investigation could not have been more thorough, especially when it has turned out that Jason was unable to substantiate any of his allegations in any way. The usual approach in these circumstances would have been to reply with a polite letter saying 'We welcome your complaint, but this service is being very closely monitored and there is no evidence of the above; please do not hesitate to contact us should any further information in this regard come to your attention.' I wonder whether this might indeed have happened had I not advised Colette to refer the matter from the Premier's Department to the Cabinet Office at the very outset. It also makes me wonder how we would have fared if a real and serious problem did ever occur at the MSIC.

Fleetingly I identify with the Iraq situation; we too have had inspectors coming through the place without notice, for weeks now. Despite the provision of tomes and tomes of information, nothing ever seems conclusive enough. We too are realising just how hard it is to prove the negative.

I am feeling utterly exhausted after all this, and the real fun and games are yet to begin with the tabling of the MSIC's final evaluation report and the inevitable public community and political debate that will follow yet to happen. I don't regret having reported Jason's professional misconduct to the board as we did; it was the right thing to do. By doing that, at least no other health service will have to deal with what we did last year. But I can't help feeling that in the wash-up we've been badly done by as a result and I can understand why some health service managers would be tempted just to let someone like that go quietly and be done with it. This is a low point for me in this whole venture.

Monday, 3 March

Over the weekend the Sunday papers covered the public release of the Greens' drug policy which, in keeping with the National Drug Strategy, is underpinned by the harm-minimisation approach. However their suggesting that ecstasy and speed be available on medical prescription does seem a little 'out there'. But otherwise their policy does not appear too radically different from what currently exists. I am told that on the ABC News tonight John Brogden criticised the Greens' drug policy and this was accompanied by footage of the injecting centre (that file tape will travel). The Greens then brought us into the fray by accusing him of hypocrisy, given his previous support of the supervised injecting centre. It would seem that the illicit drugs issue is back on the political agenda in the run-up to this state election after all.

Wednesday 5 March

I gave the team an update on the investigation, informing them that we understand it's now complete and that the findings are being written up. Presumably these will be communicated to us in the not-too-distant future.

Harry had asked me to circulate a copy of the letter he recently received from Craig Knowles, the Minister of Health, approving ongoing funding for the now extended trial. This letter included acknowledgement from the minister of Harry's courage in taking this project on and applauded the professionalism of our staff. Particularly with our morale so low at the moment, it's timely to get some encouragement like this.

Today we had a serious problem with a client called Derek, following a series of previous incidents. On the first occasion he had presented in an intoxicated state and refused to be breathalysed. There is a breathalyser on site to provide an objective measure when clients challenge staff's assessment that they are alcohol-affected. When he was then denied admission he became very abusive, particularly towards 'Robyn', the nurse involved. He threatened to blow the centre up and to set fire to it, before leaving the premises. Since then he has returned on at least two occasions; however, when staff have tried to talk him through this and the other incidents, on each occasion this escalated into further abuse.

Today Derek actually pushed Branko aside and punched a hole in the wall in the reception area. The police were called and he was charged with assault and property damage. He was then bailed by police on the condition that he not come in the vicinity of the injecting centre until the case is heard.

When Branko went to the police station to give a statement, one of the police suggested that he should consider arming himself with a baton and handcuffs. Branko raised this with me, asking whether I would support this. I said that I would get back to him but, when I discussed this with the other managers, our gut feeling is not to go there. There would be the risk of complaints if ever there was the perception that excessive force had been used and how would we assess that?

I continue to believe that such crises are best managed by aggression management skills which aim to defuse the conflict, and that the presence of weapons has the potential to escalate the situation. We look back at the serious incidents that have occurred since we began and they still don't number very many. The most serious was when Eve threatened the security guard with a blood-filled needle syringe, when indeed having a baton to knock the needle syringe out of her hand might have been useful. On the other hand, this situation was well managed—police duly attended and removed her from the service without any injury being sustained by staff or other clients. I think it's more appropriate that we leave these very rare serious occasions to the police to manage. I checked this with Dave Darcy and he agrees.

Monday, 10 March

I got a call this morning from Colette to say that the Kings Cross end of Darlinghurst Road had been completely cordoned off and that a girl, known on the streets as Midnight, was standing on the roof directly opposite the injecting centre threatening to jump off. The police, ambulance and various rescue teams were all assembled in the area. Because the road was cordoned off, no clients were able to access the centre. Apparently Midnight had taken crystal methamphetamine, which caused her to become acutely paranoid, hearing voices that urged her to climb up and jump from the roof. After several hours she was finally coaxed down by the police. However, there were reports that some of our clients had been heard yelling up to her to jump so they could get back in to use the injecting centre. We trust that they weren't serious.

Monday, 17 March

I rang Harry and urged him to communicate with the licensing authorities to find out the status of the report. He was told that the letter addressed to him on this matter is now ready and awaiting a signature. He was assured that the outcome has been positive.

Thursday, 20 March

Harry arrived at the MSIC this morning bearing the letter from the licensing authorities. It states that the injecting centre has adhered to its policy and concludes that not one of the allegations could be substantiated in the course of the investigation.

However, notwithstanding this, as we had feared, no less than ten observations and a further ten recommendations regarding our operational activities have been suggested 'for our consideration'. This seems very opportunistic under the circumstances and not exactly welcome at this time.

One of the observations was that our code of client conduct, which we display in all three stages of the facility, is printed in a typeface that may be hard for the visually impaired to read. It's further been suggested that we need to translate this into different languages, even though more than 90 per cent of the people we see are of English-speaking background and we have never encountered a language problem with this client base, ever. It was even suggested that we might represent the various codes or behaviours pictorially, for those who are literacy-challenged. I have visions of wall-to-wall codes of conduct in various languages and font sizes, some with pictures depicting a range of the behaviours that we seek to minimise.

The letter also noted that the height of the counter in Stage 1, the reception area, may prevent the assessment of potentially pregnant female clients and recommended that we address this. The height of counters in health facilities such as this is dictated by occupational health and safety requirements—a physical barrier of a certain height between health care workers and clients is considered protective. For this reason we would not want to lower the counter from its current standard height. Besides, all new clients are registered in the assessment room, where the practitioner and the client sit alongside a desk with no barrier between them, enabling assessment of any 'obviously pregnant' (as it is worded in the relevant licence condition) women. Existing clients of course move right through the service so there are many opportunities in the other stages to observe if they appear to be pregnant.

We joked among ourselves that since we can't lower the height of the counter, perhaps we should make a window in the counter (which would be referred to as the 'pregnancy window') and ask female clients to stand side-on at the counter, so we could look through that window and assess whether they might be pregnant! Other suggestions included placing a block in the middle of the waiting room for female clients to stand side-on. I suppose we should be grateful that at least they appear to have heeded my advice that it would be inappropriate to ask every female client every six weeks if they are pregnant—one small win!

We laugh about these things among ourselves but in the back of all of our minds we know that, if the past is anything to go by, whenever these recommendations have been offered 'for our consideration', there has been very little willingness to negotiate and in the end we have basically had to do what we were told.

There is still not a peep from Malcolm, so we are glad that we didn't go ahead and break the story ourselves. But I know I will have yet another sleepless night tonight as I gnash my teeth contemplating how best to respond to these various recommendations.

Sunday, 23 March

Hurrah! We actually did manage to get to the election yesterday without any press coverage of the allegations against the MSIC or the ensuing investigation. We were greatly relieved about this. Of course we're still vulnerable to adverse press but at least we can now be assured that the political response is likely to be more sane and rational than in the days running up to an election, and there is an incredibly rigorous investigation that can be referred to.

Robert Oakeshott, the former National Party Member for Port Macquarie, who stood in this election as an Independent, at least partly in response to the National Party's ongoing vocal opposition to the injecting centre, won by a large majority, bigger than he had previously held, boding well. Malcolm Duncan secured only 268 votes, even less than the 280 he received in the last election. So much for his increased profile translating into votes of support. On the other hand, Clover Moore, the sitting Independent member for Bligh, polled 15 330 votes, increasing her majority by more than 1200 on a platform which included supporting the MSIC.

sixteen

Drafting the evaluation report

Wednesday, 2 April 2003

We were having a management meeting at the injecting centre when we received word from downstairs that one of the clients in Stage 2 had rung the Kings Cross Police Service. Jake went downstairs to investigate the matter further. Apparently Desiree, a well-known client, had been standing over various clients in Stage 2, demanding drugs and generally harassing them. One particular client said he'd had enough and called the police.

This was quite a historic moment—in my experience it is very rare for clients to call police to their assistance in a situation like this. But, we did have some concern about the police entering the facility under these circumstances, particularly because Branko should be able to manage this. We therefore suggested to the client that he wait on the footpath for the police to arrive and deal with this matter outside the facility. Meanwhile Desiree had left from Stage 3, so Jake and I went to check that she was not waiting outside for clients exiting to continue these standover tactics, for which she is well known.

To our horror we found that Desiree was indeed involved in an altercation with two other clients just down the road from our exit in Kellett Street. Much screaming and shouting and running up and down the street accompanied this. She saw that Jake and I were watching her, but seemed quite unperturbed, apparently oblivious to the public nuisance she was causing. I suppose from her perspective she gets up to this all over Kings Cross, so why not here? But of course everywhere else in the Cross is not near our exit, so any disturbances happening elsewhere will not be attributed to this service.

By this stage the barbers from next door were also standing watching, as was one of the staff from the Palace Brothel, next door on our other side. The brothel worker was utterly scathing, telling anyone within earshot that this was what happened all the time. The barbers were also shaking their heads, saying that they had seen Desiree earlier today break into a car and steal a mobile phone.

Jake and I returned to our management meeting, where we agreed that Desiree needs to be 'timed out' until one of the managers can speak to her about her behaviour today. While we have very limited direct control over what clients do after they leave the facility, it's obviously very bad public relations for this sort of thing to be happening and we need to do everything we can to minimise it. So we agreed that our next fortnight's theme on posters throughout the service should focus on the need for clients to appreciate that this is still a trial and that they need to be on their best behaviour to maximise the chance that the service will continue past the trial period.

We also asked Branko to increase his patrols of the Kellett Street exit and I undertook to ring the local police service to request that they increase their patrols in this part of Kings Cross too. While this kind of incident is hardly new to Kellett Street, now it is too easily linked to the MSIC—that's a reality that we can't escape.

I remember doing an interview for ABC radio before we opened, during which I walked through the facility explaining what would happen in each of the service stages. When we came out of the exit onto Kellett Street two very obviously drug-affected people staggered past. I then made the point on-air that drug-related activities were clearly already happening in Kellett Street, but that after we opened it was likely that some in the community would hold us responsible for all drug activity here and probably for every drug-affected person in Kings Cross. And indeed, that's what has come to pass. However, the survey we recently undertook of the Kellett Street residents and businesses had encouraging results. Only eight of the 140 delivered were returned, suggesting that this is not a burning issue for the majority, and of those, five actually said things had improved in terms of drug-related activities, even in this very immediate vicinity of the MSIC.

I also asked Colette to drop in at the barber's to check how things are going and to inform them of the various steps we have taken to deal with this issue. Likewise she says that she will visit the brothel next door, although we've noticed that it does not normally seem to open until after we close.

Monday, 14 April

I have been out of the country for the last eleven days, in Chiang Mai in northern Thailand, attending a second meeting of the UN Global Reference Group on HIV Prevention and Care among Injecting Drug Users, followed by the 13th International Conference on the Reduction of Drug-related Harm. I presented data to the conference regarding the 329 heroin overdoses that were managed at the injecting centre in the first eighteen months of its operation. It was the first systematic analysis of drug overdose cases in a supervised injecting centre setting ever presented anywhere. Wearing my KRC hat, I was also involved in a symposium organised by WHO, at which I presented this as a best-practise health service delivery model to provide HIV treatment to IDUs in resource-poor settings.

While I was away I received an email from Colette saying that there had been a phone call from the NSW Health Care Complaints Commission (HCCC) asking for the full name of the 'fat nurse' who worked here. Colette had asked the male caller why he wanted to know. He then explained that he was from the HCCC and was handling a complaint about this particular nurse and needed to know her name so that the complaint could be forwarded to her. Colette realised that this probably involved Derek, given that 'you, big, fat c . . . s' was one of the many insults he hurled at staff on the night he was refused entry on the grounds of intoxication. Understandably, Robyn was quite rattled by this, particularly because Derek had also threatened to 'get her' when she left work that night. The security guard accompanies staff to their cars in this situation as he did that night. But this is another reason staff working in this field never wear badges with their full name and some decide to have silent phone numbers, as I did after receiving inappropriate calls from a particular client some years back now. So Colette was not about to disclose Robyn's full name to this person and suggested that the complaint be sent to the service and we would deal with it.

Derek is in his late thirties and has spent a large part of his life in the correctional system. He is currently on parole and knows that if he is found guilty of the charges we have laid, which is very likely, he will go back to prison. He seems particularly anxious about this prospect; maybe he has enemies on the inside whom he doesn't want to come in contact with again. We have already had calls from various bodies, including the Criminal Justice people, seeking to mediate this situation, asking if we would consider withdrawing the charges. However, our previous attempts to discuss the matter with Derek have all resulted in further abuse, so we have decided that we cannot continue to expose our staff to any more of this sort of behaviour from this particular client. He has been 'timed out' for a period of three months, subject to review at the end of that time.

He has now landed at the HCCC. While we support the role of the HCCC and of course the right of anyone to complain about their health care, the only two complaints that have been lodged against this service have both been vexatious. While, according to the HCCC's information pamphlet, they do not pursue 'vexatious or frivolous complaints' it would seem that they can't be assessed to be vexatious or frivolous until they have been fully investigated. We are still feeling rather burnt out from the last episode and the thought of having to be subject to more service audits and provide more reports over this incident adds insult to existing injury.

Monday, 28 April

I attended a four-hour meeting at the National Drug and Alcohol Research Centre today. The evaluation team presented their preliminary results. Unfortunately, as had been feared, the heroin shortage has had such a dramatic effect on all of the drug-related indicators in Kings Cross (and the rest of the country), it has made it technically more difficult to tease out what effect the MSIC may have had during this time. It is not that the injecting centre hasn't necessarily made a difference, but that it can't be easily demonstrated because of the lower baseline figures as a result of the heroin shortage, which started about six months before the MSIC opened. I know that communicating the technicalities of statistical significance through the media is going to be near to impossible and don't doubt that our detractors will draw attention to the fact that the reduction in ambulance call-outs and overdose deaths in the Kings Cross area cannot be unconditionally attributed to our efforts. So this does not bode well.

On the other hand, the crime statistics are encouraging. It seems that drug-related crime started to head downwards at the time of the injecting centre's opening. While this reduction also occurred in the rest of NSW—so again, it's probably linked to the heroin shortage, which has contracted the size of the overall IDU population over time—this downward trend will certainly be more helpful than an upward trend would have been.

Of course it has never been anticipated that the injecting centre would have an effect on crime one way or the other. Drug users attending supervised injecting centres still need to purchase their drugs on the illicit market as they always have, so these centres do not directly reduce drug-related crime as methadone and heroin prescription programs have been shown to. However, clients may reduce their drug use as a result of being referred by us to drug treatment programs, so it is only in this indirect way that the centre might reduce crime rates. The only way injecting centres might increase crime in an area would be if they attracted drug users to the area who would not otherwise be there, which has been referred to as the 'honeypot' effect. But this would then be more of a displacement of drug-related crime from elsewhere, rather than causing a net increase.

Thankfully there is no evidence of this so-called 'honeypot effect' either. As we already knew, the main reason drug users are in this area is to buy drugs, not to use the MSIC. We service providers often dream of clients from afar getting on trains and buses to attend our worthwhile services, but that just doesn't happen with this population, which almost by definition tends not to consider its personal health a priority. This is why we also have to employ outreach strategies to ensure that this population has access to relevant public health advice.

Most encouraging, community support for the centre among the 500 local residents surveyed in Kings Cross has increased from an already high 68 per cent before the trial to 78 per cent. Support among the 200 local businesses surveyed increased from 58 per cent to 63 per cent. I had been concerned by the high levels of community support measured at baseline (never happy!), thinking that they would be hard to improve on. But, amazingly, community support has increased even further.

One of the perceptions we have been unable to shake off, even among supporters, is that the local community is not supportive of the centre. Despite the baseline polling results and us saying repeatedly in the media that there was a very high level of support, the Chamber of Commerce, which is always on hand to contradict this, has successfully planted the idea that we face significant community opposition. I hope that these new findings will finally put paid to this misperception.

Clive Small also attended the meeting. Prior to his secondment to the Premier's Department, Clive was the regional police commander in the area that included Cabramatta. Admitting that he was just playing devil's advocate, he asked how we would defend the service against the argument that the results in Cabramatta (where there has been a bigger decrease in the number of needle syringes dispensed to IDUs), using a policing strategy without an injecting centre, are more encouraging than those in Kings Cross. I said that I would be cautious in using the reduction in needle syringes distributed in Cabramatta as an indicator of 'success' since it can also be an indicator that people are re-using and sharing their injecting equipment with other drug users more than before. So unless one could be sure that this reduction in the needle syringes distributed in Cabramatta was not accompanied by an increase in the incidence of blood-borne viruses such as HIV, and hepatitis B and C, this might be far from an encouraging result.

After the meeting I contacted Dr Lisa Maher, an ethnographic researcher from the Faculty of Community and Public Health at the University of New South Wales, who has done a lot of research in the Cabramatta area among injecting drug users. Lisa confirmed that a recent study undertaken during the heroin shortage showed that the incidence of hepatitis C in Cabramatta was about 47 per hundred person years. Our work at KRC indicates that in Kings Cross it is about 20 per hundred person years during this same period. What this means is that, among drug users in Cabramatta who were hepatitis C negative, say, a year ago, an incredibly high 47 per cent will have acquired the infection since then, compared to 20 per cent in Kings Cross. These higher rates of hep C infection in Cabramatta may support the theory that heavy policing in an area tends to merely displace drug users, often pushing them underground, affecting their access to public health services such as needle syringe programs. This then results in increased injecting risk behaviour, in particular in the reuse of injecting equipment. This may be evidence that having a more balanced approach, combining public health and public order strategies, has a better net effect compared to just using a zero tolerance policing approach.

But I appreciated Clive raising this issue with us because it is very likely that some in the Opposition will be tempted to employ wedge politics as they did one year ago during the debate on the extension of the trial, citing the Cabramatta situation as an example of government success. The government will of course be reluctant to deny that its handling of Cabramatta's drug problem was a success, placing it in an invidious position.

Meanwhile I have drafted a letter for Harry to send to the licensing authorities in response to their correspondence after the investigation into Jason's allegations. I had hoped that, particularly with the passage of time, I might be feeling less bitter about all this, but I still cannot find it within me to prepare a response to every single one of the observations and recommendations made. So instead I write a letter suggesting that the current process of ongoing random spot checks (now referred to by staff as 'dawn raids'!), follow-up review meetings and correspondence to verify that action has been taken as required would be the appropriate process to refer this new set of recommendations to. Since some of the recommendations would involve significant database changes, I also propose that perhaps it would be reasonable to put these on hold until we know that the service will continue beyond the current trial period.

Monday, 5 May

In state parliament the Reverend Fred Nile asked John Della Bosca one of his favourite chestnuts: exactly what percentage of clients attending the injecting centre during the trial are now completely drug-free? The minister gave a very comprehensive answer indicating that, even if only a very small percentage of people saw a very small increase in their quality of life as a result of attending the centre, this would be a very significant achievement. I was impressed with the depth of understanding of the MSIC's role demonstrated in his answer and hope that this may be an indication of ongoing support from the Government more generally for our work. For the very first time, Fred referred to the injecting centre as a 'Medically Supervised Injecting Centre' rather than as a shooting gallery, which has been his usual way. Apparently Minister Della Bosca has been ardent in correcting his terminology every time and it would seem that at last this has had effect.

Tuesday, 6 May

We were so busy today that it wasn't until after lunch that Colette realised it was our second birthday and rang me at KRC to let me know. We agreed to buy a birthday cake for the staff.

Even before we realised it, our birthday was also heralded by yet another random spot check by the licensing authorities' representatives this morning. We had faintly hoped that, given there had been a six-week investigation during the three months since our last random spot check, maybe we might be given some grace but, alas, no.

I would love to be able to record that on this eighth random spot check everything was absolutely perfect but—*quelle horreur!*—the inspectors found a mop in a bucket of water in the sluice room. We might be able to save lives, but we just don't seem to be able to organise those bloody mops to be in their proper place. This was duly noted and we assured them that heads would roll!

This evening there was another community consultation committee meeting. I tabled the eighth quarter's activity results and it was noted that in the last three months, since we extended our operating hours from 60 to 80 hours a week, the number of visits hosted has increased by 50 per cent. The total number of individual clients we had contact with each month during this period has also increased from about 800 to 900. Clearly by extending our hours we are now reaching more individuals, who hopefully will use the centre at other times of the day too. The number of overdoses has remained stable from the previous quarter, suggesting that the rate has probably dropped back a bit, in line with my hope that the client population should gradually learn more about how to prevent drug overdose.

I tabled the draft findings of the evaluation team and explained how the heroin shortage has muddied the waters quite considerably. Tom MacMahon reminded me that from a lay perspective it sometimes sounds like we are against the shortage, which is of course far from the case. The heroin shortage has been a great thing when you consider how many fewer people have died of heroin overdose in the past two years compared to the few years before that. The apparent contraction in the size of the injecting population is also a very positive thing. If only it could be sustained. But from the perspective of the MSIC evaluation it has really confounded things. The before and after MSIC evaluation methodology always had its limitations but, when such an important variable changes so dramatically throughout, it really limits what can be confidently concluded in terms of both success and failure.

It is currently anticipated that the evaluation will release the final version publicly in about mid-June. I am due to speak at a conference in London in the first week of July. When I accepted this invitation months ago, it was expected that the report would be tabled in April, well clear of this conference, so I am hoping there will be no further delays.

Friday, 9 May

I got a call from Colette that one of the nurses had sustained a needlestick injury. Apparently a client broke off the tip of their needle syringe and it was not disposed of along with the syringe in one of the sharp safes that sit on each of the stainless steel booth tables. When the nurse wiped down the table afterwards the small broken-off tip of the needle could not easily be seen against the stainless steel table, and it pricked her finger. We realise that we haven't had a needlestick injury for some time now, which is good.

Breaking the tips off needles after use is a very entrenched behaviour, particularly among older injectors, who do this to stop other people reusing the needle syringe in the event that it ends up in a public place. But there is of course no risk of that at the MSIC, so we make this the theme of our next fortnight's health promotion campaign. We have run this one before, but clearly we need to remind clients again.

Wednesday, 14 May

Tonight I was attending a dinner at the Academy of Forensic Sciences when I received two calls. The first was to let me know that there'd been a serious overdose at the centre—Narcan had been needed, but the resuscitation was successful. Half an hour later I received another call from Andy, who started out by saying that there was bad news—somebody had died of an overdose. My heart skipped a beat; I was speechless, shocked by this news. He then went on to say that this death had occurred at the Tudor Hotel next door to our entrance on Darlinghurst Road. An ambulance had been called and they had worked on this person for about half an hour before declaring him dead. The police were then called, which is the procedure when someone dies like this. The person is not known to the injecting centre or to any of the clients who had gone to the Tudor Hotel to investigate. Andy also went there and spoke to the ambulance officers, one of whom was in tears. He helped debrief this officer while other staff simultaneously managed yet another overdose—which also required Narcan—at the injecting centre. This would suggest that there is a strong batch of heroin being sold tonight, so we put the word around that IDUs need to take extra care.

Two serious overdoses successfully managed with naloxone at the MSIC versus one serious overdose resulting in death right next door at the Tudor Hotel proves something to my way of thinking. It's a pity that the evaluation won't be reporting on episodes like this, but it is clear to us where the safest place to be was tonight.

Someone may well ask why that person went to the Tudor Hotel when the injecting centre was open and right next door. Of course not everybody is eligible to use the injecting centre, because of their age, pregnancy, intoxication and so on. And some people, particularly if they are from out of town, may not know about it or where it is. Furthermore, we have a registration procedure that takes at least fifteen minutes, which might be off-putting for some, especially if they are in the area just for the night. Particularly for people who want to retain their anonymity, the injecting centre may also not appeal—to facilitate supervision our injecting booths are open, so it is impossible not to be seen by other clients at some stage of the visit.

On the other hand, these 'private hotels' have closed rooms, and injecting also often occurs there in the context of commercial sex in which the sex worker is paid extra to procure drugs and to inject their customer. This can be particularly lethal if he hasn't used heroin before, especially if he is also intoxicated, which is not uncommon in these circumstances. The $10 price charged to rent rooms such as those in the Tudor Hotel on a short-term (15–30 minute) basis is not prohibitive when you have an expensive drug habit. Drug supply is also sometimes based in such establishments, making them 'one-stop shops'. Sometimes I wonder why anyone uses the injecting centre with all its rules—it hardly seems like a social, fun place to be doing something like that. But then the drug users we see aren't usually injecting drugs for fun.

Thursday, 15 May

We have received a letter from the HCCC regarding Derek's complaint. Curiously enough, it concerns a previous visit when he claims a friend of his overdosed and the nurses all stood around doing nothing, so he was forced to do the resuscitation himself! He also complains that the MSIC allow people to inject temazepam, which he believes is illegal there (it isn't).

I have now learnt that the HCCC only pursues matters considered to be important to the provision of health care more broadly, for example systemic problems that would have the potential to impact negatively on others using the health system in future. So Derek's non-admission to the injecting centre on the basis of intoxication would not have qualified—which also explains all this nonsense about our overdose management and temazepam policy. We have now also learnt that the same HCCC person who rang wanting to know who the fat nurse was, actually wrote the complaint for Derek. I wonder how he could have missed the fact that Derek is a seriously dangerous person who is a safety risk to health-care workers. I remind myself that he is employed to be an advocate for whoever turns up to complain, and it is not his role to judge the veracity of these complaints upfront.

Monday, 19 May

I am going to spend the rest of this week collating case studies to be incorporated into the evaluation report. A year ago I met with Richard Mattick and Jo Kimber to discuss how the evaluation might be able to capture the more qualitative aspects of our work, particularly in relation to outcomes of our referrals to drug treatment programs. I agreed that providing several case studies was a good way to do this. However, the difficulty with trying to chase up case studies of people who have successfully gone on to lead drug-free lives is that such people necessarily stop coming to the injecting centre. But sometimes clients write to us from their new lives. I include here a letter just received from Mindy, a female client of the MSIC.

This is a belated thank you to all the staff during Nov/Dec 2002 and Jan 2003. During the lowest point in my life you provided the only stability I knew. A time at which I didn't know where I'd be sleeping from night to night, where the next meal was coming from or whether I was going to live or die (by choice or otherwise). Having a safe place to go with people I felt I could trust was a life-line. I am forever grateful to you all, as a team, for having such a positive effect on my life. I'd like you to know that the greatest quality, which you all showed, was the ability to make me feel that I was not being judged. Pretty amazing considering the 'state' I was in. Thanks for the tea and biscuits too! Keep up the good work. I'm sure you have helped many others as well. I'm sure you guys are a large part of the reason I'm still alive. I remain a mixed-up, shook-up girl (to quote M. Spiby) but now I'm a drug-free mixed-up, shook-up girl, ha ha! Love Mindy.

Mindy's letter shows much insight, particularly about still having issues to deal with, despite now being drug-free. We sometimes don't understand why clients achieving 'drug-free' status seems to be the only indicator of success for people like Fred Nile. It is just the very first step. As long as Mindy remains mixed-up she will be at high risk of relapsing to problematic drug use. But at least she seems to realise that, which is the second step. Let's hope she is able to get through the next 100 or so steps necessary to stay drug-free for the rest of her life.

Thursday, 29 May

The HCCC has referred Derek's complaint to the Private Health Care Branch. So we met about that today and I was again quizzed about how we manage overdoses and the use of temazepam at the MSIC. We provided all of the relevant policies and access to client files to be audited in this regard. Like Jason, this client has already caused us significant aggravation, and now here we are again being distracted by the need to respond formally to his complaint. But at least we're becoming more familiar with the drill these days!

Later in the afternoon I received by courier the first draft of the final evaluation report. As a member of the evaluation committee I am asked to provide comments on it within the next week. This draft does not include the chapter on the economic assessment of the service nor the final discussion and conclusion section. It is nonetheless a report of 206 pages and I realise that I'm going to need to put a lot of care and attention into this in the next few days.

Sunday, 1 June

I set aside time today to start going through the report with a fine-tooth comb. I made a few written comments about the first two chapters, which were generally fine, but when I got to Chapter 3—the chapter on the impact of the injecting centre on opioid overdose—I was first of all struck by its very negative tone. This is bound to be the most important chapter in the entire evaluation report.

The introduction to Chapter 3 refers to the unrealistic claims made by various advocates for the injecting centre in terms of the lives that it might save. It specifically references an interview with Dr Alex Wodak on the *7.30 Report* back in 1999 (when he was going to be the medical director of the centre under the Sisters of Charity Health Service) wherein he apparently said that he estimated that thirty lives would be saved per year of service operation. It is unusual to reference what someone said in a media interview so many years ago in a scientific report, and rightly so I think. Over the last few years I have well and truly come to appreciate just how often one is misquoted, quoted out of context or quoted without any of the riders one has stipulated. Besides, the context then was pre-heroin shortage, so Alex's predictions in this regard might well have been reasonable for that time. The rest of the chapter seems to be a well-constructed argument to systematically demonstrate just how very wrong these claims were, specifically referring to them no less than three more times. In contrast, the chapter on crime does not refer in the same way to the much more outlandish early predictions by our opponents—for example, that drug users and drug dealers would gravitate to Kings Cross from all over the country and crime rates would go through the roof—and nor should it. Surely service evaluations should not aim to disprove what were unlikely outcomes anyway; in my opinion they should avoid buying into any political hyperbole that might exist and instead set realistic benchmarks, and then assess how well a service has been able to meet these.

The chapter describes two different methods to determine how many, among the 329 heroin overdose cases successfully treated at the MSIC during the 18-month trial period, would have otherwise resulted in death. The first method used, which seems quite valid to me, estimates that up to 13 deaths may have been averted. However, the second method only factors in the 81 heroin overdoses where naloxone also needed to be administered, disregarding the other 248 overdoses completely, and estimates that about 6 deaths were averted, which is therefore necessarily an underestimate to my way of thinking. The report then goes on to opt for the latter estimate of six as being 'most plausible'. Then, to top it off, it translates that into a rate of four deaths averted per year. Annualising the results of an 18-month trial period like this is also irregular, especially if the period wasn't likely to be representative of ongoing activity and this was definitely the case with the evaluation starting on Day One of our operations, when we were only open for four hours a day and were yet to build up a client base etc.

It was towards the end of the weekend when I was reading this, and perhaps I am a bit tired, but I feel completely gutted and have a growing sense of panic. I realise that I need to stay calm and to approach this matter as dispassionately as I can. I decide to express my concerns formally in a letter to Richard Mattick, the lead author of this chapter. Naturally I recognise that I will be assumed to lack objectivity—I suppose I have to reluctantly admit that anything short of a report stating that this is the Best Service In The World Ever would always have been a bit of a disappointment to me! Nonetheless I feel that the methodology of Chapter 3 has obvious weaknesses. While arguing over whether we saved four or six or thirteen lives does appear rather unseemly, I predict that this is very likely to be the focus of debate once this report is made public.

Wednesday, 4 June

I have completed my letter to Richard, commenting on the methodology employed and suggesting some different ways to analyse the data. I also noted that the tone of this chapter seems different to the rest of the report, and recommended the complete removal of all the references to 'exaggerated claims by advocates'.

Sunday, 8 June

I received a phone call from Richard to tell me that he has taken my comments on board. He will consider undertaking some of the analyses I have suggested. He also indicated that Chapter 3 is being rewritten in response to others' comments anyway and that the reference to Alex's *7.30 Report* interview will be reconsidered. I feel very relieved, glad that I spent as much time as I did composing the letter.

Friday, 13 June

This afternoon Richard phoned about the timing of the release of the report. He indicated that he is keen to get it over and done with. If only it was the end for us too, but the report's release is likely to mark the beginning of a new phase of debate and controversy for us. As luck would have it (again), the preferred time for the report's release is now the very week—the only week—that I will be away, in the UK. I have had this growing anxiety, as the evaluation report has been delayed, delayed and further delayed, that eventually it would land during this particular week. I impressed upon Richard the importance of me being in Sydney at that time and urged that it be released when I return the week after. He said he'd to get back to me about this.

Next, I heard the case histories recently added to the evaluation report would be removed. The considerable time and effort I spent bringing these together flashed through my mind, but I tried to set that aside. I had agreed that they would add an important qualitative dimension, allowing people to better understand the challenges involved in referring people with such complex needs into drug treatment programs, which is not at all apparent just from reading the various tables about client numbers and demographics, but the evaluators had decided against including them after all. So at the end of the day I was left with a sinking feeling that things were not going our way. Today has turned out to be quite a Black Friday.

Monday, 23 June

I arrived at work wearing jeans, thinking that I will need to be dressing more formally more consistently very soon so it would be nice to get around in my preferred uniform during this calm before the storm. I then received a phone call from Pat Kennedy asking, 'Ingrid, have you heard the news?' Apparently this morning the Salvation Army launched their Drug Action Week activities with a press conference in which it was stated that, in the two years to date, there has not been a single referral from the injecting centre to any of their various rehabilitation programs.

Apparently they don't usually get much of a turnout for these launches, but the media had been tipped off that the Salvation Army would also be launching a broadside against the injecting centre, so they came in droves. They were now all flocking to Pat seeking our response. It was agreed that I would speak to the various TV news journalists, in Fitzroy Gardens near the El Alamein fountain in Kings Cross.

I did a few short grabs on 2UE and 2GB news before midday, then I quickly drove home to doff the jeans and put on my proper doctor clothes for the interviews at one o'clock. In the interim I checked with the counsellors and nurses at the injecting centre what our referral experience has been of late. Our statistics indicate that on over 800 occasions we have referred people to the wide range of drug treatment and rehabilitation services available, including those of the Salvation Army. Staff inform me that one client currently staying in a Salvation Army facility at Morisset had in fact rung up over the weekend to let us know that he was doing well.

I knew where this was coming from. Over a year ago Major Brian Watters told me that one afternoon, when he didn't have anything better to do, he'd decided to ring around their facilities to ask if they'd received referrals from us. He said that they'd all indicated they hadn't. Of course, I'd thought at the time that it was unlikely that there would ever be any one person in a facility who would be able to reliably know where every client had been referred from. So I knew there had never been any systematic review by the Salvation Army of the source of referrals. I also thought it possible that clients from the injecting centre might not necessarily want to identify themselves as coming from the MSIC. And also that whoever took Brian's phone call might not have conducted too thorough a search for referrals from the injecting centre because they could have known the answer Brian wanted to hear.

It also has to be recognised that the population of drug users seen at the injecting centre is very heavily dependent on heroin; they are usually in no position to be referred immediately to the kind of non-medicated/drug-free rehab program the Salvation Army runs. Unless they have undertaken detox first—a process that can take at least a week—they would go into acute opioid withdrawal ('cold turkey'), which such facilities are usually not set up to cope with. So the standard approach is for drug dependent people to first detox (the easy part) and then to enter a rehab program (the hard part, especially when you can't organise for this to occur back-to-back), and this is reflected in our referral data, with most being to drug detoxification services. And of course, apart from all that, it's a case of horses for courses and not all clients like their particular style of rehabilitation, particularly not the religious focus.

The public statements by the Salvation Army today were made in the context of an admission by them that they have a 20 per cent vacancy rate in their rehab programs; the implication seemed to be that somehow the MSIC was to blame for this because we were holding people back and, worse still, that this was in retaliation for the Salvation Army's explicit opposition to the injecting centre. I found these implications particularly abhorrent; as professionals, we would never let philosophical differences influence our clinical decision-making. The MSIC's approach, as reflected in our practice, is to be eclectic, embracing the full range of treatment options—from abstinence, 12-step programs and naltrexone, right through to those with more of a controlled use emphasis.

I was particularly disappointed by these accusations because I know that Brian Watters is well aware that this has always been my approach. The only silver lining from our perspective was that the admission of a vacancy rate in their treatment and rehab programs undermines any future arguments that the money spent on the injecting centre would be better spent on treatment and rehab. Clearly with such a high vacancy rate they wouldn't be spending the money they already receive from the government and therefore could hardly justify calls for a transfer of funding as has occurred in the past.

By nightfall I had spoken to virtually every radio outlet, print media and television station. Our message was simple—we have evidence that we have referred people to their programs. The problem is that the Salvation Army enjoys something of a sacred cow status within the community generally and most journalists and politicians will assume that they would never launch a pre-emptive sortie like this on us. So we didn't expect to fare too well when it got down to our word against theirs. I wished I could send the film crews to interview our client in the Morisset facility right now, but of course I knew that this would be entirely inappropriate.

Friday, 27 June

It has finally been decided that the report will be released by the government on 9 July, which is two days after I return from London, the week after next.

As I left for the airport I noticed two ambulances parked in front of the injecting centre. Apparently another person had died from a heroin overdose at the Tudor Hotel next door. This is the second death on those premises in recent times and I pondered somewhat facetiously whether perhaps this hotel should have been used as the control condition during the trial to better assess just how many lives we have saved at the injecting centre.

While waiting in the Qantas lounge I recognised Archbishop George Pell there. I recalled his alleged involvement in the Vatican's decision to have the Sisters of Charity Health Service withdraw from this project and the implications that has had for me from a professional perspective ever since. I was tempted to introduce myself but decided against it.

seventeen

The public release of the evaluation report

Monday, 7 July 2003

I arrived back from London in Sydney at 5 o'clock this morning. The conference presentation had gone well; the UK is interested in our clinical model, injecting centres being mooted there too in recent times. It's now exactly two days until the press conference to announce the release of the final evaluation report but, despite this, when I went in to work today, there was still no advance copy of the final version of the report available for us to read.

I spoke to Julie at John Della Bosca's office; she said they had not received the final report yet either. Apparently the evaluators were still working on one of the chapters over the weekend and the final version was now at the printers. She only had the last draft version, but agreed to make copies of this and courier one to me at the injecting centre and one to Harry. In the meantime, she informed me that the report concludes that it is likely the injecting centre averted at least four deaths per year.

I was speechless. In my letter to Richard I had argued that the second method used, which rendered the four, necessarily underestimated the number of deaths averted because it only considered the 25 per cent of heroin overdoses at the MSIC in which naloxone was administered and shouldn't be used at all. While the use of Narcan is undoubtedly an indicator of the severity of a heroin overdose, which is in turn a predictor of death, where the overdose would have otherwise occurred is also very relevant. Even a mild overdose not needing Narcan can eventually lead to death in an unsupervised situation, as highlighted by my friend Karen's tragic death almost two years ago. I have no doubt that some of these other 248 overdoses in which Narcan wasn't used would have resulted in death if they had occurred in other circumstances.

What's more, this method directly compares the MSIC's rate of naloxone usage with that of the ambulance service without adjusting for the differences in the respective clinical protocols and the earlier stage in the natural progression of the overdose that we initiate treatment at the MSIC. My letter had suggested that rather than stating that there had been *four to nine deaths averted per annum*, this should be expressed as being *up to thirteen deaths averted during the 18-month trial period*. Instead, it has gone quite the other way, no longer even expressed as a range. It would appear that the only suggestion that was accepted was the removal of all the references to 'advocates' exaggerated claims'.

Julie indicated that everyone there in the minister's office was also quite surprised by this rather modest number. Particularly given that the MSIC managed 329 heroin overdoses during the 18 months, it seems incredible that this would amount to an annual rate of just four deaths prevented.

While the other 80 overdoses—involving drugs other than heroin, including 60 cases of cocaine toxicity—are referred to in the report's text, there is no attempt to quantify the deaths averted by successfully treating those at the MSIC. The evaluation's protocol was of course developed prior to the heroin shortage, not predicting this or the subsequent shift across to cocaine injecting, so there was no methodology developed for this.

My other concern is that the executive summary states that the proportion of ambulance attendances to opioid overdoses in the Kings Cross area that took place during the hours of MSIC operations *changed little* during the evaluation period, whereas the later conclusions section states quite categorically that the analysis of overdoses attended by ambulances when the centre was open and when it was closed showed *no effect* on ambulance attendances because of the operation of the MSIC. Here the wording is relevant, with the term 'changed little' being directly translated into 'no effect'. The usual convention in research would be to conclude that no effect could be detected using the methodology employed, thereby not necessarily implying that this was the same as proving no effect. But I know that I will only be able to communicate such subtleties to the research community and not the rest of the community through the media.

Apart from how this finding has been expressed, the finding itself just doesn't stand to reason. Given the large number of overdoses managed in the facility, a proportion of these would have to have resulted in ambulance call-outs if we hadn't been there. So surely we must have had quite a significant effect in this regard? To my way of thinking, if ambulance call-outs didn't decrease during the evaluation period, then presumably they would have increased had we not been operating.

All of the case histories have indeed been removed and, while the economic analysis chapter has still not been included, I know that this low estimate of deaths averted will also be what has to be used to analyse the cost-benefit of the MSIC overall, so the damage will flow on to the next most crucial aspect of this evaluation. It is really all looking about as bad as it could possibly get. I'm very, very distressed. It's as though everything is going in slow motion. If only that were the case! We are now just one day away from the public release of these evaluation findings. Perhaps the jetlag is contributing to my feeling of unreality.

Tuesday, 8 July

I woke up this morning having had only three hours' sleep, but I felt slightly calmer, less strung-out than yesterday. All last night I kept hoping that perhaps Julie had somehow misread the report. But when the copy of the final draft reached me today, it confirmed that indeed the heroin overdose deaths averted have been expressed as she had said. The rest of staff at the injecting centre were also incredibly upset when they learnt this. They were there; they know it was a lot more.

Colette and I met with Harry at the injecting centre to discuss our approach for tomorrow. We decided to come across positively, saying that we are generally happy with the report's findings for the first 18 months. But we will also send a second message, that all of these results need to be translated into current service utilisation rates. Right now there are almost three times as many visits each day to inject heroin as during the evaluation period, presumably also further increasing all of the impacts as a service.

If push comes to shove, the report's methodology may have to be challenged but I know that I would have limited credibility doing this myself without looking as though it was just a case of sour grapes on my part. So I rang Alex Wodak, seeking his support as another medical spokesperson to back up these concerns. When I explained about the methodology used, directly comparing the MSIC's Narcan use with the ambulance service's, Alex understood immediately, saying it was like comparing oranges with apples, and agreed to be available as a more independent medical spokesperson.

However, he's flying out to America for two weeks tomorrow at midday, so he will only be available during the first part of the day. Nevertheless Colette dropped a hard copy of the last draft of Chapter 3 in to his office so he could fully acquaint himself with the exact methodology used in this regard.

We received a copy of the final report by courier from Minister Della Bosca's office at 5 o'clock. Later on I received the final draft of the press release to go out from the minister tomorrow, which states that he sees no reason not to recommend to Cabinet that the trial be continued. We were somewhat disappointed by the word 'trial' in the press release, but were buoyed by his support for its continuation.

I brought the final report home with me but I have found it very difficult to concentrate on any one specific section, flicking backwards and forwards as various anxieties pop into my head. I realise that perhaps I need to stop trying to absorb all of the minutiae of this very long and detailed report and focus on the bigger picture if I am to be okay under pressure tomorrow. Taking a step back, I could see that most of the report's findings were actually quite positive. It was just that they seemed to be expressed in a very understated way and I felt that perhaps the evaluators were trying too hard to avoid exaggerating the positive results in case the conservatives accused them of bias, which may well be a real risk. I also rang Clover Moore tonight, to inform her of the report's release tomorrow and to brief her about where we seem vulnerable. She asked me to email her some of the key findings so that she can prepare her own press release for tomorrow. I also left a message for Tony Trimingham of the Family Drug Support organisation, to give me a ring—I always rely on Tony for support in these situations, particularly to put a human face on the discourse.

Wednesday, 9 July

I had more difficulty sleeping last night. When I woke up I had a sense of being a soldier going into battle, but I was surprisingly calm. I started to wonder if we had perhaps developed too high a level of expectation in the general community for a positive outcome from this evaluation; almost everyone seems to assume it is all a foregone conclusion given how smoothly things have gone.

All along I had avoided ever saying we had been a success, always deferring to the evaluation as being the real report card for this initiative. But I had always been confident that, as long as the service became well utilised, and it did, then the evaluation of its impact would reflect this. It was the one area that I didn't think would need to be managed from a damage control perspective.

I now worried that our supporters, in particular, would be disappointed and I had a sense of having let them down, especially those lobbying for this type of facility elsewhere. I felt similarly about other injecting centres elsewhere in the world—if we couldn't demonstrate that we'd saved enough lives when we'd managed more drug overdoses than anywhere else during this time, how were they going to continue to justify their ongoing existence? The forces of darkness operate at a global level too, and they would all be on the lookout for the verdict of this evaluation report and be applying it widely if they could construe it as being anything other than very positive.

I was pessimistic about how today would go, with all the worst case scenarios running through my mind, but I also know that this is the way that I cope with potentially disastrous situations. If I can still face things after going through that process, it can only get better!

The main press conference was conducted by Harry Herbert and John Della Bosca at ten-thirty at Parliament House. On his way in, Harry bumped into Lee Rhiannon from the Greens. She asked where he was off to and he explained. She must have about-faced and gone straight back to her office because statements from her own press release demanding that, in view of the great success of the injecting centre, this strategy be rolled out to regional areas in NSW, were carried by almost all media by late morning and for the rest of the day.

Colette was handling the requests for TV interviews because, of all the days when we needed Pat most, he was conducting a media training course, which couldn't be changed when we finally heard when this would all take place. He was of course very disappointed about this too. We had decided to use the injecting centre as the location because this was our turf and it was less vulnerable to the elements than doing it outdoors in Fitzroy Gardens as I'd done before. Because of the limited space, it also allowed us to insist that I be interviewed by the media one at a time. I was pretty anxious about how this story was going to roll out, and I didn't want to expose myself to the risk of getting something wrong in front of multiple media at the same time. This way we would have more control and I would get a chance to settle into things.

Pat Kennedy had advised Colette to book the TV stations in for interviews according to their ratings if possible, with SBS given the first slot and Channel Nine the last on the assumption that one's performance gets more polished as one go along. However, Channel Nine rang first and SBS didn't ring at all. Colette gave Channel Nine the last slot and Seven and the ABC slots before that. Unsurprisingly, it turns out that these people all speak to each other, especially when they've all been at the same press conference in Parliament House, so it didn't take Channel Nine long to work out that, despite phoning first, they had been given the last slot—something they were very unhappy about. They rang back to say that Channel Seven would let them do their interview alongside them in their earlier slot. We explained that there wasn't the space to have two news crews interviewing at the same time but we managed to bring forward the Channel Nine interview, so they were at least a little less unhappy with us.

The media people we spoke to at the MSIC all said that the press conference at Parliament House had gone well and that, as far as they were concerned, it's a one-day story because everybody is agreeing. At the injecting centre we were listening to the various radio stations—all the news stories seemed to be very positive, leading with the fact that the minister had supported our continuation. Meanwhile Tracey emailed Martin, her husband, telling him that his wife might still have a job. Moments like this remind me of the impact of this decision on the day-to-day lives of other staff. Of course I have my job at KRC to go back to full-time if this thing folds. In fact going back to just being the director of KRC, instead of squeezing it in part-time in tandem with this job, seems like a very attractive option right now, making me momentarily wonder why I would want this thing to continue at all!

As the news reports remained favourable, our fear and anxiety started to dissipate. As the day went on more and more media made contact; their opening words were usually something like 'You must be very pleased at how positive the report is.' If only they had seen me last night, they would have realised just how displeased I was, but this is not the moment for such disclosure.

Meanwhile we heard that Brian Watters was holed up on Magnetic Island with Marie Byrne, an Irish drugs campaigner who is also fervently against strategies such as injecting centres. This may be why the prime minister came out with an announcement later today that his government would never support a trial of heroin prescription or supervised injecting centres. This gave the story more impetus and more national relevance, which means it may become more than the one-day story predicted.

Towards the end of the day I agreed to do an interview on Richard Glover's drive-time program on 2BL over the phone in my office. Richard has interviewed me quite a few times and has always given me a fair run. This time he provided me with the perfect opportunity to praise our staff's efforts. I felt this was particularly important right now, given how they had been affected by the report's assessment of the overdose cases managed. When I finished this interview, the last one scheduled for the day, I came out into the tea room area and only then realised that the staff had all been huddled around the radio, listening in. They cheered as I came out. I was delighted that they had heard me acclaim their efforts. Maintaining morale is so important. Without hard working front-line staff, there would be no clients attending the service and everything else would be academic.

Colette, Andy, Jake and I arranged to meet up back at my place to debrief after work. Unfortunately Tracey couldn't join us because she badly sprained her ankle a few weeks ago, and needed to go home for more rest and elevation, having just come in for the big day. But we rang her there and had a joint toast while she was on the other end of the line. We watched the news on every TV channel. There were all sorts of figures being used as to the number of deaths averted, from 6 to 13 to 25. It would appear that our strategy of muddying the waters with our more recent activity statistics has worked, and the number 'four' was buried amongst it all, at least in the short term. But we also realise that tonight is probably as good as it will get. So good that it also risks a backlash, especially as people start wading into the actual report, which most have not had time to do yet. We had felt that it was strategically important to serve an ace first up, to put us in a good position to win the set, but it ain't over yet.

Thursday, 10 July

The press this morning is full of it. Rachel Morris's story in the *Telegraph* was pretty positive but against this was David Penberthy's column, in which he cited the client with the most visits—646 times—and asked whether this person should get a medal. The *Telegraph*'s editorial was also negative, demanding the immediate closure of the facility given that we had no effect on ambulance call-outs and only a modest number of lives were saved. We predicted this would happen, but it's still disappointing to see it there in black and white.

The *Australian* and the *Sydney Morning Herald* ran more positive articles but have not published editorials on it yet. Sally Loane's ABC radio program focused on us for the second day in a row, now exploring whether the heroin shortage has lifted. On her program yesterday someone claiming to be a client of the MSIC had rung in to say that he was on a methadone program and now only very occasionally still used. He said he had come to the facility about once a month, but had never been offered counselling. Odd, because clients are usually grateful for that! From what he said about his situation he wouldn't have been prioritised by staff as necessarily needing such an intervention, but Sally was shocked.

Jink was driving along on her day off when she heard this interview and was so outraged, she stopped at the first service station to ring into the program. The phone there wasn't working, so she drove on to the next service station, and there managed to get on air, to explain just how the injecting centre operated in this regard. This seemed to reassure Sally Loane that we were indeed taking every opportunity to offer assistance to those who needed it.

Sally also managed to contact Dave Darcy, who was apparently just drying himself off after a swim on a beach on the Gold Coast, where he is holidaying with his family. He disagreed that there has been any major easing of the shortage in recent times, saying that this easing had commenced early last year. He then went on to say that he fully supports the injecting centre, believing that it complements police efforts in the area.

When asked about drug dealing in front of the facility, he reiterated the report's findings that there has been no increase in drug-related criminal activities in the area or the immediate vicinity as a result of the injecting centre. It is great that he is willing to put this on the record in the media. But then he went one step further, saying that the location of drug dealing is directly related to policing operations and that, if dealing does occur in front of the injecting centre, it suggests that the police may be undertaking an operation somewhere else, displacing the dealing towards the injecting centre.

A police person admitting that their activities may displace during dealing must be almost historic. Sally also seemed reassured by Dave saying that we share intelligence information, such as which drugs are being sold on the streets and their perceived purity, with the police. There is sometimes an assumption that people working on the harm reduction end of the continuum of health care not only don't support police efforts to stop drug supply but actually promote drug supply. It is depressing to realise that some people think that you're not only not helping things, but you are actually making them worse. (I wonder if cardiologists are ever accused of supporting cigarette companies?)

Jim Porter from the local ambulance service was also interviewed on ABC radio this morning and he confirmed that the injecting centre has improved things for ambulance officers in the area. He said that they notice when the injecting centre is closed because of the increased call-outs to the area. Of course this is in sharp contrast to the findings of the report.

We received transcripts from Alan Jones's talkback radio program, but we have been previously advised not to respond to him unless we wanted to have a lifelong fatwa placed upon us! On no less than three occasions this morning Jones had a go at us—also picking up on David Penberthy's theme of the client who came so many times but still obviously wasn't 'cured'. He also kept repeating that Harry Herbert had stated that there were now almost three times as many people attending to inject heroin and he asked over and over whether Harry wanted a medal for this. Harry, of course, only said this to provide a perspective on the evaluation results, which related just to our activities until the end of October last year. Perhaps Alan Jones is already waging a fatwa against Harry and the Uniting Church!

Jones also mistakenly repeated over and over again that 56 000 injecting drug users have attended the centre during the trial. In fact, that is the total number of visits that have been made; about 3800 injecting drug users attended during the first 18 months. It was surprising that, despite the number of times that he reiterated this misinformation, it didn't occur to him that there couldn't possibly be 56 000 injecting drug users in the state, let alone in Kings Cross, attending the injecting centre. We also heard that the other talkback radio DJs, such as Ray Hadley, were all getting stuck into us.

Friday, 11 July

I spoke to Julie Sibraa, who was pleased overall with how things are going, but they were unhappy about an interview Brian Watters did with John Laws yesterday, and sent us the transcript. Brian told Laws: 'You can't expect to have drug users all around the place and have a respectable community.' So much for encouraging drug users to feel part of their community! He went on to say: 'I've seen injecting rooms overseas and I don't like them, but at least in some of those there's a humane dimension, where people can have a shower and get clean clothes. There's a doctor there and they can be given in-depth counselling and they can be given some support and build up the relationship. You don't build up a relationship with people in 15 minutes. That's a nonsense. If we're going to do anything with these very difficult people out there, we should be setting up a facility where they can feel welcome and you've got trained staff who know how to work and help these people.'

When I heard this, I was truly appalled; there are quite a few other services in Kings Cross that provide amenities such as showers and clean clothes, so we didn't need more of that up here. But the centre, if nothing else, most certainly has a humane dimension and clients feel very welcome. We have built up lots of relationships; it is very rare that people would only stay for 15 minutes. Judging from the Client Comments book, they overwhelmingly value the respectful and caring way they are treated by every member of staff, who are all specifically trained to work with and help 'these people'. Brian really has crossed the line this time as far as I'm concerned, more so than ever before. He must be very nervous indeed.

John Della Bosca's office was particularly disappointed by Brian's suggestion that the NSW Government must have put a lot of pressure on the evaluators to come out with such a good report. We wish! In the next breath, however, he goes on to say that the report is not so good, if you read it more closely. So there seemed to be little consistency in what he said, but nonetheless John Laws concluded the interview by describing him as a 'good thinker'.

The *Australian* newspaper ran a negative editorial today, also demanding that the service be closed, given the waste of money since we're not affecting ambulance call-outs or saving sufficient lives. The *Australian* ran another story reporting that all the other jurisdictions in Australia—apart from Canberra—had already excluded the possibility of considering injecting centres. It is disappointing to see the *Australian* become so conservative in recent times, particularly since the conflict in Iraq. I had developed a great professional relationship with one of their most senior journalists, Sian Powell, who had a particular interest in the project right from the start. I briefed her about our progress on a regular basis for over two years, and she had a very in-depth understanding of almost all aspects, but earlier this year Sian was posted to Indonesia as their foreign correspondent. There was no time to start briefing someone else from scratch, so our coverage in the *Australian* varies greatly now.

The *Sydney Morning Herald* published several letters to the editor, mostly supporting the MSIC. It also ran an Internet poll asking whether people are in favour of the injecting room in Kings Cross; although there wasn't a large response, indicating that this is not considered a major issue at the broader community level, 83 per cent voted in favour, 15 per cent voted against and 2 per cent were undecided. These are great results but we do appreciate that people accessing *The Sydney Morning Herald* online are probably a middle-class, educated demographic, which is more likely to support this initiative.

The *Telegraph* ran mainly negative letters, including one about 'well-intentioned workers who are nonetheless misguided'. Accompanying this was a picture of me captioned a 'well-intentioned worker'—a particularly bad photo with me gazing smilingly into a packet of needle syringes. In the two years since this photo was taken, I have at least learnt not to agree to photographers taking any more photos of me in stupid poses like that!

At the end of today I spoke with Julie Sibraa again and asked her to convey to her minister that our staff did appreciate his courage in continuing to support this initiative. She said she would, then added that the report's finding that there was no negative law and order impact had probably also helped ensure the government's ongoing support, presumably because it gave no opportunity for the Shadow Police Minister to weigh in. I continue to gain many insights into what matters most politically.

Sunday, 13 July

Piers Ackerman in his *Sunday Telegraph* column described the centre as a $2.8 million flop. I'm never sure where Piers gets his figures from; in fact we spent less than $2 million this year, although this doesn't include the extraordinary expenditure of about $400 000 for insurance cover each year, which hopefully will not continue if the MSIC is operating as a more mainstream health service in future. I really don't understand why we are charged so much in this regard, particularly when you consider some of the high-risk cardiac and neuro surgical procedures that go on in the rest of the health system. We aren't even administering a drug like methadone clinics do—just supervising something that otherwise would have happened in a back street—but I suppose we live in increasingly litigious times.

Monday, 14 July

I arrived at the injecting centre this morning to be told that the inspectors from the Health Department and Kings Cross Police were in attendance. Alas, no rest for the weary!

This is the tenth random inspection in two years and is only two months after the last inspection, proving just how very wrong I was to have orignially thought that, if we went with the flow, these might ease up over time.

Thursday, 17 July

At this morning's meeting to review the random inspection check three days ago, the reps of the licensing authorities announced that they had been unable to find anything in the facility that required attention. We were pleased that after ten visits we'd finally scored a ten out of ten. Hallelujah!

Friday, 18 July

I had lunch today with Professor Ian Webster, having asked for his advice about how best to proceed with my concerns about the report's findings the drug overdoses managed at the MSIC. Ian was the Head of the School of Community Medicine when I was a medical student at the University of NSW, more than 20 years ago. He is an Emeritus Professor now, chairman of the NSW Expert Advisory Committee on Drugs, a member of the Australian National Council on Drugs and holds various other senior appointments in the field. Ian has always remained in touch with the clinical coalface and still conducts a weekly medical clinic for homeless alcoholic men at the

Matthew Talbot Hostel in Woolloomooloo, which he has done for the last 25 years. I admire him enormously.

He had read Chapter 3 of the evaluation report very closely and agreed that the methodology employed was a conservative one. It's a great relief, when I speak to other people with a medical background, to hear their ready agreement with my concerns about this.

I do realise that I have been obsessing about the number four in recent times, and that I need to keep it in perspective. After all, 95 per cent of the report was very positive. It's just that small part that wasn't. Pity that it was the most important part of the report.

Ian suggested that it would be appropriate and constructive for the service itself to be initiating further research into the impact of drug overdoses managed at the facility. Given our clinical proximity to what is actually happening there day-to-day, this insight would help enrich and deepen the overall understanding of this important public health issue. He further suggested that I should also involve other medical colleagues in such research so as to reduce my personal exposure to any accusation of a lack of objectivity. He emphasised to me the importance of keeping one's powder dry.

I later remembered how, soon after I was appointed to the position of medical director, Ian congratulated me, saying that I got this position because I had managed to keep my powder dry to date in a field where this is often difficult. I really appreciate having professional and personal support from Ian Webster. He is a great mentor.

eighteen

Decision, decisions

Monday, 21 July

The government is currently undertaking a statutory review of the Drug Summit Legislative Response Act, which the MSIC operates under, seeking submissions from relevant stakeholders including both licensing authorities, the NSW Health and Police, and the Department of Community Services. This review is actually a requirement of the original legislation, but we have been given less than two weeks to respond.

Today I discussed with Harry the issue we have with the age limit in this original legislation pertaining to the injecting centre. I have provided him with the case study of Jane, the young user who had passed herself off as being twenty. Jane was assessed to be an exceptionally high-risk IDU. After 38 visits our staff were able to clinically engage her and persuade her to enter methadone treatment. We don't believe this would have happened if we had known her real age when she registered and she had then been excluded from attending the service. We appreciate she was an extreme case but nonetheless we believe it illustrates the need for us to be allowed to use clinical discretion in extreme cases of people who are under eighteen. I recommend that in these instances the under-age person should be assessed by two staff members, and that a case management approach be adopted, where therapeutic goals are set and the client's progress is reviewed over time.

We also decided to recommend that there should only be one, and not two, licensing authorities and that this should be the Director General of NSW Health. As a health service, we find it irregular that the NSW Police Commissioner is one of the authorities, something I gather the NSW Police Service itself also finds unusual. Particularly in the instance of the investigation following Jason's complaint, we felt that the police's involvement made it feel like a criminal investigation, which was inappropriate. In particular, when this authority is delegated to the local police patrol level—thus placing Dave personally in a regulatory role—it potentially interferes with the partnership relationship between Health and Police, which is considered important at a local community level. For similar reasons, having local sworn officers as part of the random spot-check team has been problematic.

We also suggested that there be a review of how investigations of complaints are carried out in future, since this is not specified in the relevant legislation.

Meanwhile Harry has also received a response to our letter suggesting that the various observations and ten recommendations, following the complaint investigation in February, be referred to other existing processes. While the list has been scaled back from the original we have now also been asked to provide a specific strategy on how to enhance the policing of the division of drugs on the premises. Given that joint purchase and ownership of drugs is part of the prevailing drug culture, it is the policy we are least optimistic about policing. Peter Zahra has advised us that the only way to be able to accommodate it would be to exempt people from being charged with drug supply while on the premises, just as the self-administration of a drug and possession of a personal quantity are not crimes at the MSIC. But of course this would be politically unacceptable and undesirable from our perspective too. So it looks like we will have to continue to operate in the grey zone on this issue. It's a pity that we can't have discretion to determine what is drug supply as opposed to joint possession, but even the police don't have this.

We assure the authorities that every client is made aware that they are not allowed to divide drugs on the premises when they first register. It is included in the code of conduct displayed in each service stage throughout the premises, and all clients must sign that they agree to comply with this. We also act on any overt signs of drug division or supply (which is extremely rare), sanctioning clients as necessary. There is nothing more we can do short of sitting alongside every client while they are preparing their drugs to inject, which wouldn't be feasible for us or acceptable to the client base.

Tuesday, 5 August

Jink, the nurse in charge tonight, phoned me at home at nine-thirty to let me know that there have been eight overdoses during the day, two of which required naloxone. This is by far the greatest number of overdoses that have ever occurred at the injecting centre on one day. I asked Jink whether people were reporting that the quality of the heroin is higher than usual today, but she said no. It would seem the main factor is higher than usual concurrent use of temazepam.

Despite the easing of the heroin shortage in Kings Cross this has persisted, which is unsurprising. IDUs having now discovered how much temazepam increases the effect of heroin, there would be no reason to forego that, just because heroin is back in town. So we now have the worst of both worlds and this shows how the net result of a fluctuating drug supply may be worse than having a high but stable drug supply across time.

We have yet to hear back about KRC's submission to the Therapeutic Goods Administration in the ACT to have the temazepam gelcap formulation removed from the pharmaceutical market altogether, but at least one of the biggest over-prescribers has had their authority to prescribe this class of medication suspended only a few weeks ago. The Pharmaceutical Services Branch of NSW Health tells me that all five of their investigators have been kept busy for months as a result of our reporting in this regard, which is good news.

Wednesday, 6 August

Late today Dave Darcy phoned me to let me know that the tenants of the Tudor Hotel, the private hotel which essentially operates as a shooting gallery next door to us, have been informed that the police will be targeting these premises. Dave is very concerned about the two overdose deaths on the premises there last month. Apparently the Tudor only changed hands some months ago. According to Dave, the new owners didn't realise that drugs were injected in the premises they had bought. This seems surprising—you only have to stand in the reception area for about five minutes, and see who comes and goes, to work it out. That such a rundown premises can attract a weekly rent of around $2500 is the other clue. People in this community often lament why there are no dress shops and the like on the main street as there were 25 years ago. Well there's your answer—you have to move a mighty lot of dresses to afford rents like that, and this is what the market will bear these days on the main street of Kings Cross.

I also spoke to Julie Sibraa, who tells me that the legislation, which will just be an amendment of the original legislation, rather than new legislation, is likely to be presented as a bill to parliament in September. I do look forward to October.

Monday, 11 August

This afternoon Harry and I went to a meeting with Minister John Della Bosca. The minister referred to the evaluation report as seeming a bit ambivalent, but we agreed that in a strange way perhaps this has worked in our favour because it seems to have something in it for everybody, both supporters and detractors, although I still wish it didn't.

The minister confirmed his intention to recommend to Cabinet that the trial be extended by four years. This decision also effectively puts the lid on the question of other facilities being established elsewhere in NSW, which of course remains politically risky. Mind you, at this point there probably isn't a pressing need for such a centre elsewhere with heroin overdose rates in all other areas still being right down on what they were. Also, there isn't solid local community and political support, which you really need, in the only places where one might consider it. But these things can change quickly, so it would have been good for there to be enabling legislation already in place that would allow other injecting centres to be established should the need arise. It would also be really nice to have some company in this; we would really like not to be the very special only child anymore!

Harry and I expressed our concern about there being two licensing authorities and in particular the police being one of these but in the end the minister said that, while he could see where we were coming from, he doubted he could convince his Cabinet colleagues. He said that while we may see the MSIC as a health service, others see it as being more akin to licensed premises serving alcohol, and of course the police are the licensing authority for these.

We also raised our continuing concern with the age restriction but again the minister indicated that he thought it unlikely this could be amended given that this was needed to secure the political support necessary to pass the original legislation to establish the injecting centre. However, he felt there might be some willingness to remove the additional licence condition prohibiting pregnant women, because there is an appreciation of the risks to the mother and the foetus in the event of the female overdosing in a less safe situation elsewhere.

The minister then asked me whether I thought we could improve our rates of referral into treatment services. I said that I didn't think this was possible and that maybe it would be better to address instead the problem that perhaps the injecting centre's potential in this regard had been over-interpreted and over-sold. When it is claimed that injecting centres have the potential to be a 'gateway', what is really being referred to is the potential for net-widening, i.e. bringing more drug users into contact with health personnel at the injecting centre, rather than beyond that to other services per se. The mere fact that almost 60 per cent of the people who have registered to use the injecting centre have never been in contact with any of the other low-threshold health services in Kings Cross should be evidence enough that the service has widened the net and very much succeeded in being a gateway to the health service sector.

The minister accepted that perhaps the gateway concept had been over-sold but he nonetheless wanted to discuss how we could improve the MSIC's referral rate. I confessed my fear was that, if anything, over time our referral rates will drop back as we have already dealt with a lot of the backlog of need amenable to referral among many of our registered clientele. But he asked whether with additional resources we couldn't improve our performance. Harry started to say that no amount of additional resources would make a difference until I glared at him for having just committed the cardinal sin for all service providers, the rule being that you never say no to any offers of more resources, regardless of your situation!

Seriously though, this is also in part a resource issue. A significant limitation on us at this stage is that a different drug user is turning up to use the centre every few minutes and at current staffing levels, we are finding it tough to cope with that. Each referral takes up to an hour to arrange. You first have to assess the person in terms of their drug use, to decide what type of treatments might be most appropriate. Then you have to make the phone calls to arrange the appointments, then write the formal letter of referral and finally document everything in the client's medical file and on the database. Needless to say, when it's very busy, the demand for this type of assistance also increases, while our ability to meet it drops right away.

So, funding an additional position, which would not be involved in the minute-by-minute operational aspects and could be identifiable by the client base as the best person to speak to about such matters, might well improve the rate and effectiveness of this aspect of our work. Such a person would also be in a good position to maintain the most up-to-date information on what treatment services are on offer at any given time and how to fast-track people into these services. They might also be able to accompany clients to the treatment facility, remind them about appointments and check that these have been followed through. The fact that the evaluation report showed that those clients who attended more than ten times were almost eighteen times more likely to be successfully referred to other relevant services verifies that such ongoing engagement is important.

I also discussed the value of extending the service to include an outreach element, explaining that there are still premises in Kings Cross like the Tudor Hotel where sex workers inject, sometimes also with their customers and that training staff in those premises in drug overdose management would be worthwhile. Outreaching to drug users who continue to inject on the streets, to increase recruitment back to the injecting centre, would also be good to do.

We then discussed the need for ongoing evaluation and opportunities for research in general. I indicated that I thought there was still much untapped potential in this regard, and that I was keen to pursue this, particularly from the clinical side in relation to overdoses. There also seemed to be support for this in principle.

The meeting went for about an hour. At its conclusion Harry and I expressed that we were very happy that the minister would be recommending a four-year extension to Cabinet, which is almost tantamount to permanent tenure. No service in the health system is ever guaranteed permanence—just look at how many hospitals have been closed over the years. As Minister Della Bosca was leaving, I thanked him again on behalf of the staff and the clients at the injecting centre for his apparently heart-felt support and courage in sticking with us throughout. I also told him that I appreciated that the ambivalence of the final evaluation report had provided a ready exit for him, had he wanted to take it. He seemed somewhat taken aback, surprised to be thanked.

Tuesday, 12 August

At 9 am I was back at Governor Macquarie Tower on a different level (although they all look the same). I was there today for a meeting with Geoff Barnden and Maree Thomas from the Cabinet Office of Drug Policy, and Dr Denise Robinson, the Deputy Chief Health Officer of NSW Health. The discussion about increasing the rate of referral into drug treatment continued.

I was quick to reject a suggestion that we flag clients' files every hundred visits so they could be pulled to the side and asked where they were up to as far as getting into a drug treatment program. This seems to be responding to the theme developed by David Penberthy in his recent column in the *Telegraph,* when he referred to the client who had attended 646 times, and implied that he should surely have been well and truly cured before then. But what are we to do? Are we really going to say: *Okay, you've had your chance to get into a treatment program and squandered it, so back out onto the streets you go?* I can't see how that approach would benefit either this person or the community.

I explained that, through their regular use of the service, clients develop a rapport with particular staff members, who can then assess the readiness of that client to change their lifestyle and what sort of intervention would be most appropriate for them at that particular time. It is a very intuitive, organic process, which would not be enhanced by a policy which arbitrarily decides the frequency of addressing this issue with individuals. Such an approach would even have the potential to undermine the processes already established. Further, it would be like requiring clients to contract with us to go into treatment at some stage down the track, which is contrary to the whole spirit of supervised injecting centres, which are intended to be low-threshold in that they should have as few barriers to access as possible. Being unconditional in approach is considered essential to attract the most marginalised part of the actively drug-using population and thus 'widen the net' of people with whom we as health professionals are in contact. As it is, this facility has the highest threshold, in terms of hoops clients must jump through, of any injecting centre in the world.

When I described some of the indicators which guide us in our engagement with clients and suggest to us that they may be appropriate for referral to treatment, Denise asked if I would be able to document this for them. I agreed to do this, of course, but I also felt an increasing sense of despair. It would seem that the last sphere of activity in which our staff can use their clinical judgement and intuition is now about to be codified, and no doubt added to the procedures that the licensing authorities already police on a regular basis.

It's at times like this that I wonder whether my public health approach—of trying to reach the largest part of the most heroin-dependent population as possible and to achieve a high throughput, thereby maximising the centre's impact at the community level—has been misguided. Perhaps we would have been better off just recruiting forty of our favourite clients and trying to meet all their various needs over time, and then to have been able to promote each one of them as a model case study. I think most people relate more easily to individual client care approaches rather than broader population-based public health approaches and I'm not sure how to address this.

I also discussed our ongoing staffing issues and my fear that, now that we are becoming less new and pioneering, it will be increasingly difficult to retain staff. Day-to-day the work can be very same-ish, but, worse still, it is interspersed with moments of high drama when clients overdose or become erratic. Having to be hyper-vigilant while doing mundane tasks can be quite stressful in an insidious way . . . Staff would like to be involved in other aspects of clients' care too. So rotating staff between the MSIC and KRC (it being the other service in Kings Cross clients most use) would potentially increase professional satisfaction while also improving continuity of care for clients.

I suggested that it would be useful to consider an arrangement with KRC whereby clinical staff were contracted across to the MSIC on a part-time basis (sound familiar?). I am already seconded from KRC to be the medical director here on a half-time basis. Jake, Colette and Andy, plus a further 40 hours of nursing, are likewise seconded to the injecting centre, so this would merely be a more formal extension of what is already in place. Denise suggested that I draft a service agreement between Kirketon Road Centre and the injecting centre and also requested written submissions for the case manager position and the outreach workers, along with the paper describing how the counselling staff engage the clients for treatment referral. I am also going to forward the case studies to give a better idea of just how complex the health and psycho-social issues are at the individual client level. While I agreed to a fair bit of work during this meeting, things seem to be heading in the right direction.

When I got back to the MSIC I asked Tracey to retrieve the medical file of Mr 646 Visits Man to see how many visits he has actually made by now (the 646 visits were just in the first 18 months!) and whether he had ever been referred to a drug treatment program. This client, Lachlan, has now in fact visited the injecting centre no less than 1150 times but—what do you know—he was referred to a residential rehab program in July this year and hasn't used the injecting centre since, although he has been back just to let us know how well he is doing these days. Reading through his clinical notes I saw that he was being counselled by staff quite a lot all along, and there were various attempts to refer him to treatment across that time.

I read one referral letter from the beginning of 2002. It stated that Lachlan had rung a rehabilitation program in northern NSW on no less than ten occasions—every Tuesday—as is apparently the requirement, both to show motivation and to ensure that you get to the top of the waiting list. On the tenth occasion he had finally reached the top of the waiting list but then needed $400 up-front to be admitted to the program, which at that particular time he didn't have. When you read this person's notes you get a real idea of just how high and rocky a mountain they must climb in order to actually get into a rehab program. If only this was as easy as I suspect some people out there imagine it to be.

Tuesday, 19 August

At 9 pm I got a phone call from Jink telling me that there had been another eight overdoses during the day, four of which required the administration of naloxone. They had been so busy resuscitating people that Jink had not had a chance to ring me before now. I joked with her that perhaps she should be called Jinx instead of Jink.

It would seem that this time the spate of overdoses, some quite severe, was indeed due to a sudden increase in the quality of the heroin being sold on the streets today. I instructed her to alert other health services in the area and the police. We also put up signs in the injecting centre reception area warning clients that the quality of heroin was higher than usual so the overdose risk was higher too—meaning they needed to be extra careful when using it. The harm reduction advice in this instance is to inject only a small amount first up (referred to as a 'taste shot'), then judge the purity and, if okay, inject the rest. But this advice is rarely taken.

Especially because heroin has been of such poor quality during the shortage, clients want to inject as much as possible each time, to maximise what's called 'the rush', which is the feeling experienced as the concentration of heroin in the blood and then the brain rapidly increases after injecting it. It's this feeling that people seem to want to reproduce over and over again, and is why injecting drugs is associated with more compulsive 'addictive' behaviour than all other modes of drug administration, apart from smoking, which gets it to the brain via the lungs even faster.

Monday, 1 September

Minister Della Bosca made a public announcement that Cabinet has approved his recommendation to extend the trial by four years. Pat Kennedy arranged for the various TV news crews to interview me at the fountain in Fitzroy Gardens in Kings Cross again at 2 pm today. I was interviewed for about 15 minutes and, as Colette and I walked back to the injecting centre, we wondered which seven seconds of the 15 minutes taped would be aired. Later I discovered that at least two of the stations chose exactly the same seven seconds. If only they knew ahead of time which seven seconds they wanted, they would have saved a lot of everybody's time!

Tuesday, 2 September

I attended a meeting of the Ministerial Hepatitis Advisory Committee meeting, of which I'm a member. During this meeting from the Health Department reported that a further $100 000 per year has been allocated to the MSIC for ongoing service evaluation over the next four years. This was news to me and I wondered how this was going to be administered.

Meanwhile, apparently yesterday AAP reported that Minister Della Bosca had said at his press conference that only 1 in 41 visits to the injecting centre resulting in a referral to another service is not enough and that the operators agreed. This had already been picked up by the *Sydney Morning Herald*, the *Telegraph, Canberra Times* and the *Age* that we knew of. I was horrified. We most definitely don't agree with this. I actually think the fact that 1 in 41 visits results in a referral is nothing short of a miracle. This is a rate of about six referrals a day—to be handled by our staff in amongst the current average of 240 visits and two overdoses per day. I decided to call Julie Sibraa to find out how this could have been said.

Julie said she didn't know if this was indeed what the minister had said yesterday but could understand why this report would upset me. However, she urged me not to write a letter to the *Telegraph*, as I suggested, to deny that I had agreed with the minister's statements on this. She went to great lengths to assure me that she and the minister did understand how hard the staff had worked to achieve client referrals. So I suggested that, in view of today's media, it would be great if the minister could find an opportunity to put this on the record and she agreed.

I agreed not to write the letter mainly as a personal favour to Julie, whom I really like and respect. Julie is a real *mensch*, who has managed to retain perspective despite the rarefied political environment she works in and has provided a lot of support to me over the last few years. But I did also indicate to her that, if anybody started re-running the line that even the operators aren't happy with the rate of referral at the MSIC, I would need to publicly deny this. In fact that hasn't happened, at least not yet. Only my colleagues expressed their bewilderment that I would be agreeing to such a notion, and I was quick to assure them that no, this was far from my opinion on the matter.

Later on this evening John Della Bosca was being questioned by the Cost Estimates Committee in Parliament again and the issue of our referrals to drug treatment came up. As part of his reply he said: 'I take this opportunity to make the comment that the staff at the Medically Supervised Injecting Centre and the licensee of the service have done a fantastic job in fulfilling all the different parts of the brief . . . These people have taken on a very hard brief in a very difficult set of circumstances in an attempt to live up to a set of high expectations . . . and I think that the service has actually performed better than could reasonably be expected as a gateway to treatment.' I circulated a copy of this reply to all the staff at the MSIC, and all is forgiven.

Today I received congratulations from both Jo Kimber and Dr Margaret MacDonald from the evaluation team for our four-year extension. People keep congratulating me but my feelings are not that optimistic right now. I have often found in this project that, when people assume that we must be very happy, it has often been at times when we've been very unhappy, especially during the big investigation, which we needed to keep under wraps.

I am currently having to grapple with what my own personal bottom line is as far as how this service goes forward into the future. On the question of ongoing evaluation I don't think I have very much room to compromise at all. It is weird enough as it is right now, seeing conference programs include presentations in which the evaluators discuss the impact of the service but don't always involve anyone from the actual service. Until now I have had no control over the evaluation methodology and yet as medical director I have to accept all the responsibility for its findings. That this arrangement could go on for the next four years is unappealing to me right now. I need to have a central role in the ongoing service evaluation and future research, as I have always had at KRC, and is the norm for service directors, particularly because I think that the real benefits of the service have not been fully explored and documented yet. I hope the arrangements about how the ongoing service evaluation will be conducted are clarified soon.

Inevitably, I see this service as being the culmination of my life's work, and letting go of it would be very hard for me. When I think about it, I realise that I never have. I am still in my very first career position as director of Kirketon Road Centre. Maybe it's about time that I did learn to let go of something. It doesn't feel right though.

nineteen

And so ended the first trial

Friday, 5 September, 2003

I was the first speaker this morning at the Pharmaceutical Society of Australia's Symposium on Dependence and Addiction. The title of my talk, given to me by the organiser, was 'Separating Truth from Fiction'. I began by focusing on a letter in today's *Sydney Morning Herald* from Brian Watters, in which he referred to the centre as costing '$8 million to save three or four lives'. I explained that the operating expenses for the first two years were about $4 million, not $8 million; that during that time we managed 554 overdoses, which would translate into the saving of many more than three or four lives (even using the final evaluation report's conservative methodology for calculating this).

Harry had a letter published last week in the *SMH*, which contrasted the federal government's criticism of religious leaders for expressing their views on asylum seekers and other social justice issues with its apparent willingness to allow Major Watters to speak out publicly in support of its Tough on Drugs policy. It was a valid point but, as soon as I saw it, I figured it would only be a matter of time before Brian would retaliate with something against the injecting centre and here it was in the form of his letter.

When I returned to the MSIC, Andy said forlornly: 'Gosh. And there we were just coming to terms with the number four and Brian's taken it down further to three.' We laughed. The number four has gained great symbolism for us—as well as averting four deaths annually (according to the report) we've now been extended for four years. Somebody told me recently that the number four in some Asian cultures has the same significance as the number 13 in our culture. Such things are taking on additional significance for us these days. Maybe we all need a holiday?

Tuesday, 9 September

I received a phone call from a journalist in Vancouver who is covering the story of the injecting centre that is soon to be opened there. I have already seen a few headlines coming through from Canada and have noticed that they are very similar to the sort of headlines that we've had to endure, such as 'Safe Haven for Junkies' etc. I shared with this journalist some of the early experiences that we encountered when we first opened the centre nearly two and a half years ago, which now seems a lifetime away.

Thursday, 11 September

At 6.30 pm there was a Police Accountability Community Team meeting, which included Clover Moore and me on the panel, as well as our common adversary Malcolm Duncan. A representative of the 2011 Residents' Association was attempting to connect the MSIC with the advent of a 'drug centre' in the Tudor Hotel next door. I've really had enough of the MSIC taking the blame for all drug use, supply and now shooting galleries in Kings Cross. So I suggested that she inspect the ambulance data from 1999, which shows that at that time there were more than 300 call-outs to cases of drug overdose within 100 metres of where we are currently located (there were almost 700 for the whole of the Kings Cross postcode). These included the Tudor Hotel and numerous other locations on the main street of Kings Cross. If this did not convince her that such activities occurred here before the injecting centre was established and would no doubt continue if we were closed, I suggested that she read the transcripts of the Wood Police Royal Commission of 1996.

Clover once told me that there was a 50 per cent turnover among the constituents in the Bligh electorate from one election to the next. Perhaps this influences some people's appreciation of the centre's impact, many not actually knowing just how bad it used to be in terms of street-based drug-related activity before the centre opened. This is likely to increase with the gentrification of the area as a result of several of the longstanding hotels being converted into up-market apartment buildings (hardly a sign that the place has gone to the wall since the MSIC either).

I felt somewhat relieved when an elderly woman sitting in the front row, who described herself as being eighty-three and having lived in Springfield Avenue for the last ten years, said that in the past she had been appalled by the levels of drug-related activities, in particular seeing people overdosed and ambulances attending in public places. But she said that this had all ended since the injecting centre started two years ago. I spoke to her afterwards, and she turned out to have been a social worker at Sydney Hospital quite some years back now. I thanked her for speaking out, and instructed her that she has to come along to all community meetings from now on!

Tuesday, 16 September

I attended Parliament House to provide a briefing to the cross-benchers of the Upper House. I was ushered into one of the rooms and sat down at a table facing two people, one of whom I didn't recognise and the other being the easily recognisable Reverend Fred Nile. Malcolm Duncan was just leaving as I arrived, and we joked about having run into each other quite a lot lately. During the next half-hour Ian Cohen from the Greens and Arthur Chesterfield-Evans from the Democrats popped in and out, and there was a group of political staffers sitting off to the side taking notes. But for most of the time I faced questioning from this nameless person and Fred Nile.

It became very clear, almost immediately, that this person did not support the injecting centre—no sooner would I start to answer one of his questions than another one was fired at me. I had briefed some of the cross-benchers at the injecting centre, back in May last year before the legislation to extend the trial by a year was up for parliamentary debate. This had all been very civil, so I was unprepared for this onslaught. Even Fred looked a bit embarrassed, giving me reassuring glances from time to time.

It seemed that the moment the second hand hit the end of my half-hour slot, despite my being mid-sentence, this person cut me off, saying, 'That's enough—you can go now.' I looked across at Ian and Arthur, who seemed equally taken aback at this abrupt end to the briefing session. I bundled my things together and, just as I started to walk towards the door, I turned back and asked him who he was. I was intrigued to know.

Fred immediately said: 'Oh goodness, we should have introduced ourselves.' The man replied that he was the Honourable Reverend Gordon Moyes. Everything then became crystal clear. The Reverend Moyes has recently replaced Elaine Nile as the second member of the so-called 'Christian Democratic Party (Fred Nile Group)' in the NSW Legislative Council and has been a vocal opponent of the injecting centre ever since Harry took it on.

the injecting centre he was interviewed on ABC-TV's *Compass* and actually suggested that the reason Uniting*Care* wanted to oversee this project was that it and Ray Richmond were 'financially motivated'. Not even the Chamber of Commerce has ever made such an outrageous claim. Uniting*Care* is of course a not-for-profit organisation, and any unspent monies from the MSIC's budget go straight back to the NSW State Treasury at the end of each financial year. So there's nothing in this for Uniting*Care* except headaches.

Wednesday, 17 September

In the late morning I received a phone call from Clover Moore letting me know that the bill has passed through the Legislative Assembly. Later on I received a similar call from Julie Sibraa, who said I had been lucky to be where I was because having to listen to 3½ hours of disingenuous political debate had been rather excruciating for her and her colleagues. Julie said that Clover delivered a particularly good speech, as did various other MPs, including Linda Burney, the Labor member for Canterbury and the first Aboriginal woman elected to the NSW parliament, back in the March election this year. John Brogden didn't make a speech but crossed the floor to vote in favour of our continuation. Likewise Judy Hopgood, the MP for Hornsby, who is also a Liberal and a nurse with hospital emergency centre experience, voted in favour as she did last year. I let Harry and the staff at the injecting centre know that we are halfway there.

We decided that it would be timely to celebrate the decision to extend the injecting centre trial with a party on 31 October, the last day of the current licence, which fortuitously falls on a Friday night. I asked Tim, one of our staff, to design an invitation, this time specifically stipulating that it's not to have any needle syringes popping up from a birthday cake or anywhere else! Instead, he designed quite an innocuous invitation with a few balloons; not even a champagne glass was allowed. We have decided to hold it at the Lord Roberts hotel in East Sydney, the same place where we had our one-year birthday party, but this time we intend to invite more people, particularly all the people who have supported us through the difficult times over the last 3½ years. We will again provide some finger food and put some money on the bar, funded by the remainder of the advance for this book.

Thursday, 18 September

I was phoned by Maree from the Cabinet Office. She said that Gordon Moyes had addressed a parliamentary question without notice to Minister Della Bosca regarding the provision of needle syringes at the injecting centre, claiming that 30 000 had been distributed there despite this being 'forbidden'. While apparently this question shouldn't have been allowed, since the Bill pertaining to the injecting centre is already before the parliament, the Speaker didn't pick up on this.

This is a line Malcolm Duncan has been propagating lately, despite the evaluation report stating quite clearly that we are able to provide needle syringes to clients actually using the service. (What *isn't* allowed is for us to operate an NSP from the front of the service to IDUs who are not using the MSIC.) Why otherwise would our database have been designed to collect this information for the evaluators to report on a regular basis, if such activity was forbidden? As it turned out, only 1 in 20 clients avail themselves of this service anyway. So I provided the information about this modest level of usage to Maree and I also reminded her that we should in fact be promoting this as another good thing the MSIC does. She agreed and said that they would also be mentioning the recently published Return on Investments study, which quantifies to the tune of billions of dollars just how much is gained at the national level as a result of the needle syringe program, by preventing HIV and other blood-borne infections in the IDU population. Since there have been literally hundreds of needle syringe outlets operating throughout the state for the last 15 years, I don't understand why anyone would question the injecting centre also distributing such equipment to its drug-using clientele, who obviously inject elsewhere too, particularly at times when we're closed.

Later in the evening, debate began in the Upper House on the Bill to extend the MSIC trial, but the House rose for a recess of three weeks before a vote could be taken, so we are going to have to remain on tenterhooks until parliament resumes. However, on Tuesday, while being debriefed after my encounter with Gordon Moyes, I was assured by Ian Cohen that more than enough cross-benchers will be supporting the bill so there is really no risk of it not going through.

We still haven't had any confirmation about how the MSIC will operate in future, particularly not about how the ongoing evaluation will occur. I suppose they don't want to pre-empt the passage of the bill, even though this seems assured.

Today we set yet another record—345 visits accommodated during a 12-hour shift without a hitch. We wonder when the numbers will start to level off. Street-based drug use, like all outdoor activities, tends to increase across the warmer, summer months in Kings Cross, so we predict that we will continue to see more and more people, at least until the end of the year. I hope the staff will be able to cope with this as well as they have so far.

Tuesday, 23 September

I spoke to Julie Sibraa and discussed with her the importance of the ongoing service evaluation aspect to me. She assured me that at the political level there isn't quite the same sensitivity about ongoing research needing to be completely external, but she nonetheless suggested that others should perhaps also be involved in this. I assured her that, to guarantee the broad research skills base necessary, I would have to collaborate with lots of other researchers from the various respected national centres including those involved in the evaluation to date. I suggested that we should form a Scientific Advisory Committee, which would include representatives of the National Centre in HIV Epidemiology, Clinical Research and the National Drug and Alcohol Research Centre and the NSW Bureau of Crime Statistics and Research, which were all involved in this evaluation. I would also like to involve the National Centre in HIV Social Research to look at the more qualitative aspects of our work, not yet examined to any great extent. I also assured her that all future research should be subjected to formal peer review and be approved and monitored by the Chief Health Officer of the NSW Health Department.

Monday 29 September

Very sad news. Dr Margaret MacDonald died today after a sudden illness. I have known Margaret for over ten years; she has been involved in many of the research efforts at KRC during this time, and was a key member of the evaluation team for the MSIC. Everyone in the field is devastated. She had such a lot of integrity as a researcher; she will be greatly missed by all of us.

Tuesday, 30 September

I got a phone call from the Director of the Office of Drug Policy. He said that he would like me to ponder the implications of the invitation recently sent out to announce that we would be celebrating the four-year extension of the trial. He suggested that perhaps this was a little premature, given that the legislation had not yet passed through the Upper House.

When we set the date, we had assumed that the legislation would have been fully passed before the parliamentary recess, and hence before the invitations went out. I suppose we could have postponed the party, but that would have meant losing the symbolism of it being on the last day of our existing licence and brought us into the Christmas period, when venues are harder to secure. So I'd decided to leave it as arranged. While there seemed little risk that the legislation wouldn't pass through the Upper House, I suppose one can't be absolutely sure until it actually happens.

He also expressed concern about the location—if people found out that we were celebrating in a place that served alcohol, this might prompt criticism. After the debacle regarding last year's party invitation, I couldn't believe this was happening again—what was it with the MSIC and parties? I jested that at least there were no needle syringes on the invitation so we thought we had got it right this time. But obviously not. Regarding the venue, we would have been happy to have been invited to Parliament House to celebrate our achievement in the rather nice dining room there, but perhaps that invitation was still in the mail! He reiterated that he just wanted me to think about it. But I figured that the minister and his government should be able to survive whatever came out of this, so I didn't think about it too much.

Tuesday, 14 October

Soon after 9 pm I received a text message on my mobile from Julie telling me that the Bill had just been passed by the Legislative Council with a vote of 23 to 14. She rang me half an hour later, when she was out of the House, and seemed almost as excited and relieved as I was. We had not expected the debate on this Bill to resume until tomorrow so it all came as quite a surprise. I rang Colette at home straightaway, and we congratulated each other.

Wednesday, 15 October

I rang Pat first thing after 7 am to warn him that the legislation had gone through sooner than we expected and that we needed to be on standby for any resulting media inquiries this morning. I also rang Harry, whose response was, 'Well, Ingrid, I suppose you can have your party now.' And indeed we can, and we will.

In fact the ABC and 2UE were the only radio stations this morning to carry the news that the legislation has passed and they added no commentary. They probably picked this up from very small snippets in both the *Sydney Morning Herald* and the *Telegraph*, likewise simply stating that the legislation had passed.

There was no other media today. Incredible really—in many ways this was the biggest announcement that we have had since the very beginning and yet it attracted virtually no media interest at all. But we weren't complaining about this.

I decided that our regular health promotion meeting with staff this afternoon would instead be a celebration of this momentous occasion. We bought a couple of bottles of champagne to toast our success. The last time we drank champagne at the injecting centre was after our first night of operation. Malcolm Duncan had apparently said then that more champagne was drunk than the number of clients seen that night. He was not quite right. But I can definitely record here that, with an average of 262 visits going through the injecting centre each day at the present time, we definitely didn't match that in terms of the number of bottles of champagne we drank today!

Friday, 24 October

Princess Anne visited Kings Cross Police Station today. When Dave Darcy first asked me to make a presentation about the injecting centre, as part of this visit, I thought that I must have misheard what he had said. There had been lots of press about Prince Harry recently arriving on these shores during his 'gap' year, but nothing about Princess Anne. But when I spoke to him again, he confirmed that we would indeed be presenting to a group that would include her. I had not met royalty before and hoped there would be no need for any curtsying—as Annita Keating had previously shown, the Dutch don't curtsy, not even for their own royals, let alone somebody else's!

When I arrived at the police station today people were all standing around in Fitzroy Gardens waiting for the Princess to arrive. There seemed to be quite a few of these tall, grey-suited men with wraparound sunglasses poking about around the garbage bins and so on. Even one of the street sweepers seemed to be fiddling with something in his ear, apparently speaking without anyone being within earshot. But then quite a few people do that in Kings Cross.

Finally two cars arrived and it seemed that, even before they came to a halt, another set of grey-suited men had jumped out and were sweeping the Princess along up the stairs to meet Dave and Gary Groves, another policeman involved in their community programs. She introduced herself to me and thankfully stuck her hand out for it to be shaken, not even with a glove on! (I was told later that it's only at official functions that royalty wear gloves and receive curtsies.) Despite my staunch republicanism, I found myself quite in awe of her and a bit nervous, even though I have presented this information many times and know it inside out.

She was here as the patron of a group of people from various countries within the Commonwealth on a study tour focusing on leadership. Dave had thought that the MSIC provided a good case study of the need for community leadership, in terms of needing to assure the local community that the injecting centre would not undermine policing efforts in Kings Cross.

I had promised Dave that I would not run over time but I didn't even get halfway through before I was facing a barrage of questions. Really good questions; the group seemed to be absolutely fascinated by the concept of the supervised injecting centre. The Princess herself also seemed quick to grasp the concept, apparently having a personal interest in social welfare issues and how different policing approaches can affect public health. She later told Dave that she was aware of a study in the UK which compared HIV rates among injecting drug users in two areas; one where the police used the possession of injecting paraphernalia as evidence to charge people with drug use, and somewhere else where they didn't. Apparently the rate of HIV was far lower in the area where police didn't interfere with drug users' access to clean injecting equipment.

I was pleased with how the presentation went but slightly disappointed for the police that the MSIC had hijacked the agenda somewhat. In the subsequent media reports there was most mention of the fact that the Princess had heard a presentation about the MSIC. Most people assumed that she actually visited it, the news reports dragging out that file tape of the MSIC with Andy as the drug user yet again. She did walk through the streets of Kings Cross and also visited the Street Retreat Project for young people in Woolloomooloo.

Friday, 31 October

This was the last day of our existing licence. Tomorrow we start on our new licence for the next four years. We decided to close the service for the evening so that all staff could attend our celebration.

We kicked off at 6 o'clock; I was keen to get the speeches over and done with before too long and Harry agreed. So at about 7 o'clock we rounded everyone up together with Harry going first. Then Colette intervened and presented me with a huge bunch of white lilies from the management team, thanking me for having the vision and, through my tenacity and leadership throughout the project, making it work. I was deeply touched. Quite choked up in fact. I certainly wasn't expecting this.

It was then my turn. Last time we had a party like this I had to use a microphone because I had such severe laryngitis. Thankfully, this time I didn't but I had nothing prepared, partly because I'd been busy, partly because I'm lazy, but mostly because I think that speeches that come from the heart work better than prepared speeches. I figured I was pretty well positioned to speak from the heart about this particular milestone.

I went down the perilous road of actually trying to thank everybody individually, starting with Harry. I mentioned his courage in taking this responsibility on and talked more generally about the courage of church-based organisations in supporting these initiatives around the world. Even though the various churches often include in their membership some of our fiercest opponents—Watters, Moyes and Nile being cases in point—they are also the institutions that have stuck their necks out and been involved in civil disobedience exercises, putting injecting centres firmly on the political agenda in various places around the world. In Sydney it was the efforts of the Wayside Chapel's Reverend Ray Richmond that ensured that the NSW Parliamentary Drug Summit focused on this issue, which led to the critical resolution in favour of establishing a Medically Supervised Injecting Centre being put to the Summit and carried. It was then the Sisters of Charity who had the courage to offer to establish and run it. After their withdrawal, the Uniting Church of Australia stepped forward.

I also mentioned how glad I was to find that Harry and I shared a healthy irreverence towards the Powers That Be and that, whenever I'd wanted Harry to speak out about a concern we had, he'd always been willing to, even if this meant ruffling a few feathers. We almost always see things the same way including all other social justice issues, and am proud when he speaks out on these too.

I thanked the frontline staff from the injecting centre; without people willing to do what they do, day in day out, there would be no service, and all the lofty goals of public health advocates like me would remain just that. I also thanked staff from Kirketon Road Centre, and particularly the management team there as they have had to put up with me seemingly never being in the right place at the right time or with my body being in one place and my spirit in the other. They have been very tolerant of this, and have not only never complained but offered support when I was distracted by whatever the latest crisis at the MSIC was.

I thanked the management team at the MSIC too, specifically Tracey, Jake and Andy, and acknowledged the great personal support that I had received from Colette in particular—she has been a true friend and ally as well as an impressive health professional. We've been working together for seven years now, and I expressed my hope that our fruitful partnership would continue. I referred to the politicians present, including Tanya Plibersek and John Mills (Anne Symonds sent her apologies), and thanked Clover Moore in particular for her support right throughout. I spoke of the importance of the media support we had enjoyed and thanked Pat Kennedy and those media reps present along with organisations like the Hepatitis C Council of NSW and Family Drug Support, which have backed us every step of the way.

I finally ended up by saying how proud I was to be working among those in this field. Not because of its glamour—goodness knows, it must be the least glamorous field in health—but because they believe that what we are working towards is right and it *is* right. I congratulated everybody there for that.

It really is a great privilege to be involved in work for which you have a strong commitment and a tremendous passion. In what after all is an ongoing campaign, on this night we were able to celebrate a battle won. It was a wonderful evening.

Postscript

A report prepared by the Legal Affairs Section of the United Nations Office on Drugs and Crime for the INCB, published in the *Sydney Morning Herald* in late 2003 following further allegations that the MSIC contravened the UN's drug control treaties, stated the following: 'It would be difficult to assert that, in establishing drug injection rooms, it is the intent of parties to actually incite or induce the illicit use of drugs, or even more so, to associate with, aid, abet or facilitate the possession of drugs. On the contrary, it seems clear that in such cases the intention of governments is to provide healthier conditions for IV drug [users], thereby reducing risk of infections with grave transmittable diseases and, at least in some cases, reaching out to them with counselling and other therapeutic options.'

In February 2004, the Supreme Court [Equity Division] issued an order for the winding up of the Kings Cross Chamber of Commerce and Tourism after it discontinued payments to reimburse Uniting*Care*'s outstanding legal costs, a result of the Chamber's case challenging Uniting*Care*'s legal status to hold the licence to operate the MSIC. A liquidator was appointed who subsequently reported that there were no assets or records. The file was closed and the Chamber no longer exists as a legal entity.

In March 2004, fourteen candidates stood for Lord Mayor of the City of Sydney Council, including State MP Clover Moore, who won. When I told her she was crazy taking on a second job she responded, 'Yes it is, but what could I do?' I know the sentiment, but it's still crazy! Her team also won half of the positions on the council with the rest going to the ALP, the Liberals and the Greens, all of whom were explicitly in support of the MSIC.

Also in March 2004, production of the gelcap form of temazepam was ceased and there was an immediate, dramatic reduction in its associated harm among IDUs attending the MSIC.

In May 2004, Major Brian Watters AO was appointed to the International Narcotics Control Board for a 5-year term to commence in March 2005. Prime Minister Howard's press release stated: 'This tremendous result reflects the high regard in which both Major Watters and the Australian Government are held in the field of drugs policy.'

In August 2004, Paul Haege, from the former Chamber of Commerce, rang to ask me if his 16-year-old daughter and three of her Year 10 classmates could drop into the centre to discuss MSIC. He said that they were doing a project on the MSIC and that while his daughter had heard his views, he thought it only fair that she heard about it from our perspective too.

Acronyms

ACON	AIDS Council of New South Wales
AIVL	Australian Injecting and Illicit Drug Users' League
ANCD	Australian National Council on Drugs
AVO	Apprehended Violence Order
CDAT	Community Drug Action Team
CNS	Central nervous system
EAR	Expired Air Resuscitation
HREA	Health and Research Employees' Association
IDUs	Injecting drug users
INCB	International Narcotics Control Board
KRC	Kirketon Road Centre
MSIC	Medically Supervised Injecting Centre
NCHECR	National Centre in HIV Epidemiology and Clinical Research
NDARC	National Drug and Alcohol Research Centre
NSP	Needle syringe program
TGA	Therapeutic Goods Administration
UNDCP	United Nations Drug Control Programme